THE BRITISH
ARMY GUIDE

2016 – 2017

Editor – Charles Heyman

ISBN 978 1 47384 547 3

Price £9.99

Pen & Sword Books Ltd
47 Church Street
Barnsley S70 2AS

Telephone: 01226-734222 Fax: 01226-734438
www.pen-and-sword.co.uk

The Information in this publication has been gathered from
unclassified sources.

Front Cover: T Hawk UAV clearing a route of improvised explosive devices
as part of the 'Talisman' route clearance system. (Copyright MoD 2015)

Rear Cover: Soldier manning a .50 cal heavy machine gun mounted on a Jackal 2
All Terrain Vehicle. (Copyright MoD 2015)

CONTENTS

CHAPTER 1 – OVERVIEW

GENERAL INFORMATION

Population – European Union – Top Five Nations

(2015 Official national estimates)

Germany	81.1 million
France	64.3 million
United Kingdom	64.5 million
Italy	61.0 million
Spain	46.3 million

Total European Union population is estimated at 507 million. For comparison other population estimates include: China 1,350 million; India 1,250 million; United States 321 million and Russia 144 million.

Finance – European Union – Top Five Nations (2015 IMF Estimates)

In billions of US$; Euros and UK £

	GDP (US$)	GDP (Euros)	GDP (£)
Germany	3,300	3,630	4,953
United Kingdom	3,002	3,302	4,503
France	2,935	3,228	4,402
Italy	2,152	2,367	3,228
Spain	1,421	1,563	2,131
		US$1 – €1.10	US$1 = £1.50

GDP (Gross Domestic Product) is an annual figure that values all of the goods and services produced by a country in that year. GDP is a very simple indicator of national wealth.

International Monetary Fund (IMF) projections for GDP in 2019 will be approximately:

European Union 22,328; United States 22,149; China 15,519; Japan 5,433; Germany 4,558; United Kingdom 3,704; France 3,393; India 3,182. *(Figures are in billions of US$)*

2011 Census UK Population

England	53 million
Scotland	5.3 million
Wales	3.1 million
Northern Ireland	1.8 million

UK Population Breakdown – Military Service Groups

UK Office for National Statistics (2011 census figures – figures rounded to the nearest hundred)

	Males	Females	Total
0–14	5,600.000	5,400.000	11,100.000
15–64	20,700.000	20,900.000	41,600.000
65+	4,500.000	5,800,000	10,300.000

UK Area

(in square kilometres)

England	130,423
Scotland	20,766
Wales	78,133
Northern Ireland	14,160
Total	243,482

Note: Comparisons include Germany 356,854 sq kms and France 550,000 sq kms. The total area of the European Union is 4,324,782 sq kms. The United States is 9,826,630 sq kms; Canada 9,984,670 sq kms; China 9,640,821 sq kms; India 3,166,414 sq kms and Russia 17,098,242 sq kms.

GOVERNMENT

The executive government of the United Kingdom is vested nominally in the Crown, but for practical purposes in a committee of Ministers that is known as the Cabinet. The head of the ministry and leader of the Cabinet is the Prime Minister and for the implementation of policy, the Cabinet is dependent upon the support of a majority of the Members of Parliament in the House of Commons. Within the Cabinet, defence matters are the responsibility of the Secretary of State for Defence.

National Security Council (NSC) This council is where the UK Government decides on the national defence and security objectives and the best way in which these objectives can be met using national resources. The National Security Council is chaired by the Prime Minister, and generally meets weekly with representation from across the major Departments of State. The Secretary of State for Defence attends as does the Chief of the Defence Staff when the need arises.

MILITARY TASKS AND DEFENCE PLANNING ASSUMPTIONS OF THE UK'S ARMED FORCES

The 2010 Strategic Defence and Security Review (SDSR) stated that the contribution of the UK Armed Forces to the national security effort is defined by a number of Military Tasks (MT) and Defence Planning Assumptions (DPA).

Military Tasks (MT)
The seven military tasks are:

◆ Defending the UK and its Overseas Territories
◆ Providing strategic intelligence
◆ Providing nuclear deterrence
◆ Supporting civil emergency organisations in times of crisis
◆ Defending the UK's interest by projecting power strategically and through expeditionary intervention
◆ Providing a defence contribution to UK influence
◆ Providing security for stabilisation

Defence Planning Assumptions (DPA)
These assume that in the future the UK Armed Forces will have the size and shape that will enable them to conduct operations of the following type:

An enduring stabilisation operation at around brigade level (possibly up to 6,500 personnel) with maritime and air support as required, while also conducting:

One non-enduring complex intervention (up to 2,000 personnel), and
One non-enduring simple intervention (up to 1,000 personnel):

or alternatively:

Three non-enduring operations if the UK Armed Forces are not already engaged in an enduring operation:

or

For a limited time period, and with sufficient warning, committing all the UK's effort to a one-off intervention of up to three brigades with air and maritime support at a level of about 30,000 personnel.

Having largely worked through the effects of the restructuring and budgetary cuts imposed by the 2010 Strategic Defence and Security Review (SDSR) the UK Armed Forces await the publication of the 2015 SDSR with analysts expecting some reductions in the UK's defence capability. However, we believe that recent events in the Ukraine and the Middle East have prompted an urgent 'across the board' rethink of the global threat and it is possible that any further reductions are unlikely.

FUTURE FORCE 2020

In general terms the planning framework provided by the Military Tasks and Defence Planning Assumptions provides an outline for structure which the UK Government aims to establish by 2020. The proposal is for the Future Force 2020 to have three main combined service elements:

- ♦ The Deployed Force
- ♦ The High Readiness Force
- ♦ The Lower Readiness Force

This force will consist of 82,000 trained regular personnel and 30,000 trained reserves – an army consisting of 112,000 personnel.

The Deployed Force
This will consist of those forces that are actually engaged in operations. Therefore aircraft engaged in operations (including the defence of the UK's airspace), forces involved in operations in the South Atlantic, forces operating in support of friendly nations and other expeditionary operations, plus the nuclear deterrent will all form elements of The Deployed Force.

The High Readiness Force
This force will consist of a range of maritime, air and land based units capable of deploying at short notice to meet the requirements of the Defence Planning Assumptions. Such forces would enable the UK to react quickly to a range of scenarios that might threaten our national security interests. These force elements would be capable of operating with allies or where necessary on 'stand-alone' UK operations.

The High Readiness Force will include an enhanced Special Forces capability.

In the main Joint Forces Command will have operational control of the majority of future High Readiness Force (Deployed Force) operations.

The Lower Readiness Force
The Lower Readiness Force would consist of elements that have either recently returned from operations, or those that are preparing and training for inclusion in The High Readiness Force. Many Lower Readiness Force units (especially logistic) would be involved in supporting The Deployed Force on operations.

Land Forces

Land force capabilities will be based around eleven brigades as follows:

A Reaction Force of three multi-role brigades in 3 (UK) Division each consisting of around 6,500 personnel that are comprised of main battle tanks, armoured reconnaissance units, armoured, mechanised and light infantry elements, plus artillery, engineers, army aviation units in support and a complete range of logistic support units. One brigade would always be part of the High Readiness Force and where necessary these brigades could be self supporting.

16 Air Assault Brigade would be the fourth brigade and would provide parachute and air assault units for rapid intervention operations at very short notice. This brigade would be self supporting for short duration operations.

All of the above could form part of a much larger organisation (possibly divisional size) under the command of a deployable UK divisional headquarters. For multinational operations the headquarters of the Allied Rapid Reaction Corps (HQ ARRC) would be available.

Another seven brigades in 1 (UK) Division. These brigades would be equipped at lighter scales and be composed of a mix of regular and reserve personnel. They would be at a lower state of readiness, and if required individual units could be attached to formations in the Reaction Force. Many of the units in these brigades would be able to provide 'depth' in any enduring operation.

The Royal Marines 3 Commando Brigade (a Royal Naval formation) would be available for Land Force operations as required.

There are plans for all UK Army units to have been withdrawn from their bases in Germany by 2020 (combat units should have been withdrawn by the end of 2016). A majority of land force units will be returned to the UK well before that date.

Royal Navy

Under the terms of the Future Force 2020 proposals the Royal Navy will provide a continuous nuclear deterrent system at sea, maritime defence of the United Kingdom and defence of territories in the South Atlantic. Forces assigned to these roles will include:

The Vanguard submarine force equipped with Trident submarine launched inter-continental ballistic missiles. Current plans are for the Vanguard class submarines to be replaced in the late 2020s (with the first submarine possibly being delivered in 2028).

Seven Astute class nuclear powered hunter killer submarines equipped with Tomahawk land attack cruise missiles. Astute class submarines are capable of operating at sea indefinitely.

Two new aircraft carriers, one of which will be kept at extended readiness. The aircraft carrier at sea will be equipped with Joint Strike Fighters and a range of helicopters that (depending on the operational requirement) could include Apache attack helicopters and possibly Chinook and Merlin support helicopters.

A balanced surface fleet of 19 frigates and destroyers.

Up to 14 mine counter- measures vessels to be based on the existing Hunt and Sandown class vessels. In addition there will be an ice patrol ship and an oceanographic survey capability.

The Royal Marine's 3 Commando Brigade will provide an important maritime response capability to the High Readiness Force. 3 Commando Brigade will be able to land significant forces anywhere in the world.

Strategic transport will be provided by a force of up to 6 x roll-on, roll-off ferries.

The Royal Fleet Auxiliary will continue to supply and refuel Royal Naval vessels at sea worldwide.

Royal Air Force

The Royal Air Force will continue to provide the air defence of the United Kingdom and territories in the South Atlantic. To meet this requirement, in the longer term, a fast jet force of both Eurofighter Typhoon and Joint Strike Fighter aircraft will provide air defence, precision ground attack and combat ISTAR capabilities.

In the short term elements of the Tornado fleet will be retained to support operations in Iraq and elsewhere should the operational requirement arise.

The Royal Air Force will also provide a fleet of strategic and tactical airlift aircraft based around approximately 7 x C-17, 22 x A400M and 14 x Airbus A330 tanker and transport aircraft. The Chinook helicopter fleet will be increased by 12 new aircraft and Merlin helicopters will be retained.

ISTAR capabilities will be enhanced to include a range of unmanned air systems that will complement existing manned aircraft. The UK may purchase 3 x KC-135 Joint Rivet signals intelligence aircraft to improve the existing ISTAR capability.

CURRENT FORCE LEVELS

Total British Armed Forces (mid 2015)

All Services: 160,460; Army 92,000; Royal Navy 33,450 (including about 7,000 Royal Marines); Royal Air Force 35,030. (Figures are for trained and untrained and includes small numbers of Full Time Reserves).

Army figure includes about 2,700 Gurkhas.

By 2020 Regular Forces levels are planned to be about: Army 82,000; Royal Navy 30,000; Royal Air Force 33,000.

Reserves: Army 20,480; Maritime 1,940; Royal Air Force 1,500. There are probably over 50,000 Regular Reserves who could be recalled in a major emergency.

MOD Civilians: 61,630 (mid 2015)

Strategic Forces: 4 x Vanguard Class submarines capable of carrying up to 16 x Trident II (D5) Submarine Launched Ballistic Missiles (SLBM) deploying with 40 x warheads per submarine. If necessary a D5 missile could deploy with 12 MIRV (multiple independently targetable re-entry vehicles). Future plans appear to be for a stockpile of 120 operationally ready warheads and 58 missile bodies. Strategic Forces are provided by the Royal Navy.

Current plans appear to be for the Vanguard Class submarines to be replaced in the '2030s'.

Army: 83,340 (trained strength mid 2015): 1 x Corps Headquarters (HQ ARRC – NATO Deployable HQ); 1 x Reaction Force Divisional HQ (1 x Headquarters plus 5 x Brigades including 1 x Air Assault Brigade and 1 x Logistic Brigade); 1 x Adaptable Force Divisional HQ (1 x Headquarters plus 8 x Brigades including 1 x Logistic Brigade); Force Troops Command (1 x Headquarters plus 8 Brigades); 8 x Regional Headquarters; 1 x District HQ (London District).

These figures include:

Formations: 3 x Armoured Infantry Brigades, 1 x Air Assault Brigade; 7 x Regional Infantry Brigades; 3 x Logistics Brigades; 1 x Artillery Brigade; 1 x Engineer Brigade; 2 x Signal Brigades; 1 x Medical Brigade; 1 x Intelligence & Surveillance Brigade; 1 x Military Police Brigade.

Major Units: 9 x Armoured Regiments; 31 x Infantry Battalions (plus 1 x public duties company); 13 x Artillery Regiments; 10 x Engineer Regiments/Major Units; 11 x Signal Regiments; 4 x Army Air Corps Regiments; 6 x Equipment Support Battalions; 12 x Logistic Regiments; 9 x Medical Regiments/ Field Hospitals; 3 x Intelligence Battalions; 4 x Military Police Regiments.

Major Royal Navy Elements: 30,200 (trained strength – mid 2015 – including some 7,000 Royal Marines): 4 x Nuclear Powered Ballistic Missile firing (UK Strategic Deterrent); 6 x Nuclear Powered Submarines (attack type); 4 x Amphibious Assault Ships; 6 x Destroyers; 13 x Frigates (future combined total of 19); 15 x Minehunters and Minesweepers (future total of 14); 9 x Fleet Air Arm Squadrons (front line); *New construction:* 5 x Nuclear Attack Submarines; 2 x Aircraft Carriers. 6 x Destroyers Planned to enter service from 2018).

Royal Marines: 7,000; 1 x Commando Brigade Headquarters; 3 x Royal Marine Commando (Battalion Size); 2 x Commando Assault Helicopter Squadrons; 1 x Commando Regiment Royal Artillery (under command); 1 x Commando Squadron Royal Engineers (under command); 1 x Commando Logistic Regiment; 4 x Commando Assault Squadrons (Landing craft); 1 x Fleet Protection Group; 4 x Nuclear Security Guarding Squadrons; 4 x Special Boat Service Squadrons.

Major Royal Air Force Elements: 32,180 (trained strength – early 2015) ; 11 x Strike/Attack/ Fast Jet Squadrons; 2 x Unmanned Air Vehicle (UAV) Squadrons; 2 x Airborne Early Warning Squadrons; 2 x ISTAR Squadrons; 5 x Transport Squadrons; 3 x Air to Air Refuelling Squadrons; 7 x Support Helicopter Squadrons; 2 x Search and Rescue Squadrons; 8 x Ground (Field) Defence Squadrons (RAF Regiment). With the following aircraft (numbers approximate): 112 x Typhoon (total of 160 on order); 90 x Tornado GR4/4A; 60 x Hawk (all types); 12 x Voyager (total of 14 on order; 4 x Sentry AEW; 3 x Sentinel; 5 x Shadow R1; 24 x Hercules C1/3/4/5 8 x C-17; 5 x Reaper; 52 x Chinook (JFH); 24 x Puma (JFH); 22 x A400M Atlas will replace Hercules C1/C3 later in the decade; RAF Chinook and Puma helicopters are assigned to the Joint Force Helicopter (JFH); RAF Merlin helicopters were transferred to the Royal Navy's Commando Helicopter Force in 2014.

Joint Forces: 1 x Joint Forces Command HQ; **Joint Helicopter Command:** 4 x Royal Naval Helicopter Squadrons; 4 x Army Aviation Regiments (already listed in the above Army entry plus 1 x Reserve Regiment); 7 x Royal Air Force Helicopter Squadrons (including 1 x RAuxAF Helicopter Support Squadron). **Joint Special Forces Group:** 1 x Regular Special Air Service (SAS) Regiment; 2 x Volunteer Reserve Special Air Service Regiments; 4 x Special Boat Service (SBS) Squadrons; 1 x Special Reconnaissance Regiment; 1 x Special Forces Support Group; 1 x Joint Special Forces Air Wing; **NBC:** Defence CBRN Wing: **Defence Medical Services:** Ministry of Defence Hospital Units; The Royal Centre for Defence Medicine: The Defence Medical Rehabilitation Centre (Headley Court); Defence Medical Services Training Centre; Defence Dental Services; Defence Medical Postgraduate Deanery.

National Police Forces: England and Wales 128,000 Scotland 17,000, Northern Ireland 7,200.

BRITISH ARMY EQUIPMENT SUMMARY

Armour: 227 x Challenger 2 (MBT).
AIFV: 400 x MCV 80 Warrior.
APC: 800 x Fv 432/430 family (Bulldog); (possibly 100 more available); 300 x Spartan; 115 x Warthog.
PPV: 400 x Mastiff; 400 x Foxhound; 179 x Vector; 125 x Wolfhound; 350 x Husky; 100 x Ridgeback.
CLV: 400 x Panther.
Recce: 220 x Scimitar; 11 x Fuchs (NBC); approx 200 Jackal (all types).
Anti Tank: 1,500+ x Javelin; possibly 20 x Spike (some SP).
Artillery and Mortars: 90 x 155 mm AS 90 (probably at least 50 in store); 50 x 227 mm MLRS/GLMRS; 100 x 105 mm Light Gun; 400 x 81 mm mortar (including about 100 x self- propelled); 1,000 x 51 mm Light Mortar.
Air Defence: 24 x Rapier C Fire Units; 100 x Starstreak (LML); 60 x HVM (SP on Stormer).
Army Aviation: 66 x WAH-64D Apache; 30 Lynx Wildcat (plus 6 for light assault); 50 x Lynx AH 7/9; 35 x Gazelle; 6 x BN-2; 4 x EC 365N3.
Engineer: 80 x CRARRV; 40 x Warrior ARRV; 33 x Titan (AVLB); 33 x Trojan; 38 x M3 (SP Bridge); 60 x Terrier (AVRE)'
UAV: 30 x Watchkeeper (our estimate): 10 x Hermes 450 (our estimate).

MINISTRY OF DEFENCE (MoD)

In 1963, the three independent service ministries (Admiralty, War Office and Air Ministry) were merged to form the present MoD.

The UK MoD is the government department that is responsible for all defence related aspects of UK National Policy. This large organisation, which directly affects the lives of about half a million servicemen, reservists and MoD employed civilians, is controlled by The Secretary of State for Defence.

The Secretary of State for Defence has the following principal deputies;

♦ Minister of State for the Armed Forces.
♦ Minister of State for Defence Procurement.
♦ Parliamentary Under Secretary of State and Minister for Personnel and Veterans.
♦ Parliamentary Under Secretary of State and Minister for Reserves.
♦ Parliamentary Under Secretary of State and the Lords Spokesman on Defence.

The Secretary of State for defence is assisted by two advisers, one a civilian and the other a senior military officer:

Permanent Under Secretary of State (PUS): The PUS is responsible for policy, finance and administration in the MoD. As the MoD's Principal Accounting Officer he is personally responsible to Parliament for the expenditure of all public money voted to the MoD for Defence purposes. The PUS is the most senior civilian in the MoD.

Chief of the Defence Staff (CDS): The CDS acts as the professional head of the Armed Forces and he is the principal military adviser to both the Secretary of State and to the Government.

Both the PUS and the CDS have deputies; the Second Permanent Under Secretary of State (2nd PUS), and the Vice Chief of the Defence Staff (VCDS). The VCDS acts as the Chief Operating Officer in the Armed Forces Chain-of-Command.

DEFENCE COMMITTEES

In general terms defence is managed through a number of major committees that provide corporate leadership and strategic direction:

Defence Council – chaired by the Secretary of State for Defence
Defence Board – chaired by the Permanent Secretary
Chiefs of Staff Committee – chaired by the CDS
Service Boards (Admiralty Board, Army Board and Air Force Board)

Defence Council

The Defence Council is the senior committee which provides the legal basis for the conduct and administration of defence and this council is chaired by the Secretary of State for Defence. The Defence Council reflects the constitutional principle that the defence forces are commanded by a Member of Parliament. The composition of the Defence Council is as follows:

Secretary of State for Defence.
Minister of State for the Armed Forces.
Minister of State for Defence Procurement.
Parliamentary Under Secretary of State and Minister for Defence Personnel and Veterans.
Parliamentary Under Secretary of State and Minister for Reserves.
Parliamentary Under Secretary of State and the Lords Spokesman on Defence.
Permanent Under Secretary of State
Chief of the Defence Staff
Vice-Chief of the Defence Staff

Chief of the Naval Staff and First Sea Lord
Chief of the Air Staff
Chief of the General Staff
Chief of Defence Materiel
Chief Scientific Adviser
Director General Finance
Second Permanent Under-Secretary of State for Defence

Defence Board
Chaired by the Secretary of State for Defence this board is the MoD's main corporate board providing senior leadership and direction to the implementation of defence policy. It is responsible for the full range of Defence business other than the conduct of military operations.

The current membership of the Defence Board is:

Secretary of State for Defence.
Minister of State for the Armed Forces.
Permanent Under Secretary.
Chief of the Defence Staff.
Vice Chief of the Defence Staff .
Chief Executive Defence Equipment and Support.
Director General Finance.
Audit Committee Chair (Non Executive Director).
Investment Approvals Committee Chair (Non Executive Director).
Appointments Committee Chair (Non Executive Director) .

The MoD describes the objectives of the Defence Board's core tasks as follows:

◆ Role of Defence: To help define and articulate the Department's strategic direction, and provide a clear vision and set of values for defence.
◆ Targets and Objectives: To establish the key priorities and defence capabilities needed to deliver the strategy.
◆ Resource Allocation: To ensure that Defence priorities and tasks are appropriately resourced.
◆ Performance Management: To manage corporate performance and resources in-year to deliver the required results.

The Defence Board is supported by three sub-committees:

◆ The Defence Audit Committee.
◆ The Investment Approvals Committee
◆ The People (Personnel) Committee.

Chiefs of Staff Committee
This committee is chaired by the CDS and is the MoD's senior committee that allows the CDS to gather information and advice from the single service chiefs of staff on operational matters and the preparation and conduct of military operations.

Single Service Boards
There are three single service boards: Admiralty Board, Army Board and the Air Force Board all of which are chaired by the Secretary of State for Defence. In general the purpose of the boards is the administration and monitoring of single service performance. Each of these three boards has an executive committee chaired by the single service chief of staff; Navy Board, Executive Committee of the Army Board and the Air Force Board Standing Committee.

MOD HEAD OFFICE

The MoD Head Office allocates resources to Top Level Budget Holders (TLB) who are then accountable to the Chief of the Defence Staff and the Permanent Under Secretary. TLB holders are responsible for the way in which their resources are allocated.

There are seven TLB holders:

◆ MoD Head Office & Corporate Services
◆ Land Command
◆ Navy Command
◆ Air Command
◆ Joint Forces Command
◆ Defence Equipment & Support
◆ Defence Infrastructure Organisation

In general terms the Head Office structure resembles the following:

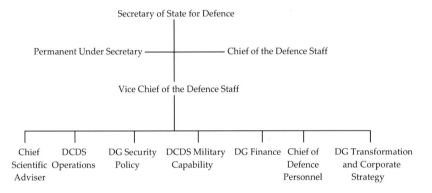

Secretary of State for Defence

Permanent Under Secretary —————————————— Chief of the Defence Staff

Vice Chief of the Defence Staff

Chief	DCDS	DG Security	DCDS Military	DG Finance	Chief of	DG Transformation
Scientific	Operations	Policy	Capability		Defence	and Corporate
Adviser					Personnel	Strategy

CHIEF OF THE DEFENCE STAFF

The Chief of the Defence Staff (CDS) is the officer responsible to the Secretary of State for Defence for the coordinated effort of all three fighting services. He has his own Central Staff Organisation and a Vice Chief of the Defence Staff who ranks as number four in the services hierarchy, following the three single service commanders. The current Chief of the Defence Staff is:

GENERAL SIR NICHOLAS HOUGHTON GCB CBE ADC GEN

General Nick Houghton was born in 1954 in Otley, West Yorkshire. He was educated at Woodhouse Grove School in Bradford, RMA Sandhurst and St Peter's College, Oxford, where he completed an in-service degree in Modern History.

Commissioned into the Green Howards in 1974, he had a variety of Regimental and Staff appointments before attending the Army Command and Staff Courses at both Shrivenham and Camberley. Thereafter he was Military Assistant to the Chief of Staff British Army of the Rhine and a member of the Directing Staff at the Royal Military College of Science, Shrivenham. At Regimental Duty he was both a Company Commander in, and Commanding Officer of, 1st Battalion The Green Howards in the Mechanised and Airmobile roles, and in Northern Ireland.

General Houghton was Deputy Assistant Chief of Staff, G3 (Operations & Deployment) in HQ Land Command 1994–1997 and attended the Higher Command and Staff Course in 1997. He commanded 39 Infantry Brigade in Northern Ireland from 1997 to 1999 and was the Director of Military Operations in the Ministry of Defence from December 1999 to July 2002.

He was Chief of Staff of the Allied Rapid Reaction Corps from July 2002 to April 2004 before becoming the Assistant Chief of the Defence Staff (Operations) from May 2004 to October 2005. He was the Senior British Military Representative Iraq and Deputy Commanding General of the Multi-National Force-Iraq from October 2005 until assuming the appointment as Chief of Joint Operations at PJHQ (UK) in March 2006.

From 2009 General Houghton was the Vice Chief of the Defence Staff and in July 2013 he became the Chief of the Defence Staff.

General J N R Houghton GCB, CBE, ADC Gen. (MoD Crown Copyright 2015)

Vice Chief of the Defence Staff

Where appropriate the Vice Chief of the Defence Staff deputises for the Chief of the Defence Staff. On a day to day basis he is responsible through the Central Staff for running defence business (with the Second Permanent Under-Secretary).

As of May 2013 the Vice Chief of the Defence Staff is Air Chief Marshal Sir Stuart Peach who was previously Chief of Joint Operations/Commander Joint Forces Command.

CHAIN OF COMMAND

The Chief of the Defence Staff (CDS) commands and coordinates the activities of the three services through the following chain of command:

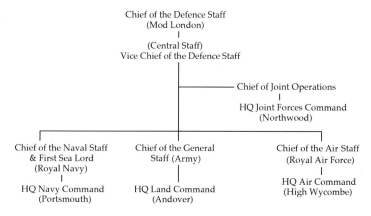

The three single service commanders exercise command and control of their services through their respective headquarters. However, the complex inter-service nature of the majority of modern military operations, where military, air and naval support must be coordinated, resulted in the establishment in April 2012 of Joint Forces Command (JFC). More detail regarding the JFC can be found in Chapter 4.

DEFENCE EQUIPMENT AND SUPPORT (DE&S)

Following the establishment of PJHQ (now Joint Forces Command) at Northwood it became important to combine the separate logistics functions of the three armed forces. As a result, in 2000 the three distinct separate service logistic functions were fused into one and the Defence Logistic Organisation was formed.

From 1 April 2007 the Defence Procurement Agency (DPA) and the Defence Logistic Organisation (DLO) were merged to form Defence Equipment and Support (DE&S). More detail regarding the DE&S can be found in Chapter 4.

THE UNITED KINGDOM AND DEFENCE FINANCE

"You need three things to win a war,
Money, money and more money".

Trivulzio (1441–1518)

In general terms defence is related to money, and a nation's ability to pay for its defence is linked to its GDP (Gross Domestic Product) as measured by the sum of all economic activity within a country. Estimates for the world's top ten GDP rankings for 2014 (in billions of US$) and the latest year for which accurate (International Monetary Fund) figures are available are as follows:

GDP 2014 *(US$ billions)*

European Union	18,451 (1)
United States	17,426
China	10,335
Japan	4,770
Germany	3,820
France	2,902
United Kingdom	2,838
Brazil	2,244
Italy	2,159
Russia	2,050

Note:

(1) This is the sum total of the GDP of all 28 European Union nations.

UK DEFENCE EXPENDITURE

In the 2015–2016 Financial Year (FY) the UK Government plans to spend £34.8 billion on defence.

For comparison purposes defence expenditure is often expressed as a percentage of GDP. Expenditure in FY 2015–2016 will represent just over 2 per cent of GDP. In 1985 UK defence expenditure represented 5.2 per cent of GDP.

The estimated total UK government expenditure for FY 2015–2016 is £747 billion.

Major spending departments include:

Department for Work and Pensions	£155 billion
Department of Health	£135 billion
Social Security	£112 billion
Department for Children, Schools and Families	£92 billion

Some interesting comparisons can be made when looking at estimates for the world's top defence budgets for 2014 (in billions of US$ (and the latest year for which accurate figures are available) are as follows:

Defence Budgets 2014 *(US$ billions)*

United States	581 billion
China	129 billion
Saudi Arabia	81 billion
Russia	70 billion
United Kingdom	62 billion
France	53 billion
Japan	48 billion
Germany	44 billion
India	37 billion

UK – TOP LEVEL BUDGETS

Under the early 1990s 'New Management Strategy' the UK defence budget was allocated to a series of 'Top Level Budget Holders' each of whom were allocated a budget with which to run their departments. The money allocated to these Top Level Budgets (TLBs) constitutes the building bricks upon which the whole of the defence budget is based.

As previously stated there are seven Level Budget holders and the last figure we can identify relating to actual TLB expenditure is for Financial Year (FY 2012–2013):

Royal Navy Command	– £3.93 billion
Army Command	– £7.97 billion
Air Command	– £4.03 billion
Joint Forces Command	– £0.32 billion
Defence Equipment and Support	– £11.29 billion
Defence Infrastructure Organisation	– £3.33 billion
Head Office and Corporate Services	– £2.09 billion

Note: Army Command TLB includes Service Children's Education; Defence Equipment & Support TLB includes Defence Storage and Distribution Agency; Central TLB includes Defence Vetting Agency, MoD Police and Guarding Agency, People Pay and Pensions Agency and Service Personnel and Veterans Agency.

Within the TLBs, there are approximately 29 reporting entities, known as management groupings, producing detailed management accounting information as part of the annual financial management.

In addition to the major TLBs there are three Trading Funds as follows: Defence Support Group, Defence Science and Technology Laboratory, Hydrographic Office.

THE DEFENCE EQUIPMENT PLAN

Over the 10 year period from April 2014 to April 2024 the MoD plans to spend £163 billion on defence equipment.

MoD Equipment Budget 2014–2024 (*£ billions*)

Ships	18.2
Submarines	40.0
Land Equipment	15.4
Weapons	12.6
Combat Air	17.9
Air Support	13.8
Helicopters	11.1
ISTAR	4.9
Information Systems & Services	16.9
Other Support	6.6

Some of the total programme costs for a selection of the MoD's major equipment programmes are amongst the following:

A400M	Large transport aircraft	£2.7 billion
Astute Class	Attack submarines	£9.4 billion
Strategic Tanker	Air-to-air refuelling & passengers	£11.4 billion
Lightning II	Fighter/attack aircraft	£5.0 billion
Queen Elizabeth Class	Aircraft carriers	£6.1 billion
Scout Vehicle	Armoured fighting vehicle	£1.4 billion
Typhoon	Fighter aircraft	£18.2 billion
Warrior	Capability sustainment programme	£1.3 billion

The high unit costs of individual items of equipment also serves to illustrate the problems faced by defence planners when working out their annual budgets. Some of the following prices illustrate the costs:

Storm Shadow (Air to Ground) Missile)	–	£500,000
Kinetic Energy Round for Challenger	–	£3,500 each
155 mm High Explosive Round	–	£900 each
Individual Weapon (IW)	–	£800 each (estimate)
5.56 mm round for IW	–	£1.25
Tomahawk Cruise Missile (Block IV)	–	£600,000
One Rapier Missile	–	£60,000
One Challenger 2 MBT	–	£4.5 million (approx)
Combat High Boot	–	£95 per pair
Starstreak Missile	–	£110,000 each
Attack Helicopter	–	£42 million (region)
Eurofighter	–	£60 million (estimate)
Merlin Support Helicopter	–	£34 million
F-35B Lightning II	–	£90 million (recent estimate)
Panther CLV	–	£500,000
Astute Class Submarine	–	£1.3 billion (average cost)

Another interesting table shows the relationship between the defence budget and the numbers of active service personnel in a number of selected countries.

Country	Defence Budget 2014 (US$ billions)	Total active service personnel (mid 2014)	Cost per serviceman (US$ billions)
United States	581 billion	1,360,000	427,205
China	129 billion	2,285,000	56,455
Russia	70 billion	845,000	82,840
United Kingdom	62 billion	159,600	388,471
France	53 billion	215,000	246,511
Germany	44 billion	180,200	233,444

BRITISH ARMY STATISTICS

UK Armed Forces – Army (mid 2015) – Trained and Untrained Strength

	2015	1995	1990
Total	83,340	104,600	137,200

The Army 2020 plan calls for 82,000 trained regular personnel and 30,000 trained reserves – an army consisting of 112,000 personnel.

UK Armed Forces – Army (mid 2015) – Trained Strength

Officers	12,300 (includes 110 Gurkha officers)
Soldiers	71,040 (includes 2,540 Gurkhas)
Total	83,340 (3,950 under the requirement)

UK Armed Forces – Army (mid 2015) – Untrained strength

Officers	760
Soldiers	5,860 (includes 70 Gurkhas)

UK Armed Forces – Army – Intake to the Training Organisation – (Year ending 31 Dec 2014)

	(2014)	(1980/81)
Officers	540	1,489
Soldiers	6,840	27,382
	7,380	**28,871**

Note: 1980/81 figures are given for comparison.

UK Armed Forces – Army – Outflow – Year ending 31 Dec 2014)

	(2014)	(1990/91)	(1980/81)
Officers	1,150	1,860	1,497
Soldiers	10,940	20,964	20,422
	12,090	**22,824**	**21,919**

Note: Table includes trained and untrained personnel.

Strengths by Arm and Service

The following table is somewhat dated (mid 2012) but is the most recent available. Although dated, the table provides a rough guide to the approximate current strengths of the Arms and Services.

Trained regular personnel by arm and service	Strength
Staff	760
The Household Cavalry / Royal Armoured Corps	5,490
Royal Regiment of Artillery	7,330
Corps of Royal Engineers	9,840
Royal Corps of Signals	8,140
The Infantry	25,840
Army Air Corps	2,000
Royal Army Chaplains Department	140
The Royal Logistics Corps	14,760
Royal Army Medical Corps	3,000
Royal Electrical and Mechanical Engineers	9,660
Adjutant General's Corps	6,120
Royal Army Veterinary Corps	370
Small Arms School Corps	160
Royal Army Dental Corps	340
Intelligence Corps	1,680
Army Physical Training Corps	460
Queen Alexandra's Royal Army Nursing Corps	880
Corps of Army Music	780

Service Personnel Deployed in the UK (mid 2015): 136,054

Service Personnel Deployed/Stationed outside the UK mainland (Early 2015)

Germany	– 10,550
Ukraine	– 35 (training mission)
Cyprus	– 2,420 (includes 300 UNFICYP)
Gibraltar	– 160
Other Europe	– 700
Sierra Leone	– 10 (+800 on temporary deployment)
Kenya	– 200
Iraq	– 145
Saudi Arabia	– 120
Other Middle East	– 140
Belize / Caribbean	– 10
South America	– 10
Australia	– 40
Canada	– 270
USA	– 590
Afghanistan	– 470 (Operation Resolute Support)
Brunei	– 700 (estimate – mainly Gurkhas)
Falkland Islands	– 1,200 (capable of rapid reinforcement)

Army Cadet Force (at 1 April 2014)

Total Army Cadets   – 50,480 (includes 9,440 adult volunteers)

The Army Cadets are run and administered by the MoD. There are another 45,760 in the Combined Cadet Force (CCF) that has Army, Navy and Royal Air Force contingents. CCF units are usually attached to schools

Dogs and Horses

During early 2015 we believe that there are about 550 military working dogs and 485 horses in service with the UK Armed Forces. There appear to be a further 400 dogs in service with the Ministry of Defence Police and other guarding agencies.

Over 100 Years Ago – Strength of the British Army at 1 Jan 1905

Regular Army	– 195,000
Colonial Troops or Native Indian Corps	– 14,000
Army Reserve	– 80,000
Militia	– 132,000
Yeomanry (Cavalry)	– 28,000

Regular forces in India totalled 74,500.

The Indian Army totalled approximately 240,000 all ranks.

Three years previously Regular Army totals by Corps were:

Household Cavalry	– 1,390
Cavalry of the Line	– 20,200
Horse Artillery	– 3,483
Field Artillery	– 15,509
Mountain Artillery	– 1,200
Garrison Artillery	– 18,400
Royal Engineers	– 7,130
Foot Guards	– 5,873
Infantry of the Line	– 132,332
Colonial Corps	– 5,217
Army Service Corps	– 3,555
Ordnance Staff	– 920
Armourers	– 352
Medical Services	– 2,993
Total	– 218,554

A force reduction was in place due to the drawdown following the end of the war in South Africa.

CHAPTER 2 – ARMY ORGANISATIONS

Under the direction of the Defence Board (described in Chapter 1) management of the Services is the responsibility of the Single Service Boards; in the case of the Army the Army Board is the senior management directorate.

THE ARMY BOARD

The routine management of the Army is the responsibility of the Army Board the composition of which is as follows:

Secretary of State for Defence
Minister of State for the Armed Forces
Minister of State for Defence Procurement
Parliamentary Under Secretary of State and Minister of State for Defence Personnel and Veterans
Permanent Under Secretary
Second Permanent Under-Secretary of State (Secretary of the Army Board)
Chief of the General Staff
Assistant Chief of the General Staff
Adjutant General
Quartermaster General
Master General of the Ordnance
Commander-in-Chief Land Forces
The Army Board generally meets formally twice a year

Executive Committee of the Army Board (ECAB)

Attended by senior UK Army commanders, ECAB dictates the policy required for the Army to function efficiently and meet the aims required by the Defence Council and government. The Chief of the General Staff is the chairman of the Executive Committee of the Army Board.

Army Board and ECAB decisions are acted upon by the military staff at the various headquarters worldwide.

The Chief of the General Staff (CGS) is the officer responsible for the Army's contribution to the national defence effort. He maintains control through the commanders and the staff branches of each of the various army headquarters organisations.

CHIEF OF THE GENERAL STAFF – GENERAL SIR NICHOLAS CARTER

General Sir Nicholas Carter was commissioned into The Royal Green Jackets in 1978. At Regimental Duty he has served in Northern Ireland, Cyprus, Germany, Bosnia and Kosovo and commanded 2nd Battalion, The Royal Green Jackets from 1998 to 2000.

He has attended the Army Staff College, the Higher Command and Staff Course and the Royal College of Defence Studies.

At staff duties General Carter has been the Military Assistant to the Assistant Chief of the General Staff, Colonel Army Personnel Strategy, spent a year at HQ Land Command writing the Collective Training Study, and was Director of Army Resources and Plans. He also served as Director of Plans within the US-led Combined Joint Task Force

General Sir Nicholas Carter.
(MoD Crown Copyright 2015)

180 in Afghanistan and spent three months in the Cross Government Iraq Planning Unit prior to the invasion of Iraq in 2003.

General Carter commanded 20th Armoured Brigade in Iraq in 2004 and the 6th Division in Afghanistan in 2009/10. He was then appointed as the Director General Land Warfare before becoming the Army 2020 Project Team Leader. He served as the Deputy Commander International Security Assistance Force (DCOM ISAF) from October 2012 to August 2013, became Commander UK Land Forces in November 2013. He was appointed Chief of the General Staff in September 2014.

ARMY CHAIN-OF-COMMAND

The Army is commanded from the Headquarters at Andover and the Chief of the General Staff has the responsibility for preparing, training and equipping the forces under his command for operations worldwide.

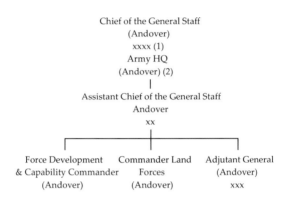

The Chief of the General Staff keeps a small 'forward headquarters' at the MoD in London.

Note:

(1) Stars denote the rank of the incumbent: xxxx General; xxx Lieutenant General; xx Major General; x Brigadier.

(2) From Mid 2009 HQ Land Forces has been located at Andover in Hampshire having moved from Wilton near Salisbury.

Commander Force Development and Capability (FDC) is responsible for training the Army, developing its overall capability, doctrine and sustainability. Previously known as Force Development and Training the Command was renamed in April 2014 as Force Development and Capability following the transfer of some of its responsibilities.

Commander Land Forces (CLF) is responsible for delivering and sustaining the Army's operational capability, whenever required. CLF commands almost all of the Army's fighting formations.

The Adjutant-General (AG) has the responsibility for all aspects of personnel policy from recruiting through career management and everyday personnel administration. In addition the AG's department is responsible for a whole mass of administrative functions such as legal and medical services that enables the system to function efficiently.

Headquarters Joint Forces Command (HQ JFC) at Northwood in Middlesex has an important input into command at the operational level. It is almost certain that any operation where Army units (or formations) are involved will be under the overall command of the Commander Joint Forces (CJF) and his subsidiary headquarters PJHQ.

STAFF BRANCHES

The Staff Branches that you would expect to find at every military headquarters from the Ministry of Defence (MoD) down to Brigade level are as follows:

Commander	– Usually a General (or Brigadier) who commands the formation.
Chief of Staff	– The officer who runs the headquarters on a day-to-day basis and who often acts as a second-in-command. Generally known as the COS.
Gl Branch	– Responsible for administration, personnel matters including manning, discipline and personal services.
G2 Branch	– Responsible for intelligence and security.
G3 Branch	– Responsible for operations including staff duties, exercise planning, training, operational requirements, combat development and tactical doctrine.
G4 Branch	– Logistics and quartering.
G5 Branch	– Plans.
G6 Branch	– Communications and IT.
G7 Branch	– Training.
G8 Branch	– Resource Management (finance and contracts).
G9 Branch	– CIMIC (Civil affairs and cooperation with other agencies).

Note: Commander – The senior officer in a large headquarters could be an Admiral, General or Air Marshal. The Army often refers to the commander as the GOC (General Officer Commanding), the Royal Air Force to the AOC (Air Officer Commanding) while the Royal Navy uses the term Flag Officer.

COMMANDER LAND FORCES (CLF)

CLF's Headquarters (HQ Land Forces) is located at Andover in Hampshire and commands almost 100 per cent of the Army's fighting capability. This capability is organised into four formations (plus London District) and are commanded by Major Generals.

CLF's role is to deliver and sustain the Army's operational capability, whenever required. For operations, CLF would deliver the required force package (drawn from formations or units under his command) to the Commander Joint Forces (CJF) for deployment worldwide.

Under his command CLF has almost all the Army's fighting equipment, including attack helicopters, Challenger 2 tanks, Warrior Infantry Fighting Vehicles, AS90 guns and the Guided Multi-Launched Rocket System (GMLRS). From late 2014 Lieutenant General James Everard is the Commander-in-Chief Land Forces.

Commander Land Forces (CLF) Structure

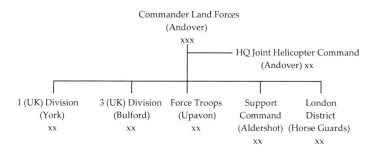

CLF has Operational Control of the Joint Helicopter Command (JHC).

CLF is also responsible for the drawdown and return to the UK of units from British Forces Germany (BFG). The majority of combat units will be stationed in the UK by the end of 2015.

Reports during mid 2015 suggest that CLF may establish another subsidiary headquarters to command formations assigned to the Field Army.

1 (UK) Division is 'The Adaptable Force' and 3 (UK) Division is the 'Reaction Force'.

The Reaction Force – 3 (United Kingdom) Division: This formation provides the high readiness elements that will undertake short notice contingency tasks and provides the conventional deterrence for Defence. Trained and equipped to undertake the full spectrum of intervention tasks, this force based upon three armoured infantry brigades under a divisional headquarters with associated support elements and an air assault brigade, will provide the building blocks for any future enduring operation. Given the high readiness nature of this force, it will comprise predominantly Regular Forces with about 10% being drawn from the Reserve Forces.

The Adaptable Force – 1 (United Kingdom Division): This formation comprises a pool of Regular and Reserve units organised during peace under seven regionally based infantry brigades for training and administrative purposes. For a given operation, force package could be selected from across the pool of Adaptable Force units. In addition to providing forces for operational tasks when required, the Adaptable Force will deliver the elements required for the Standing Commitments in areas such as Cyprus, Brunei and the Falkland Islands plus Ceremonial Duties in the UK and for UN commitments as they occur.

The Adaptable Force will also be capable of undertaking the following tasks:

◆ Overseas military capacity building – training and developing indigenous armies in order to strengthen their national defence capability and prevent future conflict.
◆ Military support to homeland resilience – this would include maintaining a contingent capability to deal with natural disasters and other tasks.
◆ Providing follow-on forces for future enduring operations. This would require the Adaptable Force to maintain institutional readiness at an appropriate level of training.

3RD (UNITED KINGDOM) DIVISION – THE REACTION FORCE

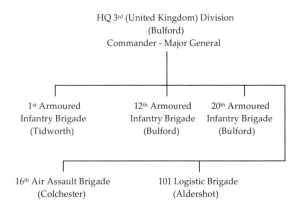

HQ 3rd (United Kingdom) Division
(Bulford)
Commander - Major General

| 1st Armoured Infantry Brigade (Tidworth) | 12th Armoured Infantry Brigade (Bulford) | 20th Armoured Infantry Brigade (Bulford) |

16th Air Assault Brigade (Colchester)   101 Logistic Brigade (Aldershot)

16 Air Assault Brigade – During operations either all, or some part of 16 Air Assault Brigade would most likely be under command of 3rd (United Kingdom) Division. The Order of Battle of this brigade is therefore given in this section.

During peace, the aviation elements of this brigade are under the command of the Joint Helicopter Command for support, administration and some aspects of training (See Joint Forces Chapter).

3 Commando Brigade – a Royal Naval formation, is available to support 3 (United Kingdom) Division if necessary. Details of the organisation of 3 Commando Brigade are given in the Miscellaneous Chapter.

3rd (United Kingdom Division) – Brigades

1st Armoured Infantry Brigade (Tidworth)

Unit	Role	Location	Affiliated reserve unit
Household Cavalry Regiment	Armoured Cavalry	Windsor	
Royal Tank Regiment	Armour (T56)	Tidworth	
1st Bn The Royal Regiment of Fusiliers	Armoured Infantry	Tidworth	
1st Bn The Mercian Regiment	Armoured Infantry	Bulford	
4th Bn The Rifles	Heavy Protected Mobility	Aldershot	

12th Armoured Infantry Brigade (Bulford)

Unit	Role	Location	Affiliated reserve unit
Royal Lancers	Armoured Cavalry	Catterick	
Kings Royal Hussars	Armour (T56)	Tidworth	Royal Wessex Yeomanry (R)
1st Bn The Yorkshire Regiment	Armoured Infantry	Warminster	
1st Bn The Royal Welsh	Armoured Infantry	Tidworth	
1st Bn The Scots Guards	Heavy Protected Mobility	Aldershot	

20th Armoured Infantry Brigade (Bulford)

Unit	Role	Location	Affiliated reserve unit
Royal Dragoon Guards	Armoured Cavalry	Catterick	
Queen's Royal Hussars	Armour (T56)	Tidworth	
5th Bn The Rifles	Armoured Infantry	Bulford	
1st Bn The Princess of Wales's Royal Regiment	Armoured Infantry	Bulford	
4th Bn The Royal Regiment of Scotland	Heavy Protected Mobility	Catterick	

16th Air Assault Brigade (Colchester)

Unit	Role	Location	Affiliated reserve unit
2nd Bn The Parachute Regiment	Parachute	Colchester	
2nd Bn The Parachute Regiment	Parachute	Colchester	4th Bn The Parachute Regiment (R) (Pudsey)
3rd Regiment Army Air Corps	Attack	Wattisham	6th Regiment Army Air Corps (R) (Bury St Edmunds)
4th Regiment Army Air Corps	Attack	Wattisham	
7th Parachute Regiment Royal Horse Artillery	Close Support	Colchester	
23rd Engineer Regiment (Air Assault)	Close Support	Woodbridge	
13 (Air Assault) Regiment Royal Logistic Corps	Logistic Support	Colchester	
16 (Air Assault) Medical Regiment	Medical Support	Colchester	
7th (Air Assault) Bn Royal Electrical and Mechanical Engineers	Helicopter Support	Wattisham	
12 (Air Assault Battery) Royal Artillery	Air Defence HVM	Thorny Island	
216 (Parachute) Signals Squadron	Comms	Colchester	

101 Logistic Brigade (Aldershot)

Unit	Role	Location	Affiliated reserve unit
1st Regiment RLC	Close Support	Bisector	
3rd Regiment RLC	Close Support	Aldershot	
4th Regiment RLC	Close Support	Abingdon	
9th Regiment RLC	Theatre Support	Hullavington	157 (Welsh) Transport Regiment RLC (R) (Cardiff)
10th Queens Own Gurkha Regiment RLC	Theatre Support	Aldershot	151 Transport Regiment RLC (R) (Croydon)
27th Regiment RLC	Theatre Support	Abingdon	154 (Scottish) Transport Regiment RLC (R) (Dunfermline) & 156 Supply Regiment RLC (R) (Liverpool)
1st Armoured Medical Regiment	Casevac	Tidworth	
4th Armoured Medical Regiment	Casevac	Aldershot	
5th Armoured Medical Regiment	Casevac	Tidworth	
3rd Armoured Close Support Bn REME	Close Support	Tidworth	105 Bn REME (R) (Bristol)

Unit	Role	Location	Affiliated reserve unit
4th Armoured Close Support Bn REME	Close Support	Tidworth	103 Bn REME (R) (Crawley)
6th Armoured Close Support Bn REME	Close Support	Tidworth	
5th Force Support Bn REME	Force Support	Cottesmore	

1ST (UNITED KINGDOM) DIVISION – THE ADAPTABLE FORCE

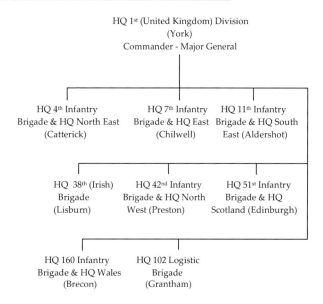

There are 7 x Brigades in the Adaptable Force (1 UK Division). This division has the responsibility of providing 2 x deployable brigades to supplement the 3 x operational brigades in the Reaction Force (3 UK Division). Therefore 3 x brigades in the Adaptable Force are intended to be kept up to strength and at a reasonably high level of readiness, as they are intended to combine to deliver 2 x deployable brigades. This structure will serve to achieve deployable brigades necessary to support an enduring operation overseas.

These three brigades earmarked for higher readiness are believed to be 4 (Catterick), 7 (Chilwell) and 51 (Edinburgh). The other 4 x brigades in the Adaptable Force will be at a lower state of readiness.

1st (United Kingdom Division) – Brigades

HQ 4th Infantry Brigade & HQ North East (Catterick)

Unit	Role	Location	Affiliated reserve unit
The Light Dragoons	Light Cavalry	Catterick	The Queens Own Yeomanry (R) (Newcastle)
2nd Bn the Yorkshire Regiment	Light Protected Mobility	Catterick	4th Bn The Yorkshire Regiment (R) (York)

Note: (R) denotes a Reserve unit.

HQ 7th Infantry Brigade & HQ East (Chilwell)

Unit	Role	Location	Affiliated reserve unit
1st Queen's Dragoon Guards	Light Cavalry	Swanton Morley	The Royal Yeomanry (R) (London)
2nd Bn the Royal Anglian Regiment	Light Protected Mobility	Cottesmore	3rd Bn the Royal Anglian Regiment (R) (Bury St Edmunds)
1st Bn the Royal Irish Regiment	Light Protected Mobility	Tern Hill	2nd Bn the Royal Irish Regiment (R) (Lisburn)
1st Bn The Royal Anglian Regiment	Light Role Infantry	Woolwich	3rd Bn the Princess of Wales's Royal Regiment (R) (Canterbury)

HQ 11th Infantry Brigade & HQ South East (Aldershot)

Unit	Role	Location	Affiliated reserve unit
1st Bn The Welsh Guards	Light Protected Mobility	Pirbright	3rd Bn The Royal Welsh (R) (Cardiff)
1st Bn the Grenadier Guards	Light Role Infantry	Aldershot	The London Regiment (R) (Westminster)
1st Bn The Royal Gurkha Rifles	Light Role Infantry	Shorncliffe	

HQ 38th Irish Brigade (Lisburn)

Unit	Role	Location	Affiliated reserve unit
1st Bn The Royal Regiment of Scotland	Light Role Infantry	Belfast	
2nd Bn The Rifles	Light Role Infantry	Ballykinler	7th Bn The Rifles (R) (Reading)

HQ 42nd Infantry Brigade & HQ North West (Preston)

Unit	Role	Location	Affiliated reserve unit
2nd Bn The Mercian Regiment	Light Role Infantry	Chester	4th Bn The Mercian Regiment (R) (Wolverhampton)
2nd Bn The Duke of Lancaster's Regiment	Light Role Infantry	Weeton	4th Bn the Duke of Lancaster's Regiment (R) (Preston)

HQ 51st Infantry Brigade & HQ Scotland (Edinburgh)

Unit	Role	Location	Affiliated reserve unit
The Royal Scots Dragoon Guards	Light Cavalry	Leuchars	The Scottish and North Irish Yeomanry
3rd Bn The Rifles	Light Protected Mobility	Edinburgh	5th Bn The Royal Regiment of Fusiliers (R) (Newcastle)
3rd Bn The Royal Regiment of Scotland	Light Protected Mobility	Fort George	7th Bn The Royal Regiment of Scotland (R) (Perth)
2nd Bn The Royal Regiment of Scotland	Light Role Infantry	Edinburgh	6th Bn The Royal Regiment of Scotland (R) (Glasgow)

HQ 160th Infantry Brigade (Brecon)

Unit	Role	Location	Affiliated reserve unit
1st Bn The Rifles	Light Role Infantry	Chepstow	6th Bn The Rifles (R) (Exeter

HQ 102 Logistic Brigade (Grantham)

Unit	Role	Location	Affiliated reserve unit
6 Regiment RLC	Force Logistic Regiment	Dishforth	150 Transport Regiment (R) (Hull)
7 Regiment RLC	Force Logistic Regiment	Cottesmore	158 Transport Regiment (R) (Peterborough)
159 Supply Regiment RLC (R)	Reserve Supply Regiment	Coventry	
2 Medical Regiment RAMC	Hybrid Regiment	North Luffenham	Comprises Reserves & Regulars
3 Medical Regiment RAMC	Hybrid Regiment	Preston	Comprises Reserves & Regulars
225 (Scottish) Medical Regiment RAMC (R)	Reserve Medical Regiment	Dundee	
254 (East of England) Medical Regiment RAMC (R)	Reserve Medical Regiment	Cambridge	
1 Close Support Battalion REME	Close Support	Catterick	102 Battalion REME (R) (Newton Aycliffe)

Unit	Role	Location	Affiliated reserve unit
2 Close Support Battalion REME	Close Support	Leuchars	106 Battalion REME (R) (Glascow)
104 Battalion REME (R)	Reserve Equipment Support	Northampton	

FORCE TROOPS COMMAND

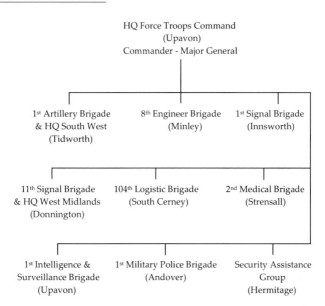

HQ 1st Artillery Brigade & HQ South West (Tidworth)

Unit	Role	Location	Affiliated reserve unit
1st Regiment Royal Horse Artillery	AS90 & GMLRS	Larkhill	
19th Regiment Royal Artillery	AS90 & GMLRS	Larkhill	
26th Regiment Royal Artillery	AS90 & GMLRS	Larkhill	
3rd Regiment Royal Horse Artillery	Light Gun	Harlow Hill	105th Regiment Royal Artillery (R) (Edinburgh)
4th Regiment Royal Artillery	Light Gun	Topcliffe	103rd (Lancashire Artillery Volunteers) Regiment Royal Artillery (R) (St Helens)

HQ 8th Engineer Brigade (Minley)

Unit	Role	Location	Affiliated reserve unit
25 (Close Support) Engineer Group (Minley)			
21 Engineer Regiment	Close Support	Catterick	Hybrid – Comprises Reserves & Regulars
22 Engineer Regiment	Close Support	Perham Down	
26 Engineer Regiment	Close Support	Perham Down	
32 Engineer Regiment	Close Support	Catterick	Hybrid – Comprises Reserves & Regulars
35 Engineer Regiment	Close Support	Perham Down	
12 (Force Support) Engineer Group (Wittering)			
36 Engineer Regiment	Force Support	Maidstone	75 Engineer Regiment (R) (Maidstone)
39 Engineer Regiment	Force Support	Kinloss	71 Engineer Regiment (R) (Leuchars)
20 Works Group	Force Support	Wittering	
170 (Infrastructure Support) Engineer Group (Chilwell)			
62 Works Group	Infrastructure Support	Chilwell	Hybrid – Comprises Reserves & Regulars
63 Works Group	Infrastructure Support	Chilwell	Hybrid – Comprises Reserves & Regulars
64 Works Group	Infrastructure Support	Chilwell	Hybrid – Comprises Reserves & Regulars
65 Works Group (R)	Infrastructure Suppor	Chilwell	Reserve Unit
66 Works Group	Infrastructure Support	Chilwell	Hybrid – Comprises Reserves & Regulars
Royal Monmouthshire Royal Engineers (R)	Infrastructure Support	Monmouth	Reserve Unit
29 Explosive Ordnance Disposal & Search Group (Aldershot)			
33 Engineer Regiment	Disposal & Search	Wimbish	Hybrid – Comprises Reserves & Regulars
101 Engineer Regiment	Disposal & Search	Wimbish	Hybrid – Comprises Reserves & Regulars
11 (EOD) Regiment RLC	Explosive Disposal	Didcot	
1 Military Working Dog Regiment	Search	North Luffenham	Hybrid – Comprises Reserves & Regulars

HQ 1st Signal Brigade (Innsworth)

Unit	Role	Location	Affiliated reserve unit
22 Signal Regiment	ARRC & JRRF Support	Stafford	
30 Signal Regiment	ARRC & JRRF Support	Bramcote	
ARRC Support Battalion	ARRC Support	Innsworth	
299 Signal Squadron	Special Communications	Bletchley	

HQ 11th Signal Brigade & HQ West Midlands (Donnington)

Unit	Role	Location	Affiliated reserve unit
1 Signal Regiment	Close Support	Stafford	
16 Signal Regiment	Close Support	Stafford	
21 Signal Regiment	Close Support	Colerne	39 Signal Regiment (R) (Bristol)
2 Signal Regiment	General Support	York	32 Signal Regiment (R) (Glasgow)
3 Signal Regiment	General Support	Bulford	
2 Signal Group (Donnington)			
10 Signal Regiment	Specialist Support	Corsham	
14 Signal Regiment	Specialist Electronics	Brawdy	
15 Signal Regiment	Information Support	Blandford	
32 Signal Regiment (R)	Reserve Unit	Glasgow	Supports 2 Signal Regiment
37 Signal Regiment (R)	Reserve Unit	Reddich	
39 Signal Regiment	Reserve Unit	Bristol	Supports 21 Signal Regiment
71 Signal Regiment (R)	Reserve Unit	Bexleyheath	

HQ 104th Logistic Brigade (South Cerney)

Unit	Role	Location	Affiliated reserve unit
17 Port & Maritime Regiment RLC	Port & Maritime	Marchwood	165 Port and Enabling Regiment RLC (R) (Plymouth)
29 Regiment RLC	Postal, Courier & Movements	South Cerney	162 Postal & Courier Regiment RLC (R) (Nottingham)
152 Fuel Support Regiment RLC (R)	Reserve Unit	Belfast	
167 Catering Support Regiment RLC (R)	Reserve Unit	Grantham	
2 Operational Support Group RLC (R)	Reserve Unit	Grantham	
101 Battalion REME	Reserve Unit	Wrexham	

HQ 2nd Medical Brigade (Strensall)

Unit	Role	Location	Affiliated reserve unit
22 Field Hospital	Major Medical Facility	Aldershot	202 (Midlands) Field Hospital (R) (Birmingham); 207 (Manchester) Field Hospital (R) (Manchester); 208 (Liverpool) Field Hospital (R) (Liverpool)
33 Field Hospital	Major Medical Facility	Gosport	203 (Welsh) Field Hospital (R) (Cardiff); 243 (Wessex) Field Hospital (R) (Bristol); 256 (City of London) Field Hospital (R) (Walworth)
34 Field Hospital	Major Medical Facility	Strensall	201 (Northern) Field Hospital (R) (Newcastle-upon-Tyne); 204 (North Irish) Field Hospital (R) (Belfast); 205 (Scottish) Field Hospital (R) (Glasgow); 212 (Yorkshire) Field Hospital (R) (Sheffield)
306 Hospital Support Regiment (R)	Reserve Unit	Strensall	
335 Medical Evacuation Regiment (R)	Reserve Unit	Strensall	
Operational HQ Support Group (R)	Reserve Unit	Strensall	

HQ 1st Intelligence and Surveillance Brigade (Upavon)

Unit	Role	Location	Affiliated reserve unit
5 Regiment Royal Artillery	Surveillance & Target Acquisition	Catterick	Honourable Artillery Company (City of London)
32 Regiment Royal Artillery	Unmanned Air Systems	Larkhill	
47 Regiment Royal Artillery	Unmanned Air Systems	Larkhill	104 Regiment Royal Artillery (R) (Newport)
14 Signal Regiment (EW)	Electronic Warfare	St Athan	
1 Military Intelligence Battalion	Military Intelligence	Catterick	3 Military Intelligence Battalion (R) (Hackney); 5 Military Intelligence Battalion (R) (Edinburgh);
2 Military Intelligence Battalion	Military Intelligence	Upavon	6 Military Intelligence Battalion (R) (Manchester);
4 Military Intelligence Battalion	Military Intelligence	Bulford	7 Military Intelligence Battalion (R) (Bristol);

Unit	Role	Location	Affiliated reserve unit
Land Intelligence Fusion Centre	Military Intelligence	Bristol	Specialist Military Intelligence Group (R) (Hermitage)
Defence Specialist Cultural Unit	Cultural Intelligence Aspects	Hermitage	
Military Stabilisation Support Group	Specialist Support	Hermitage	Media Operations Group (R) (London)
15 Psychological Operations Group	Specialist Support	Hermitage	

77 Brigade – Formed during 2015 this Brigade brings together the following units under one headquarters:

15 Psychological Operations Group (15 POG) – Psychological Warfare.

Military Stabilisation Support Group (MSSG) - Stabilisation and Conflict Prevention.

Media Operations Group (MOG) – Media Operations.

Security Capacity Building Team (SCBT) – Military Capacity Building.

We are still trying to identify 77 Brigade's location in the chain-of-command and it is possible that it comes under the overall command of Force Troops Command.

HQ 1st Military Police Brigade

Unit	Role	Location	Affiliated reserve unit
1 Regiment Royal Military Police	Police Duties	Andover	Hybrid Unit
3 Regiment Royal Military Police	Police Duties	Bulford	Hybrid Unit
4 Regiment Royal Military Police	Police Duties	Aldershot	Hybrid Unit
Special Investigation Branch Royal Military Police	Special Investigations	Bulford	Hybrid Unit
Military Corrective Training Centre	Rehabilitation & Training	Colchester	Hybrid Unit
Specialist Operations Unit Royal Military Police	Specialist Operations	Longmoor	

SUPPORT COMMAND

Support Command provides real time support to the whole of the UK Army and is the command headquarters for the UK Garrisons, also providing support and commands the UK detachments in Brunei and Nepal. The Command provides the link to the Land Forces Reserves and Cadets.

Support Command is also the Army's link to the civilian community ensuring that the requisite support is available for any unforeseen emergencies. In addition, Support Command acts as the focal point for the Armed Forces Covenant ensuring that wherever possible the aims of the Covenant are implemented throughout the UK.

The UK Regional Headquarters are co-located with a number of brigade headquarters as follows:

Regional Headquarters	Location	Co-located with
HQ West Midlands	Donnington	HQ 11 Signal Brigade
HQ North West	Preston	HQ 42 Brigade
HQ Scotland	Edinburgh	HQ 51 Brigade
HQ Wales	Brecon	HQ 160 Brigade
HQ South West	Tidworth	HQ 1 Artillery Brigade
HQ North East	Catterick	HQ 4 Infantry Brigade
HQ East	Chilwell	HQ 7 Infantry Brigade
HQ South East	Aldershot	HQ 11 Infantry Brigade

Support Command is also responsible for support to the following garrisons:

Aldershot Garrison
Colchester Garrison

Joint Helicopter Command (JHC)

The Joint Helicopter Command's primary role is to deliver and sustain effective Battlefield Helicopter and Air Assault assets, operationally capable under all environmental conditions, in order to support UK's defence missions and tasks. JHC major formations are as follows:

- All Army Aviation Units
- RAF Support Helicopter Force
- Commando Helicopter Force
- 16 Air Assault Brigade
- Combat Support Units
- Combat Service Support Units
- Joint Helicopter Command and Standards Wing

There is more detail relating to the JHC in the Joint Forces Chapter.

LAND EQUIPMENT (LE)

The Land Equipment Directorate (under the command of Defence Equipment and Support) exists to provide front line support and 'through life' equipment solutions for land operations. LE is composed of five major groups with each group having a number of subsidiary teams providing specific support to various group activities. Director Land Equipment (DLE) is responsible for the operations of these major groups which are:

Combat Tracks Group (CTG)

Systems Team (ST); Combat Tracks Group Platforms Team; Armoured Vehicle Support Transformation Team; Artillery Systems Team (AST); Platforms Team (PT); The Medium Armoured Tracks Team (MATT).

Combat Wheels Group (CWG)

Protected Mobility Team (PMT); Manoeuvre Support Team (MST); Utility Vehicle Team (UVT).

General Support Group (GSG)
Battlefield Utilities Unit (BFU); Deployable Support and Test Equipment Team (DS&TE); Expeditionary Campaign Infrastructure (ECI); General Support Vehicles (GSV); Service Provision (SP).

Individual Capability Group (ICG)
Integrated Soldier Systems Executive (ISSE); Dismounted Soldier Systems Team (DSST); Surveillance, Target Acquisition and Night Observation (STANO); Light Weapons, Photographic & Batteries Team (LWPBT).

Joint and Battlefield Trainers; Simulation & Synthetic Environments Group (JBTSE)

Other areas and tasks
Although Land Command is not responsible for running operations in Northern Ireland, the Former Yugoslavia, Afghanistan, Sierra Leone, Cyprus, the Falkland Islands and Iraq (a responsibility of PJHQ), it will provide the operational troops for these areas.

Some 500 troops are involved at any one time in MoD -sponsored equipment trials, demonstrations and exhibitions. Public Duties in London take up two/three battalions at any one time. All troops not otherwise operationally committed are also available to provide Military Aid to the Civil Authorities (MACA) in the United Kingdom.

ARMOURED INFANTRY BRIGADE ORGANISATION

The major UK operational brigades are under the command of 3 (United Kingdom) Division (The Reaction Force) and would be structured according to the task. The following diagram provides an illustration of the possible configuration of a UK Armoured Infantry Brigade on high intensity operations and includes units that could be assigned from both 2 (United Kingdom) Division (The Adaptable Force) and Force Troops Command.

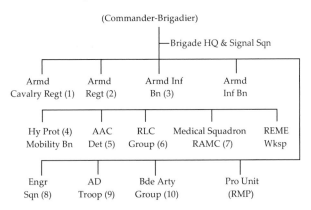

Notes:

(1) Armoured Cavalry Regiment with 3 x Sabre Squadrons each with 16 CVR(T) (being replaced with Scout). Plus 1 x Command and Support Squadron.

(2) Armoured Regiment with 56 x Challenger 2 MBT. Comprises 3 x Sabre Squadrons each with 18 x Challenger 2. Plus 1 x Command and Reconnaissance Squadron with 2 x Challenger 2 and 8 x CVR(T) to be replaced with 8 x Scout.

(3) Armoured Infantry Battalion with 45 x Warrior AIFV. Comprises 3 x Rifle Companies each with 14 x Warrior. Plus 1 x Support Company and 1 x HQ Company with 3 x Warrior.

(4) Heavy Protected Mobility Battalion with 45 x Mastiff. Comprises 3 x Rifle Companies each with 14 x Mastiff. Plus 1 x Support Company and 1 x HQ Company with 3 x Mastiff.

(5) Army Air Corps Detachment possibly drawn from 16 Air Assault Brigade. May be Lynx, Wildcat or Apache or a mix of both depending upon the mission.

(6) Royal Logistic Corps Group to stockpile and move essential supplies forward to the combat units.

(7) Brigade Medical Squadron that could comprise armoured or wheeled ambulances.

(8) Engineer Squadron that could include an armoured engineer detachment.

(9) Air Defence Detachment if required. Could be HVM mounted on CVR(T).

(10) Brigade Artillery Group. Size and composition dependent upon the mission but could be 105mm Light Gun or 155mm AS90 or 227mm GMLRS or a mix. Supported by UAVs and various artillery intelligence and artillery support elements.

Possible Brigade Totals:

56 x Challenger MBT (Possibly)
90 x Warrior AIFV
45 x Mastiff
300 x AFV 432/CVR(T)/ Spartan Armoured Vehicles (approximately)
8 x Light Gun/ AS 90
Approx 5,000 personnel

This Brigade could provide the HQs for three Battlegroups.

THE BATTLEGROUP

A division usually consists of two or three brigades. These brigades are further sub-divided into smaller formations known as battlegroups. The battlegroup is the basic building brick of the fighting formations.

A battlegroup is commanded by a Lieutenant Colonel and the infantry battalion or armoured regiment that he commands, provides the command and staff element of the formation. The battlegroup is then structured according to task, with the correct mix of infantry, armour and supporting arms.

The battlegroup organisation is very flexible and the units assigned can be quickly regrouped to cope with a change in the threat. A typical battlegroup fighting a defensive battle on the FEBA (Forward Edge of the Battle Area), and based upon an organisation of one armoured squadron and two mechanised companies, could contain about 600 men, 18 tanks and about 80 other armoured vehicles.

The number of battlegroups in a division and a brigade could vary according to the task the formation has been given. As a general rule you could expect a division to have as many as 12 battlegroups and a brigade to have up to three or four. The following diagram shows a possible organisation for an armoured battlegroup in either 1(UK) Armd Div or 3(UK) Div.
Notes:

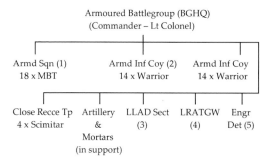

(1) Armoured Squadron
(2) Armoured Company
(3) LLAD-Low Level Air Defence – HVM
(4) LRATGW – Long Range Anti Tank Guided Weapons
(5) Engineer Detachment.

COMPANY GROUPS/TASK GROUP

Each battlegroup will operate with smaller organisations called task groups or company groups. These groups which are commanded by a Major will be allocated tanks, armoured personnel carriers and supporting elements depending upon the aim of the formation. Supporting elements such as air defence, anti-tank missiles, fire support and engineer expertise ensure that the company group/task group is a balanced all arms grouping, tailored specifically for the task. In general a battlegroup similar to the one in the previous diagram could be expected to form three company groups.

A possible Company Group/Task Group organisation could resemble the following diagram:
Notes:

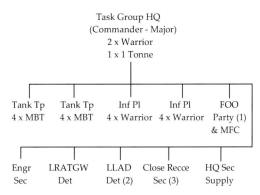

(1) Forward Observation Officer (FOO – usually a Captain) with his party from the Royal Artillery. This FOO will be in direct communication with a battery of six/eight guns and the Artillery Fire Direction Centre. The MFC is usually a sergeant from an infantry battalion mortar platoon who may have up to six mortar tubes on call. In most Combat Teams both the FOO and MFC will travel in close proximity to the Combat Team Commander
(2) Possibly 2 x Spartan with HVM
(3) Possibly 2 x Scimitar.

BRITISH FORCES GERMANY (BFG)

The 2010 SDSR stated that there was "no longer any operational requirement" to base UK forces in the country. Thus, the government decided to accelerate the re-basing of military personnel from Germany with the aim of returning half of the more than 20,000 personnel to the UK by early 2015. The withdrawal tempo was increased when the Army Basing Plan was announced in March 2013, a plan that required all but 4,400 troops should return to the UK by late 2016. The remaining personnel (mainly logistic and administrative) are earmarked to return to the UK by the end of 2018. Latest early 2015 reports suggest that the withdrawal of personnel from Germany is moving faster than originally planned.

The HQ of 1st (United Kingdom) Division moved to the UK (York) in early 2015 and this will be the first time since early 1945 that the UK will not have a divisional headquarters in Germany. At the height of the Cold War the UK had four divisional headquarters in Germany.

HQ 7 Armoured Brigade moved back to the UK (early 2015) where it was re-designated as the 7 Infantry Brigade (based in Chilwell) under the command of 1st (United Kingdom) Division. This will leave one Brigade Headquarters (20 Armoured Brigade) in Germany until late 2016 when the Headquarters will move to Bulford and come under the command of 3 (United Kingdom) Division.

The headquarters of British Forces Germany has moved from Rheindahlen to Bielefeld and 372 staff are being relocated in an effort to cut down on the £55 million cost of running the old HQ at Rheindahlen.

The estimated cost to the public purse of maintaining and operating bases in Germany in 2010–11 was approximately £190 million. It is believed that the previous net injection to the German economy from the UK presence in Germany was around £700 million and following the return of troops from Germany, a similar sum will be injected back into the UK economy.

NORTHERN IRELAND

On 1 August 2007 Op BANNER, the military support to the civilian police in Northern Ireland ended and despite some recent activity by resurgent Irish Republican factions the Province remains relatively peaceful.

The worst year for terrorist violence was in 1972 when 131 service personnel were killed and 578 wounded. At one stage in 1972 there were over 30,000 service personnel in the Province supported by another 10,000 police. Overall 763 members of the armed forces and 303 other members of the security forces lost their lives as a result of the violence in Northern Ireland.

By early 2016 it is believed that the service strength in Northern Ireland will be approximately 2,000 personnel of whom about 95 per cent will be from the Army – a figure similar to the personnel strength in 1969 before the current 'troubles' began. The core of the peacetime garrison is centred around facilities at Ballykinler, Belfast (Holywood), and Lisburn.

On 1 January 2009 HQ Northern Ireland was disbanded and HQ 38 (Irish) Brigade (Thiepval Barracks, Lisburn) became the Province's single headquarters.

CHAPTER 3 – INTERNATIONAL COMMITMENTS

"The UK belongs to more international organisations than any other country. We are party to 14,000 treaties of various kinds and magnitudes. We have been an avowed nuclear weapons state since 1952, the third (after the USA and Russia) to achieve that status. We are a permanent member of the United Nations Security Council. We are one of three states with global intelligence reach (the other two are the United States and Russia—with China coming up fast) thanks to the 1946 US-UK Communications Agreement. The UK possesses other special capabilities: for example, we are one of a small number of countries that is a top-of-the-range 'submarine nation', capable of building SSN (nuclear powered attack submarines) and SBN (nuclear powered submarines capable of launching ballistic missiles with nuclear warheads)."

From written evidence for the House of Commons Defence Committee Report (Towards the next Defence and Security Review – December 2013) from Lord Henesy of Nympsfield, FBA, Atle Professor of Contemporary British History, University of London.

THE NORTH ATLANTIC TREATY ORGANISATION

The United Kingdom is a member of NATO (North Atlantic Treaty Organisation) and the majority of the UK's military operations are conducted in association with the forces of NATO allies.

The following nations are members of the NATO Alliance.

Albania, Belgium, Bulgaria, Canada, Croatia, Czech Republic, Denmark, Estonia, France, Germany, Greece, Hungary, Iceland, Italy, Latvia, Lithuania, Luxembourg, Netherlands, Norway, Poland, Portugal, Romania, Spain, Slovakia, Slovenia, Turkey, United Kingdom, United States.

Between them these 28 nations probably have the following totals of personnel and equipment that could be mobilised in an emergency:

◆ 3.4 million active personnel (about 1.7 million army)
◆ 22 nuclear armed submarines
◆ 13 aircraft carriers
◆ 122 frigates
◆ 3,800 combat aircraft
◆ 9,400 main battle tanks
◆ 10,800 infantry fighting vehicles

During 2014 NATO nations spent a total of US$990 billion on defence. The United States spent US$581 billion with the remaining 27 nations contributing US$409 billion.

Article V of the 1948 Washington Treaty commits each NATO member state to consider an armed attack against one state to be an armed attack against all states. Non-Article 5 operations are operations that are not concerned with collective defence.

The current NATO concept is for forces that are able to rapidly deploy to crisis areas and remain sustainable, be it within or outside NATO's territory, in support of both Article 5 and Non-Article 5 operations. This concept has its largest impact on land forces. Maritime and air forces are by nature already highly mobile and deployable and are often at a high state of readiness. Most of NATO's land based assets, however, have been rather static during the past 20 years and have had limited (strategic) mobility. In the current structure, land forces should also become highly deployable and should have tactical and strategic mobility. The mobility requirements will have great impact on the Alliance's transport and logistic resources (sea, land and air based). The need for quick reaction requires a certain amount of highly trained forces that are readily available. Further, interoperability (the possibility of forces to co-operate together with other units) and sustainability (the possibility to continue an operation for an extended period of time) are essential in the current force structure.

Following a reorganisation in 2003 NATO consists of two Commands. The first is ACT (Allied Command Transformation) with headquarters at Norfolk, Virginia (USA) and the second is ACO (Allied Command Operations), with its headquarters at Mons in Belgium. NATO operations in which the United Kingdom is a participant would almost certainly be as part of a coalition force under the command and control of Allied Command Operations (ACO).

The current Supreme Allied Commander Europe (SACEUR) is General Philip M Breedlove. SACEUR, (a US officer) who is responsible for the overall command of NATO military operations and conducts the necessary military operational planning, including the identification of forces required for the mission and requesting these forces from NATO countries, as authorised by the North Atlantic Council and as directed by NATO's Military Committee.

The Deputy Supreme Allied Commander Europe (DSACEUR) is a UK officer General Sir Adrian Bradshaw who assumed the post in March 2014.

SACEUR – GENERAL PHILIP M. BREEDLOVE

General Philip M. Breedlove assumed duties as Supreme Allied Commander, Europe and Commander of US European Command in May 2013.

General Breedlove was commissioned in 1977 as a distinguished graduate of Georgia Tech's ROTC (see note) program and was raised in Forest Park, Georgia. A fighter pilot by trade, General Breedlove is a Command Pilot with over 3,500 flying hours primarily in the F-16. He has flown combat missions in Operation Joint Forge supporting the peacekeeping operation in Bosnia and Operation Joint Guardian to implement the peace settlement in Kosovo.

From 1993–1994, General Breedlove commanded the 80th Fighter Squadron in Kunsan AB, South Korea. From 1997–1999, he commanded the 27th Operations Group at Cannon AFB, New Mexico. From 2000–2001, he was the commander of the 8th Fighter Wing, Kunsan AB, South Korea. From 2002–2004, he was the commander of the 56th Fighter Wing at Luke AFB, Arizona followed by another wing command from 2004 -2005 of the 31st Fighter Wing at Aviano AB, Italy. From 2008–2009, General Breedlove commanded 3rd Air Force, Ramstein AB, Germany. From 2012–2013, he was Commander, US Air Forces in Europe; Commander, US Air Forces Africa; Commander Headquarters Allied Air Command, Ramstein; and Director, Joint Air Power Competence Centre, Kalkar Germany.

In addition to General Breedlove's command assignments he has served in a variety of senior leadership positions for the US Air Force including: the senior military assistant to the Secretary of the Air Force; the Vice Director for Strategic Plans and Policy on the Joint Staff; the Deputy Chief of Staff for Operations, Plans and Requirements for Headquarters US Air Force; and Vice Chief of Staff of the US Air Force.

General Breedlove earned a Master of Science degree in Aeronautical Technology from Arizona State University and a Master's degree in National Security Studies from the National War College in 1995.

General Breedlove also attended the Massachusetts Institute of Technology in 2002 as a Seminar XXI Fellow.

He is a distinguished graduate of both Squadron Officer School and Air Command and Staff College.

General Breedlove holds various decorations and awards, including the Distinguished Service Medal, the Defence Superior Service Medal and four awards of the Legion of Merit.

Note: The Reserve Officers' Training Corps (ROTC) is a college-based program for training commissioned officers of the United States armed forces.

General Breedlove. (US Air Force Image)

NATO COMMANDS

There are two major NATO Commands:

◆ Allied Command Operations (ACO)
◆ Allied Command Transformation (ACT)

Allied Command Operations (ACO)

Allied Command Operations, with its headquarters, SHAPE, near Mons, Belgium, is responsible for all Alliance operations. The levels beneath SHAPE have been significantly streamlined, with a reduction in the number of headquarters. The operational level consists of two standing Joint Force Commands (JFCs) one in Brunssum, the Netherlands, and one in Naples, Italy – both of these headquarters can conduct operations from their static locations or provide a land-based Combined Joint Task Force (CJTF) headquarters, and a robust but more limited standing Joint Headquarters (JHQ), in Lisbon, Portugal, from which a deployable sea-based CJTF HQ capability can be drawn. The current organisation of Allied Command Operations is as follows:

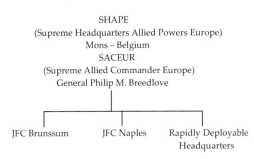

SHAPE
(Supreme Headquarters Allied Powers Europe)
Mons – Belgium
SACEUR
(Supreme Allied Commander Europe)
General Philip M. Breedlove

| JFC Brunssum | JFC Naples | Rapidly Deployable Headquarters |

Component Headquarters at the tactical level

The component or tactical level consists of six Joint Force Component Commands (JFCCs), which will provide service-specific land, maritime, or air expertise to the operational level. Although these component commands will be available for use in any operation, they will be subordinated to one of the Joint Force Commanders.

Joint Forces Command – Brunssum

HQ JFC Brunssum

| JFCC Air | JFCC Maritime | JFCC Land |
| Ramstein – Germany | Northwood - UK | Heidelberg - Germany |

Joint Forces Command – Naples

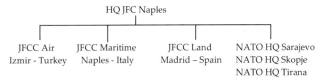

HQ JFC Naples

JFCC Air	JFCC Maritime	JFCC Land	NATO HQ Sarajevo
Izmir - Turkey	Naples - Italy	Madrid – Spain	NATO HQ Skopje
			NATO HQ Tirana

Static Air Operations Centres (CAOC)

In addition to the above component commands there are four static Combined Air Operations Centres with two more deployable as follows:

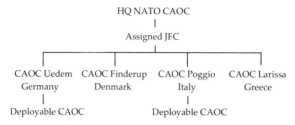

As the deployable CAOCs will need to exercise their capability to mobilise and deploy, the current facilities at Torrejon Air Base in Spain will probably be the primary site for training and exercising in that region. A small NATO air facility support staff is stationed at Torrejon to support this capability.

NATO Airborne Early Warning Force (NAEWF) – The NATO Airborne Early Warning Force provides air surveillance and command and control for all NATO commands. It is based in Geilenkirchen, Germany, and Waddington, United Kingdom.

DEPLOYABLE NATO RESPONSE FORCES AVAILABLE:

Response Forces – Maritime

There are five High Readiness Forces (Maritime) Headquarters which can command and control assigned naval forces up to the level of a NATO naval task force made up of a number of warships. Each headquarters provides the Maritime Component Command for the NATO Response Force on a rotational basis. SACEUR has available:

- Headquarters Commander Italian Maritime Forces.
- Headquarters Commander Spanish Maritime Forces.
- Headquarters Commander United Kingdom Maritime Forces.
- Headquarters Commander French Maritime Forces.
- Headquarters Naval Striking and Support Forces NATO.

Response Forces – Air

There are three deployable High Readiness Forces (Air) Headquarters provided by the United Kingdom, France and Germany, which also provide the Air Component Command for the NATO Response Force on a rotational basis.

Response Forces – Land

There are nine Land Forces Headquarters under operational command capable of graduated response. These headquarters are capable of providing support for NATO operations on a rotational basis:

- ARRC Headquarters in the United Kingdom as framework nation.
- Rapid Deployable German-Netherlands Corps Headquarters based on the 1st German-Netherlands Corps Headquarters in Münster, Germany.
- Rapid Deployable Italian Corps Headquarters based on the Italian Rapid Reaction Corps Headquarters in Solbiate Olona, near Milan, Italy.
- Rapid Deployable Spanish Corps Headquarters based on the Spanish Corps Headquarters in Valencia, Spain.
- Rapid Deployable Turkish Corps Headquarters based on the 3rd Turkish Corps Headquarters near Istanbul, Turkey.

- EUROCORPS in Strasbourg, France, sponsored by Belgium, France, Germany, Luxembourg and Spain. EUROCORPS has a different international military status than the other five headquarters but has signed a technical arrangement with Allied Command Operations and can also be committed to NATO missions.
- French Rapid Reaction Corps based in Lille, France.
- NATO Deployable Corps Greece based in Thessaloniki, Greece.
- Multinational Corps Northeast based in Szczecin, Poland

VERY HIGH READINESS JOINT TASK FORCE (VJTF)

During the 2014 NATO summit in Wales NATO leaders agreed to establish a Very High Readiness 'Spearhead Force' to enhance security in NATO border areas and increase the capability of NATO Response Forces. At a further meeting in February 2015 NATO Defence Ministers confirmed a plan to create a high readiness land brigade called the Very High Readiness Joint Task Force (VJTF).

The VJTF will be able to deploy at very short notice to counter threats against NATO sovereignty. It will consist of a land brigade numbering around 5,000 troops, supported by air, sea and special forces. The VJTF would be supported by two more land brigades as a 'rapid reinforcement capability' in the case of a major crisis. In total the enhanced NATO Response Force will amount to around 30,000 troops.

The core of the VJTF will consist of up to five manoeuvre battalions with support elements. Leading elements of the force will be capable of deploying within 48 hours and leadership of the VJTF will be on a rotational basis, with lead nations being the UK, France, Germany, Italy Poland and Spain.

An interim capability has already been established and exercises and training started in 2015.

THE ALLIED RAPID REACTION CORPS (ARRC)

The concept of the Allied Rapid Reaction Corps was initiated by the NATO Defence Planning Committee in May 1991. The concept called for the creation of Rapid Reaction Forces to meet the requirements of future challenges within the alliance. The ARRC provides the Supreme Allied Commander Europe (SACEUR) with a multinational corps sized grouping in which forward elements can be ready to deploy within 14 days (lead elements and reconnaissance parties at very short notice).

As stated by SHAPE the mission of the ARRC is: "HQ ARRC, as a High Readiness Force (Land) HQ, is prepared to deploy under NATO, EU or coalition auspices to a designated area, to undertake combined and joint operations across the operational spectrum as:

- a Corps HQ
- a Land Component HQ
- a Land Component HQ in command of the NATO Response Force
- a Joint Task Force HQ for Land-centric operations

These formations will enable support for crisis support management options or the sustainment of ongoing operations."

As NATO's most experienced High Readiness Force (Land) Headquarters the ARRC is actively engaged in the NATO Response Force (NRF) transformation initiative. Currently the ARRC trains for missions across the spectrum of operations from deterrence and crisis management to regional conflict.

Headquarters ARRC is located in Innsworth (UK) with a peace-time establishment of about 400 personnel. It comprises staff from all the contributing nations. As the Framework Nation, the UK provides the infrastructure, administrative support, communications and 60 per cent of the staff. HQ ARRC moved from Rheindahlen (Germany) to Innsworth in the UK during the summer of 2010.

The Commander (COMARRC) and Chief of Staff are UK 3 Star and 2 Star Generals and the Deputy Commander is an Italian 2 Star General. The other appointments, as with the training and exercise costs, are shared among the contributing nations.

Outline Composition of the ARRC Headquarters (Allied Command Europe Rapid Reaction Corps)

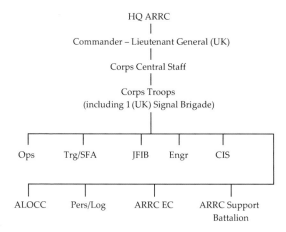

Abbreviations: Ops – Operations; Trg – Training; SFA – Security Force Assistance; JFIB – Joint Fires & Influence; Engr – Engineer; CIS – Command Information Systems; ALOCC – Airland Operations Coordination Cell; ARRC EC – Allied Rapid Reaction Corps Enabling Command.

Although having no permanently assigned formations. HQ ARRC has five Divisions affiliated for operations and training.

1st UK Division	– HQ York
3rd UK Division	– HQ Bulford
1st Danish Division	– HQ Haderslev (Denmark)
Acqui Division	– HQ San Giorgio a Cremano (Italy)
1st Panzer Division	– HQ Hanover (Germany)

The operational organisation, composition and size of the ARRC would depend on the type of crisis, area of crisis, its political significance, and the capabilities and availability of lift assets, the distances to be covered and the infrastructure capabilities of the nation receiving assistance. It is considered that a four-division ARRC would be the maximum employment structure.

The main British contribution to the ARRC is 3 (UK) Armoured Division. In addition, and in times of tension the assets of 1 (UK) Division could be allocated together with the assets of 16 Air Assault Brigade and 3 Commando Brigade. In total, we believe that should the need arise some 30,000 British soldiers could be assigned to the ARRC together with substantial numbers of Regular Army Reservists and some formed Reserve Units.

Command Posts and Deployment
Due to the need to be able to respond flexibly to the whole range of potential operations, HQ ARRC has developed the capability for rapidly deployable and modular HQs. Deployment begins with the despatch of a Forward Liaison and Reconnaissance Group (FLRG) within 48 hours of the order to move being given.

Within four days the key enablers from 1 (UK) Signal Bde would be within theatre and three days later HQ ARRC Forward and HQ Rear Support Command (RSC) Forward – as required – could be established. The forward-deployed HQs are light, mobile and C-130 transportable. While there is a standard 'default' setting for personnel numbers, the actual staff composition is 'tailored' to the task and can vary from approximately 50 to 150 staff, depending on the requirement. The 'in-theatre' task would then be supported by the remainder of the staff, using sophisticated 'Reachback' techniques and equipment.

The Early Entry HQs are capable of sustained independent operations if required but can also be used as enablers if it is decided to deploy the full HQ ARRC. This deployment concept has been tested and evaluated on several exercises and has proven its worth. In parallel, HQ ARRC is continuously looking to make all of its HQs lighter and more survivable.

ALLIED COMMAND TRANSFORMATION (ACT)

Allied Command Transformation, with its headquarters in Norfolk, US, has the responsibility for the transformation of NATO's military capabilities. In doing so, ACT enhances training, improves capabilities, tests and develops doctrines and conducts experiments to assess new concepts. It also facilitates the dissemination and introduction of new concepts and promotes interoperability. There is an ACT Staff Element in Belgium primarily for resource and defence planning issues.

ACT commands the Joint Warfare Centre in Norway, a Joint Force Training Centre in Poland and the Joint Analysis and Lessons Learned Centre in Portugal. ACT Headquarters will also supervise the Undersea Research Centre in La Spezia, Italy and the NATO School at Oberammergau in Germany. There are direct linkages between ACT, Alliance schools and NATO agencies, as well as the US Joint Forces Command. In addition, a number of nationally or multinationally-sponsored Centres of Excellence focused on transformation in specific military fields support ACT.

EUROPEAN UNION

The following 28 countries are members of the European Union:

Austria; Belgium; Bulgaria; Cyprus; Croatia; Czech Republic; Denmark; Estonia; Finland; France; Germany; Greece; Hungary; Ireland; Italy; Latvia; Lithuania; Luxembourg; Malta; Netherlands; Poland; Portugal; Romania; Slovakia; Slovenia; Spain; Sweden; United Kingdom.

Council of the European Union
The Council of the European Union represents the governments of the Union's 28 nations in the legislature of the European Union. Each nation provides one minister whose portfolio includes the subject being discussed. In the case of defence – the ministers responsible would attend (in company with their own National European Commissioner). The other legislative body is the European Parliament.

European Political and Security Committee (PSC)
The PSC keeps track of the requirements of the EU's Common Foreign and Security Policy and defines how those requirements can be incorporated into the Common Security and Defence Policy. Reporting to the Council of the EU the PSC is composed of EU Ambassadors who have the responsibility for providing a coherent response to a crisis or emergency.

European Common Security and Defence Policy (CSDP)
The EU CSDP is the successor to what used to be known as the European Security and Defence Policy (ESDP). As such the CSDP is an important component of the EU's Foreign and Security Policy (CFSP) and provides the framework for policy and plans relating to all aspects of European defence and security.

CSDP OBJECTIVES – EU HELSINKI HEADLINE GOAL 2010

The EU has adopted the following illustrative scenarios which form the basis for force planning to meet the EU Helsinki Headline Goal 2010 proposals:

◆ Stabilisation, reconstruction and military advice to third world countries
◆ Separation of parties by force
◆ Assistance to humanitarian operations
◆ Conflict prevention
◆ Evacuation operations in a non-permissive environment

To ensure that the requirements of the CSDP and the objectives of the Headline Goal 2010 are met, the following command and planning elements have been established:

Under the direction of the European External Action Service (EEAS) the following two organisations are responsible for the implementation of the Common Security and Defence Policy (CSDP).

Crisis Management Planning Directorate (CMPD)

The CMPD is part of the European External Action Service and embodies a basic part of the EU Common Foreign and Security Policy. It is one of the more recent directorates having been created in 2009, following European Council conclusions encouraging the establishment of a new, single civilian-military strategic planning structure for EU peace-keeping and humanitarian operations and missions. The CMPD works under the political control and strategic direction of the Political and Security Committee consisting of the representatives of all the 28 Member States. The CMPD also provides assistance and advice to the High Representative and the relevant EU Council bodies.

Civilian Planning and Conduct Capability (CPCC)

The CPCC plans and conducts civilian Common Security and Defence Policy (CSDP) missions under the political control and strategic direction of the EU's Political and Security Committee. The CPCC provides assistance and advice to the High Representative, the Presidency and the relevant EU Council bodies and work in close cooperation with other crisis management structures within the European External Action Service and the European Commission.

EUROPEAN UNION MILITARY COMMITTEE (EUMC)

The EUMC is composed of the Chiefs of Defence of the EU member nations. Under normal circumstances these Chiefs of Defence are represented by officers seconded to the EUMC from each of the EU member nations.

The EUMC provides advice and recommendations on all aspects of EU security and defence matters to the EU Political and Security Committee (PSC). The EUMC directs all EU military activities and provides the PSC with advice and recommendations on military matters.

The EUMC has a permanent Chairman, selected by the Chiefs of Defence of the Member States and appointed by the Council.

The Chairman is the military adviser to the High Representative of the European Union for Foreign Affairs and Security Policy on all military matters and represents the primary Point of Contact with the Operation Commanders of the EU's military operations.

IMPLEMENTATION OF THE COMMON SECURITY AND DEFENCE POLICY

Implementation of the military aspects of the CSDP is in the main the responsibility of:

◆ European Union Military Staff (EUMS)
◆ European Defence Agency (EDA)

EUROPEAN UNION MILITARY STAFF (EUMS)

Working directly to the Chairman of the EUMC the staff is composed of military and civilian personnel who are responsible for planning and coordination of EU security and defence objectives and operations within the framework of the CSDP.

DIRECTOR GENERAL OF THE EU MILITARY STAFF

Lieutenant General Wolfgang Wosolsobe (Austria)

Lieutenant General Wolfgang Wosolsobe assumed the responsibilities of Director General of the EU Military Staff, Brussels, on 28 May 2013.

Born in 1955, Lieutenant General Wolfgang Wosolsobe started his military career in 1974 at the "Theresianische Militärakademie" in Wiener Neustadt, Austria and was commissioned as an Infantry Officer in 1977. Assignments as Company Commander (infantry) and instructor at the Military Academy followed. He attended the General Staff Officers Course of the Austrian Armed Forces (1982–1985) and during two following years occupied a post in Defence Planning..

In 1987 and 1988, he joined the French "École Supérieure de Guerre Interarmées" and the "Cours Supérieur Interarmées" which offered him the full range of joint staff training and a good command of the French language. Two additional years as a Defence Planner (1989 -1990) were accompanied by functions as lecturer for strategic management methods at the Austrian Defence Academy and as Chief of Staff of the Territorial Command of Salzburg.

In 1991, he joined the Austrian Diplomatic Mission in Geneva as a Military Advisor for Disarmament. This 15 month period in Geneva offered, beyond a first experience in multilateral military diplomacy, a broad range of contacts with other Geneva based institutions, including the Graduate Institute for International Studies. His international career continued with the assignment as Defence Attaché (colonel) to France, from 1992 to 1997. Back in Austria, he took over command of the Austrian Special Forces for the period 1997–1998, where he continued the efforts of his predecessors to pave the way for the international employment of this force.

After his return to the Austrian MoD, he was appointed Director for Military Policy in 1999, a post which he occupied until 2005. He was promoted to Brigadier General in 2001. During these 6 years, he contributed to shaping the international posture of the Austrian Armed forces. During the defence reform process, conducted during this period, Brigadier General Wosolsobe largely contributed to the adaptation of Austria's defence policy to new realities, particularly to the European Security and Defence Policy (ESDP).

This laid the groundwork for his appointment as Defence Policy Director during the Austrian Presidency of the EU Council in 2006. From there, he joined Brussels as Military Representative in 2007 and was promoted to Major General in June of the same year. During his period as Military Representative, he served as Dean of the EU Military Committee in 2009 and 2010. In 2012, he was elected

Lieutenant General Wolfgang Wosolsobe.
(Photo EEAS)

to the post of Director General of the EU Military Staff. He assumed this appointment on 8 May 2013. In March 2013, he was promoted to Lieutenant General.

EUMS Outline Structure (Brussels)

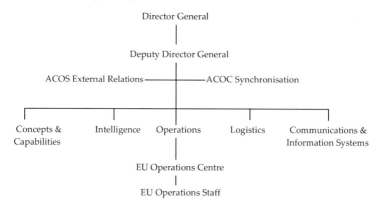

Note: ACOS External Relations has links with the UN, NATO and the SHAPE EU Liaison cell.

European Union Operations Centre

Established in January 2007 the EU Operations Centre is located in Brussels with a small core of permanent staff capable of rapid expansion as necessary to command and control operations. Extra staff required for the direction of operations would come from the Military Staff, the Crisis Management and Planning Directorate; the Civilian Planning and Conduct Capability Group; the geographical desks plus reinforcements from Member States.

In addition to the EU Operations Centre, there are 5 x national operational headquarters which have been made available for use as required by the EU for specific operations. These are:

◆ Mont Valerien (Paris)
◆ Northwood (London)
◆ Potsdam (Berlin)
◆ Centocelle (Rome)
◆ Larissa (Greece)

CURRENT MAJOR EU MILITARY OPERATIONS (MID 2015)

EUFOR (Operation Althea)

The EU launched Operation Althea in Bosnia and Herzegovina (BiH) – in December 2004. This follows the decision by NATO to conclude the SFOR mission.

The EU deployed a large force of 6,300 personnel to ensure continued compliance with the Dayton/Paris Agreement and to contribute to a safe and secure environment in BiH.

The key objectives of Operation Althea are to provide deterrence and continued compliance with the responsibility to fulfil the role specified in Annexes 1A and 2 of the Dayton/Paris Agreement (General Framework Agreement for Peace in BiH) and to contribute to a safe and secure environment in BiH, in line with its mandate, and to achieve core tasks in the Stabilisation and Association Process (SAP).

The headquarters of EUFOR is in Sarajevo and in mid 2015 the personnel strength for Operation Althea was in the region of 800 personnel from over 20 nations.

Operation Althea has been authorised by the United Nations Security Council Resolution 1575.

EURONAVFOR (Operation Atalanta)
In December 2008, the EU established operation ATALANTA to protect World Food Programme and other vulnerable shipping transiting through the Gulf of Aden. The UK has provided the Operation Commander and Operation Headquarters at Northwood since its inception and will continue to do so until the end of the mandate.

EURONAVFOR currently includes warships, support vessels, and the delivery of shipping advice and reassurance from Belgium, Denmark, France, Germany, Greece, the Netherlands and Spain. Maritime Patrol aircraft are provided by Portugal, Spain, Germany and France.

Personnel strength is in the region of 1,050 and Operation has been mandated until December 2016.

EUTM (Somalia)
During January 2010, the EU established a training mission for Somali security forces which commenced during early May. Previously training actually took place in Uganda but due to the improved security situation the Mission HQ was moved to Mogadishu during early 2015. EUTM has a personnel strength of around 100 personnel from 10 member states (including the UK). Since 2010 the mission has contributed to the training of over 4,000 Somali soldiers from the Somali National Army (SNA) with a focus on the training of Non-Commissioned Officers (NCOs), Junior Officers, specialists and trainers.

The mission also includes a liaison office in Nairobi and a support cell in Brussels.

EUTM (Mali)
Established in April 2013 EUTM Mali supports the formation and training of the Malian Army. The mission consists of about 500 personnel (includes 200 instructors) from a variety of 23 member states (including the UK).

The overall aim of the mission is to support the rebuilding of the Malian armed forces and to meet their operational requirements. Much of this training is carried out at the Koulikoro Training Camp (about 60 kms from Bamako) and as well as standard military training, modules include international humanitarian law and human rights, as well as on the protection of the civilian population. The mission is not involved in combat operations.

Other EU Operations (Mid 2015)
EUBAM Libya operates from Tunisia with about 15 personnel.
EU BAM Rafah assists in control of the Rafa (Gaza) crossing point with about 10 personnel.
EUCAP Nestor enhances the maritime capacities of five countries in the Horn of Africa with about 150 personnel.
EUCAP Sahel Niger provides advice and training to support the Nigerien authorities.
EUCAP Sahel Mali support the Malian state to ensure constitutional and democratic order with about 80 personnel.
EUFOR RCA provides support in achieving a secure environment in the Bangui area of the Central African Republic.
EUMAM RCA supports the authorities in the Central African Republic to reform the security sector and the management of the armed forces.
EULEX Kosovo is the largest civilian mission with (about 800 personnel) launched under the CSDP. The central aim is to assist and support the Kosovo authorities in the rule of law area, with a specific focus on the judiciary.
EUMM Georgia's objective is to contribute to stability throughout Georgia and the surrounding region.
EUPOL Afghanistan with about 180 staff from member nations focuses on institutional reform of the Ministry of Interior (MoI) and on the professional structures of the Afghan National Police (ANP). The mission is mandated until December 2016.
EUPOL COPPS supports the reform and development of the police and judicial institutions in the Palestinian Territories with about 170 personnel.

EUSEC RD Congo mission with about 30 personnel has been in the Democratic Republic of the Congo (DRC) since June 2005 and its major objective is the reform of the Congolese Army.

EUAM Ukraine was established in July 2014 to assist the government in Kiev in the reforms relating to the 'rule of law' and the police. EUAM Ukraine is an unarmed, non-executive civilian mission.

EUBAM Moldova and Ukraine was established in 2005 to support capacity building for border management, including customs, on the whole Moldova-Ukraine border.

EUROPEAN DEFENCE AGENCY

The European Defence Agency (EDA) was established in July 2004 following a unanimous decision by European Heads of State and Government. It was established under the Council Joint Action 2004/5 51/CFSP on the basis of Article 14 of the treaty on the European Union (Maastricht).

The purpose of the European Defence Agency is to support the Member States and the Council of Europe in order to improve European defence capabilities in the field of crisis management, and to sustain and develop the European Security and Defence Policy (ESDP).

UK Government position on membership of elements of the European defence establishment
The UK is currently a participant in the activities of the European Defence Agency. The following is an extract from a statement made by the then Secretary of State for Defence Phillip Hammond on 12 February 2013:

I am announcing today that following a review of our membership of the European Defence Agency the UK will at the present time remain a member of the agency.

In 2010 the UK reviewed its membership of the EDA following the strategic defence and security review. Subsequently, my predecessor, my right hon. Friend Dr Fox, recommended that the UK should remain a member of the EDA with a stocktake after two years.

In consultation across Government, my Department has reassessed the benefits of remaining in the EDA and reviewed progress made by the agency since 2010 against identified shortfalls.

On 6 March 2013 a question was asked in the UK Parliament regarding the decision of the UK Government to remain a member of the European Defence Agency and to the annual cost of membership. The reply by Lord Astor of Hever ((Parliamentary Under Secretary of State, for Defence) was as follows:

As set out in the Statement of 12 February, the Government have concluded that the agency has achieved some progress against identified shortfalls. There is, however, further work to be done to improve its performance. We will work with the agency and its member states to achieve this, and review our continuing membership in late 2013. Our European Defence Agency membership costs some £3 million to £4 million per annum and is calculated on gross national income.

On 7 January 2014 during an exchange in the UK House of Commons David Livington (The Minister for Europe) set out the UK Government's attitude to European Defence and continued co-operation:

On the hon. Lady's important points about Common Security and Defence Policy, the key is to understand the distinction between ownership by the EU of defence capabilities, which we do not support and have resisted successfully, and co-operation by European countries in providing greater defence and security capabilities.

The EDA has the following tasks:

◆ To improve the EU's defence capabilities in the field of crisis management.
◆ To promote European armaments cooperation.
◆ To strengthen the European defence industrial and technological base and create a competitive European defence equipment market, in consultation with the Commission.
◆

◆ To promote research, in liaison with Community research activities, with a view to strengthening Europe's industrial and technological potential in the defence field.

The Steering Committee, the principal decision-making body of the Agency is made up of Defence Ministers from participating Member States (all EU members except Denmark) and a member of the European Commission. In addition to ministerial meetings at least twice a year, the Steering Committee also meets at the level of national armaments directors, national research directors, national capability planners and policy directors.

The EDA's Chief Executive is Jorge Domecq (Spain) who was appointed in January 2015. The EDA Headquarters is in Brussels (Belgium) and there is approximately 120 staff.

The Agency had a budget of €30.5 million for 2015.

EDA Organisation

In the longer term the EDA will achieve its goals by:

◆ Encouraging EU Governments to spend defence budgets on meeting tomorrow's challenges and not, in their words, yesterday's threats.
◆ Helping EU Governments to identify common needs and promoting collaboration to provide common solutions.
◆ The EDA is an agency of the European Union and therefore under the direction and authority of the European Council, which issues guidelines to, and receives reports from the High Representative as Head of the Agency. Detailed control and guidance, however, is the responsibility of the Steering Committee.

European Union Institute for Strategic Studies (EU-ISS)

The EU-ISS is based in Paris and was established in 2002 and is an independent think tank that researches issues relevant to EU defence and security. Much of the work is published and the EU-ISS organises conferences and seminars on all aspects of EU related defence and security.

EU DEFENCE EXPENDITURE

Country	Defence Budget 2014 (Euros)
In billions of Euros except where designated in millions (m)	
Austria	2.29
Belgium	3.94
Bulgaria	537 m
Croatia	594 m
Cyprus	529 m
Czech Republic	1.57
Denmark	3.61
Estonia	402 m
Finland	2.69
France	40.0
Germany	32.4
Greece	4.0
Hungary	772 m
Ireland	885 m
Italy	17.0
Latvia	227 m
Lithuania	437 m
Luxembourg	190 m
Malta	104 m
Netherlands	8.0
Poland	38.5
Portugal	1.9
Romania	1.7
Slovakia	831 m
Slovenia	332 m
Spain	11.0
Sweden	5.05
United Kingdom	50.83
	230.32 billion (£164.51 billion)

At mid 2015 exchange rates from local currencies.

Notes:

(1) The above figures are not authoritative and had been taken from a number of sources. Many EU countries use different accounting systems to calculate their defence budgets and the above figures should only be treated as a reasonable guide.

(2) This table shows 2014 budgets – the latest year for which reasonably accurate figures are available.

(3) All EU Governments are facing financial problems and it is likely that many of the above budgets will be under pressure during the next five years.

OVERVIEW EU FORCE LEVELS

Country	Total Active Armed Forces	Attack Submarines (1)	Frigates & Destroyers	Combat Aircraft	Transport Aircraft (2)	MBT (3)	AIFV (4)
Austria	22,500	0	0	37	3	56	112
Belgium	30,700	0	2	88	11	0	37
Bulgaria	31,300	0	4	42	3	80	160
Croatia	16,500	0	0	9	0	75	102
Cyprus	12,000	0	0	0	0	134	43
Czech Republic	21,000	0	0	47	0	30	206
Denmark	17,200	0	7	45	4	55	45
Estonia	5,700	0	0	0	0	0	0
Finland	22,000	0	0	107	0	100	212
France	215,000	6	22	235	30	200	630
Germany	181,500	5	16	237	58	410	529
Greece (5)	144,900	8	13	244	23	1,354	398
Hungary	26,500	0	0	14	0	30	120
Ireland	9350	0	0	0	0	0	0
Italy	176,000	6	17	242	31	160	346
Latvia	5,300	0	0	0	0	3	0
Lithuania	10,950	0	0	0	3	0	0
Luxembourg	900	0	0	0	0	0	0
Malta	1,950	0	0	0	0	0	0
Netherlands	37,400	4	6	74	4	0	184
Poland	99,300	5	2	130	5	426	1,838
Portugal	34,600	2	5	42	6	56	0
Romania	71,400	0	3	69	11	437	124
Slovakia	15,800	0	0	20	0	30	239
Slovenia	7,600	0	0	0	0	46	0
Spain	133,250	3	11	149	7	327	144
Sweden	15,300	6	0	134	7	132	354
United Kingdom	160,460	6	19	266	33	227	400
	1,526,360(6)	51	127	2,231	239	4,368	6,223

Source: International Institute for Strategic Studies (IISS) 2015

Notes:

(1) Not included in these figures are strategic submarines capable of launching ballistic missiles. France has four and the UK has four.

(2) This figure is for medium and heavy transports. It does not include light transport aircraft.

(3) Main battle tanks.

(4) Armoured infantry fighting vehicles.

(5) Financial constraints due to the current austerity programme almost certainly mean that a significant percentage of Greek military equipment and systems are both ageing and at a low state of readiness.

(6) This is a total for active forces and does not include reserves.

Comments on the table:

The figure of over 1.5 million active Armed Forces can be misleading. Many of these personnel (possibly 10 per cent or more) will be involved in headquarters functions of one sort or another. In addition, most modern armed forces only have about 35 per cent of personnel that fall into the category of combat forces. The remainder are involved in support roles without which a modern armed force would be unable to function.

Naval vessels, submarines, frigates and destroyers are often in refit or workup. It would be reasonable to assume that only about 50 per cent of the vessel shown in the table would be available for operations at any one time.

Keeping modern combat aircraft ready for immediate operations is incredibly expensive and most air forces can only maintain a total of between 10 per cent and 20 per cent available for immediate operations. Expect another 30 per cent to 40 per cent to be available within seven days. In times of crisis or heightened tension this figure would of course be much higher.

The EU equipment inventory is inflated somewhat by quite large numbers of armoured vehicles held by nations that were once members of the Warsaw Pact. Many of these Soviet designed vehicles are now obsolete and close to being marked up for disposal.

EU MILITARY STRUCTURES

The following table sets out the main multilateral military structures outside NATO which include European Union members. A number of these also include non-EU countries. In addition, there are many other bilateral military agreements between individual EU member states.

Military agreements between other EU members are a matter for those member states' governments.

Structure	EU participants
EAG – European Air Group	Belgium, France, Germany, Italy, Spain, UK
European Airlift Centre	Belgium, France, Germany, Italy, Netherlands, Spain, UK
Sealift Coordination Centre (Eindhoven)	Netherlands, UK
European Amphibious Initiative (including the UK/Netherlands Amphibious Force)	France, Italy, Netherlands, Spain, UK
SHIRBRIG – Stand-by High Readiness Brigade	Austria, Denmark, Finland, Ireland, Italy, Lithuania, Netherlands, Norway, Poland, Portugal, Slovenia, Spain, Sweden. (Observers: Czech Republic, Hungary)
SEEBRIG – South-Eastern Europe Brigade	Greece, Italy, Slovenia
NORDCAPS – Nordic Coordinated Arrangement for Military Peace Support	Finland, Sweden, Denmark
EUROCORPS	Germany, Belgium, Spain, France, Luxembourg
EUROFOR	France, Italy, Portugal, Spain
EUROMARFOR	France, Italy, Portugal, Spain

EUROCORPS

The Eurocorps was inaugurated in January 1989 and declared operational in October 1991 and comprises military contributions from its five framework nations: Belgium, France, Germany, Luxembourg and Spain. The Headquarters is located in Strasbourg (France). Polish membership will be effective from January 2016. Austria and Finland have staff officers attached to the Eurocorps Headquarters with Greece, Italy, the Netherlands and the United Kingdom contributing liaison officers.

The Commander Eurocorps (COMEC) is a Lieutenant General (3 stars). The Deputy Commander (DCOM) is a Major General (2 stars). The staff is directed by the Chief of Staff (COS), also a Major General and he is supported by two Deputy Chiefs of Staff (DCOS) for Operations and Support, both of whom are Brigadier Generals (1 star).

The posts of Commanding General and the other general officers as well as some key functions are filled by EU framework nations on a rotational basis. COMEC, DCOM and COS are always of different nationalities. Their tour of duty generally lasts for two years.

In general terms the Eurocorps is at the disposal of the European Union and available for service in support of NATO. The command language is English.

The Eurocorps consists of formations under direct operational control and formations earmarked for assignment during a crisis or emergency:

Under direct operational control:

◆ Franco German Brigade (GE-FR Bde)
◆ Multinational Command Support Brigade (MNCS Bde)

Formations earmarked for assignment during an emergency:

French Contribution
Etat-Major de Force numéro 3 (EMF3) in Marseille (equivalent to a divisional HQ) composed of:

1 x Armoured Brigade
1 x Mechanised Infantry Brigade
Specialised support units

German Contribution
The 10th Armoured Division, with its HQ in Sigmaringen, composed of:

2 x Brigades as required
Specialised support units

Belgian Contribution
Belgian Operational Command Land, with its HQ in Evere, composed of:

1st Medium Brigade in Leopoldsburg
Support units

Spanish Contribution
1st Land Forces Command its HQ in Burgos, composed mainly of 1st Mechanised Division.

Luxembourg Contribution
Luxembourg assigns a reconnaissance company composed of about 180 personnel. During operations this unit would be integrated into the Belgian contingent.

Operational Experience

During the past decade the Eurocorps HQ has been involved in operations as follows:

SFOR (Bosnia) 1999–2000
KFOR III (Kosovo) 2000
ISAF IV (Afghanistan) 2004–2005
HQ Eurocorps Standby Element of Nato Response Force (2006–2007)
HQ Eurocorps Standby Element of Nato Response Force (2010–2011)
Afghanistan Training Deployment – 300 personnel (2012–2013)

Note: If all earmarked national contributions were committed to operations, the Eurocorps would number approximately 60,000 personnel.

Franco – German Brigade (FGB)

This is a joint formation which consists of both French and German units and under the direct command of the Eurocorps.

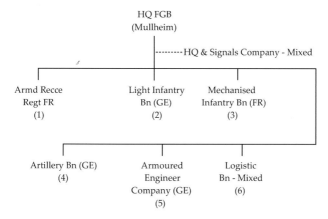

Approximately 5,200 personnel

Notes:

(1) 3e Regiment de Hussars stationed in Metz (France)
(2) Jagerbataillon 292 stationed at Donaueschingen (Germany)
(3) 110e Regiment d'Infanterie stationed at Donaueschingen (Germany)
(4) Panzerartilleriebataillon 295 stationed in Immendingen (Germany)
(5) Panzerpionierkompanie 500 stationed in Immendingen (Germany)
(6) Logistic Battalion with: Supply Company; Maintenance Company; Transport Company; Administration & Support Company; HQ & Support Company.

EU BATTLEGROUPS

In the immediate future, the EU plans to be able to provide at least one coherent Battlegroup package at any one time (usually two), to undertake Battlegroup-sized operations in support of the EU Helsinki Headline Goals.

Full Operational Capability (FOC) was reached at the end of 2007 when all Battlegroups became available. The EU now has the capacity to undertake at least two concurrent single Battlegroup-size rapid response operations, including the ability to launch both such operations nearly simultaneously.

There are usually 2 x EU Battlegroups on standby for operations and trained to respond to emerging contingencies at any one time. They would be deployed following a unanimous decision of the European Council of Ministers, with the nations providing the Battlegroup having a veto on any deployment decision.

EU Member States have indicated that they will commit to Battle Groups, formed as follows:

	Lead Nation	Participants
1	United Kingdom	Netherlands
2	France	
3	France	Belgium
4	Italy	
5	Spain	
6	France	Germany, Belgium, Luxembourg and Spain
7	Germany	Netherlands and Finland
8	Germany	Austria and the Czech Republic
9	Italy	Hungary and Slovenia
10	United Kingdom	Sweden, Netherlands, Latvia and Lithuania
11	Italy	Spain, Greece and Portugal
12	Poland	Germany, Slovakia, Latvia and Lithuania
13	Sweden	Finland, Estonia, Latvia, Lithuania, Ireland and Norway
14	Greece	Bulgaria, Cyprus and Romania
15	Czech Republick	Slovakia
16	Spain	Germany, France and Portugal as
17	Italy	Romania and Turkey
18	Poland	Germany and France

Expect a battlegroup to have between 1,500 and 2,000 personnel.

Each Battlegroup will have a 'lead nation' that will take operational command, based on the model set up during the EU's peacekeeping mission in the Democratic Republic of the Congo (Operation Artemis). Two non-EU NATO countries, Norway and Turkey participate in the EU Battlegroup program.

Battlegroups would have to be able to deploy within 5–10 days and be sustained initially for 30, but possibly up to 120 days while operating up to 6,000 km from Brussels.

EUROPEAN RAPID REACTION FORCE

As yet (mid 2015) there is no standing European Rapid Reaction Force (other than the Franco – German Brigade) nor any EU agreement to create one. What has sometimes been referred to as a 'European Rapid Reaction Force' is, in fact, a catalogue of forces which member states could make available to the EU should they choose to participate in a particular EU-led operation (possibly under the EUFOR umbrella). Any contribution to a particular EU-led operation would depend on the operation's requirements, the availability of forces at the time and the willingness of EU members to participate. However, it is likely that this will change during the next five years.

EU RELATIONSHIP WITH NATO

In a joint declaration by both the EU and NATO during 2002, a previously slightly confused relationship was clarified under a number of major headings that included partnership, mutual cooperation and consultation, equality and due regard for the autonomy of both the EU and NATO, plus reinforcing and developing the military capability of both organisations.

The 'Berlin Plus Agreement' of March 2003 allows the EU to use NATO structures to support military operations that do not fall within the remit of NATO responsibilities. In addition, there is considerable exchange of information between both organisations and they are EU/NATO liaison cells situated in the headquarters of both organisations.

Because in many cases nations that are members of the EU are also members of NATO, the same forces are often assigned to both EU and NATO missions. It is therefore likely that the EU will only act if NATO first decides that it will not do so.

FRENCH – UNITED KINGDOM DEFENCE CO-OPERATION

In a summit meeting held at RAF Brize Norton during January 2014 the UK and France agreed to strengthen defence co-operation.

French President Francois Hollande and the UK Prime Miniister set out plans for future closer defence co-operation between the two countries. Following initial co-operation agreed in 2010 the 2014 agreement should enhance security with a commitment to:

◆ Joint training of armed forces.
◆ Joint investment in the procurement of defence equipment.
◆ Continued development of the Anglo-French Combined Joint Expeditionary Force (CJEF).

Following the signing of the agreement UK Defence Secretary (at the time) Philip Hammond said that "Britain and France are natural partners for defence co-operation. We have made substantial progress since the Lancaster House treaty was signed in 2010 and today we have committed ourselves to go further still. The agreements we have reached at this summit will improve the interoperability of our forces, enhance our joint equipment procurement and build on our capacity to support security and stability in places such as Libya, Mali and the Central African Republic".

COMBINED JOINT EXPEDITIONARY FORCE (CJEF)

The CJEF is a Franco British Force conceived in 2010 with land, air and maritime elements deployable at short notice and under a unified command structure.

Using standard NATO procedures a series of exercises in 2015 and 2016 will test and validate the concept, which should achieve full operational capability during late 2016. The structures being developed should enable UK and French forces to deploy more rapidly in the event of a crisis, with greater capability than might be achieved individually.

Core tasks for the CJEF could include:

◆ Protection of shared national interests abroad.
◆ Extraction operations.
◆ Non-combatant evacuation operations.
◆ Temporary strengthening of a peacekeeping operation.
◆ Support to emergency humanitarian assistance.
◆ Crisis management, involving early entry into a potentially hostile territory (including) the initial enforcement of no-fly zones, embargoes and sanctions).

The UK and France would collaborate to provide logistic support.

The concept was tested in May 2014 when staff officers from the 3rd (United Kingdom) Division the French army's 'État-major de Force n°1' (EMF 1) formed a divisional sized CJEF Headquarters during at two-week exercise in the Champagne region of France.

This was the second time the CJEF has trained together as a fully-integrated headquarters and follows the British-led Exercise 'Iron Triangle' at RAF St Mawgan in Cornwall in December 2013.

During April 2013 the concept was tested at the formation level during Exercise 'Joint Warrior' when troops from 16 Air Assault Brigade (the British Army's rapid reaction force) and French troops from the 11th Parachute Brigade arrived by air in the West Freugh area of Scotland. The exercise scenario tasked them with stabilising an area disputed by two fictional nations divided by economic and ethnic factors.

AFGHANISTAN

Mandated by the United Nations NATO's ISAF (International Security Assistance Force) took the lead in security operations in Afghanistan from 2003 until the end of 2014. From 2011 onward, responsibility for security was gradually passed to Afghan forces. These forces took the lead in security operations culminating in a total handover in December 2014.

In mid 2011 the UK had approximately 9,500 personnel serving in Afghanistan as part of the international security Assistance Force (ISAF). The majority of these personnel served in Helmand Province where over 60 per cent of violent incidents took place.

For the record, during early 2011 there were approximately 132,000 troops in ISAF with contributions from 48 nations and national contingent strengths changing on a regular basis. Major contributors included:

◆ United States   90,000
◆ United Kingdom   9,500
◆ Germany   5,000
◆ Italy   3,800
◆ France   3,400
◆ Canada   2, 900
◆ Poland   2,500
◆ Turkey   1,800
◆ Romania   1,700
◆ Australia   1,500
◆ Spain   1,500

ISAF was supported by approximately 150,000 personnel from the Afghan National Army (ANA) and about 90,000 personnel from the Afghan National Police (ANP).

By the end of the ISAF operation in 2014 some 3,387 personnel were killed. Nations with the most casualties included the US: 2,254; UK: 453; Canada: 158; France: 88; Germany 57.

A new, smaller non-combat mission – Operation Resolute Support was launched on 1 January 2015 to provide further training, advice and assistance to the Afghan security forces and institutions.

During early March 2015 about 13,200 personnel from 40 nations were taking part in Operation Resolute Support. Major contributing nations were:

◆ United States   6,839
◆ United Kingdom   470
◆ Georgia   885
◆ Germany   850
◆ Italy   500
◆ Romania   650
◆ Turkey   503

Afghanistan – Costs

"When the army marches the treasury empties"
Sun Tzu – The Art of War (around 500 BC)

The additional costs for operations in Afghanistan (excluding salaries and ongoing costs that would have happened anyway) are paid for by the Governments Contingency Reserve fund. The next table shows annual costs from 2001 which total to just over £22 billion.

Cost of Operations in Afghanistan 2002–2011 (in million of UK £)	
2001–2002	221
2002–2003	311
2003–2004	46
2004–2005	67
2005–2006	199
2006–2007	738
2007–2008	1,504
2008–2009	2,623
2009–2010	4,187
2010–2011	4,436
2011–2012	3,458
2012–2013	2,673
2013/2014	1,877
Total	22,340

We await final accurate UK Government figures for the end of operations. Some analysts believe that the final year of operations will cost about £800 million.

CHAPTER 4 – JOINT FORCES COMMAND AND JOINT SERVICE ORGANISATIONS

JOINT FORCES COMMAND

Joint Forces Command (JFC) was established in April 2012 and reached full operating capability in April 2013. The creation of the Joint Forces Command was recommended by Lord Levene's 2011 Defence Reform Review.

The JFC was created to ensure the Joint Capabilities of all three of the UK's fighting services were fully optimised, with an additional JFC aim of creating a more direct link between front line experience and top-level planning. The headquarters of the Joint Forces Command, is at Northwood in Middlesex (just north of London) and consists of around 150 military staff and civilians.

Across the whole command, the JFC's day to day personnel total could possibly number about 30,000 military and civilian personnel, a figure that would include forces deployed on operations under command of the Chief of Joint Operations (CJO). These personnel are at locations across the UK, overseas in the Permanent Joint Operating Bases (PJOBs), and on operations world-wide.

The JFC is a Top Level Budget holder and included in the overall JFC budget are the costs of the UK forces in the Falkland Islands, Cyprus, the British Indian Ocean Territory and Gibraltar. Major operations such as the ongoing operational commitment in Afghanistan are funded separately by way of a supplementary budget, and in almost all cases, this requires government- level approval. Small operations and the cost of reconnaissance parties are funded from the standard JFC budget.

JFC responsibilities are now so wide-ranging and complex it is probably easier to comment on operational areas with which this Headquarters will not be involved. These include Defence of the UK Home Base; Integrity of UK Airspace and Seaspace; Strategic Nuclear Deterrent; Counter-terrorism in the UK; Northern Ireland and NATO General War (Article V) operations.

General Richard Barrons CBE took command of the JFC in succession to Air Chief Marshal Sir Stuart Peach in mid-April 2013.

GENERAL SIR RICHARD BARRONS CBE – CHIEF OF JOINT OPERATIONS

General Barrons was commissioned into the Royal Regiment of Artillery in 1977, prior to reading for a degree in Philosophy, Politics and Economics at Queen's College, Oxford. He then served in a variety of regimental appointments based in the UK and Germany, which included periods of training in Belize, Canada, France, Hong Kong and Brunei, and two years at the MoD in London.

He completed a Masters degree in Defence Administration in 1990 before attending the Army Staff College, Camberley in 1991.

General Sir Richard Barrons.
(MoD Crown Copyright 2015)

As Chief of Staff of HQ 11 Armoured Brigade in Minden, Germany, he was despatched at a week's notice in October 1993 to form the first HQ British Forces in Bosnia and Croatia. This was followed by a short tour in the Directorate of Military Operations as the Balkans desk officer, before assuming command of B Battery, 1st Regiment Royal Horse Artillery in 1994 for two years – including a period of Northern Ireland duty.

On promotion to Lieutenant Colonel in 1996 he served as a Military Advisor to the High Representative in Bosnia, also leading on liaison with HQ NATO and SHAPE. In 1997 he was appointed Military Assistant (MA) to the Chief of the General Staff. He assumed command of 3rd Regiment Royal Horse Artillery in Hohne, Germany in 1999, deploying the Regiment to Kosovo and Bosnia in 2001 and commanding the first KFOR deployments alongside Serbian forces.

He was promoted to Colonel in December 2001 and appointed Chief of Staff of 3rd (United Kingdom) Division, deploying to Afghanistan the next day as the Headquarters established the International Security Assistance Force in Kabul for the first half of 2002. Having attended the Higher Command and Staff Course in 2003, he deployed again with the Headquarters as the Chief of Staff of HQ Multinational Division (South East) in Basra until October 2003.

As a Brigadier, he commanded 39 Infantry Brigade, covering Belfast and South Armagh from December 2003 to December 2005 when he assumed the appointment of ACOS (Assistant Chief of Staff) Commitments at HQ Land Forces, responsible for intelligence, security and operations – especially force generation for Iraq and Afghanistan.

On promotion to Major General in 2008 he served as a Deputy Commanding General of Multinational Corps Iraq (Baghdad), leading on operations with the Iraqi Army.

He was appointed Chief of Staff of the Allied Rapid Reaction Corps in April 2009. In October 2009 he was posted at very short notice to HQ ISAF to establish a Force Reintegration mechanism.

General Barrons was appointed MBE in 1993, OBE in 1999, CBE in 2003, awarded QCVS in 2004 and 2006, and appointed as an Officer of the US Legion of Merit in 2009.

JFC STRUCTURE

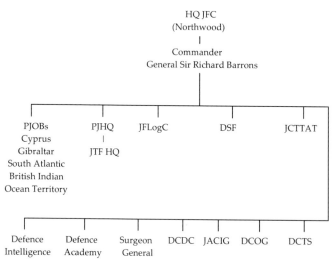

Abbreviations:

PJOBs – Permanent Joint Operating Bases; PJHQ – Permanent Joint Headquarters; JFLogC – Joint Force Logistics Component: JCTTAT – Joint Counter-Terrorist Training and Advisory Team; DSF – Director Special Forces; Def Ac – Defence Academy; DCDC – Development Concepts and Doctrine Centre; JACIG – Joint Arms Control Implementation Group; (DCTS); DCOG – Defence Cyber Operations Group; DCTS – Defence Centre of Training Support.

Notes:

(1) PJHQ and DSF are within JFC, however the commanders can also report directly to the Chief of the Defence Staff.

(2) PJHQ is commanded by the Chief of Joint Operations (CJO)

Chief of Defence Intelligence and his staff advise the MoD on all aspects of defence intelligence.

Head of the Defence Academy Group directs the activities of the various Joint Service Staff Colleges and Academies.

The Surgeon General is the professional head of the Defence Medical Services and responsible for the healthcare and medical operational capability of the Armed Forces.

Defence Cyber Operations Group leads on Cyber Security, Cyber Policy and plans.

PJOB costs during FY 2012–2013 (the latest year for which figures have been identified) were as follows:

British Indian Ocean Territory	- £2 million
Falkland Islands	- £67 million
Gibraltar	- £53 million
Cyprus (Akrotiri & Dhekelia)	- £188 Million

PERMANENT JOINT HEADQUARTERS (PJHQ)

An essential element of the JFC, Permanent Joint Headquarters (PJHQ) was established as a headquarters for joint military operations at Northwood in Middlesex in April 1996. This headquarters is the UK's national operational level command and contains elements of a rapidly deployable in-theatre Joint Task Force Headquarters (JTF HQ), that has the capability of commanding front line forces.

PJHQ is commanded by the Chief of Joint Operations (CJO), Lieutenant General John Lorimer DSO MBE (appointed January 2015) who is responsible for the planning and execution of joint, or potentially joint, national and UK-led multinational operations conducted outside the UK. CJO can reports directly to the CDS for advice on a number of matters including the conduct and resourcing of military operations.

CJO commands UK forces assigned for a specific operation and is responsible at the operational level for the deployment, direction, sustainment and recovery of deployed forces. CJO acts as the Joint Force Commander and is usually based at Northwood. Forces in the operational area are commanded by a Joint Task Force (JTF) Commander or in cases where the UK is operating alongside allies, the UK National Contingent Commander.

Principal Additional Tasks of PJHQ Include:

♦ Monitoring designated areas of operational interest
♦ Preparing contingency plans
♦ Conducting Joint Force exercises
♦ Focus for Joint Rapid Reaction Force planning and exercising

Chain of Command for Joint Operations

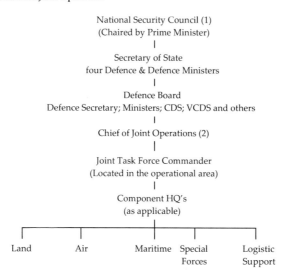

National Security Council (1)
(Chaired by Prime Minister)

Secretary of State
four Defence & Defence Ministers

Defence Board
Defence Secretary; Ministers; CDS; VCDS and others

Chief of Joint Operations (2)

Joint Task Force Commander
(Located in the operational area)

Component HQ's
(as applicable)

| Land | Air | Maritime | Special Forces | Logistic Support |

Notes:

(1) The National Security Council (NSC) is where the UK Government decides on the national defence and security objectives, and the best way in which these objectives can be met using national resources. The NSC is chaired by the Prime Minister, and generally meets weekly with representation from across the major Departments of State. The Secretary of State for Defence attends as does the Chief of the Defence Staff (CDS) when the need arises. Other attendees can include Defence Ministers, Parliamentary Under Secretary (PUS), Vice Chief of the Defence Staff (VCDS), Chief of Defence Materiel (CDM) and Director General Finance (DG Fin).

(2) CDS has the option of advice from the three service commanders and the Chief of Joint Operations.

(3) Chief of Joint Operations (CJO) is provided with force packages (as required) by the three service commanders. CJO has a civilian Command Secretary who provides a wide range of policy, legal, presentational, financial and civilian human resources advice.

PJHQ operates through the following staff branches:

J1 Personnel and Admin	J6 Communication and Information Systems
J2 Intelligence	J7 Doctrine and Joint Training
J3 Operations	J8 Finance
J4 Logistics & Medical	J9 Policy, legal and presentation
J5 Policy and Crisis Planning	

PJHQ staff includes personnel from the three armed services and the civil service who are responsible for directing, deploying, sustaining and recovering UK Joint Forces. Liaison officers from other armed forces will be represented when operations include allied nations.

JOINT RAPID REACTION FORCE (JRRF)

The JRRF is essentially the fighting force that PJHQ has immediately available. The JRRF provides a force for rapid deployment operations using a core operational group of the Army's 16th Air Assault Brigade and the Royal Navy's 3rd Commando Brigade, supported by a wide range of air and maritime assets such as the Joint Helicopter Command and the Royal Navy's Response Task Group.

The JRRF uses what the MoD has described as a 'golf bag' approach with a wide range of units available for specific operations. For example, if the operational situation demands assets such as heavy armour, long range artillery and attack helicopters, these assets can easily be assigned to the force. This approach means that the JRRF can be tailored for specific operations, ranging from support for a humanitarian crisis to missions including high intensity operations.

The 'reach' of the JRRF is enhanced by the Royal Navy's amphibious vessels HMS Albion and HMS Bulwark. Both of these vessels have the ability to carry 650 troops plus a range of armoured vehicles including main battle tanks. A flight deck allows for ship-to-shore helicopter operations.

Responsibility for providing units to the JRRF remains with the single service commanders who ensure that units assigned are at an extremely high state of readiness. Units assigned to the JRRF are trained to Joint standards and be committed to NATO, EU, UN or other coalition operations as required.

Under normal circumstances, it would be expected that the Army would ensure the following land forces were available to the JRRF: a brigade sized grouping held at High Readiness and two Strategic Reserves—the Spearhead Land Element (SLE) held at Extremely High Readiness and the Airborne Task Force (ABTF) held at Very High Readiness.

The force commander is the JTF Commander (Joint Task Force Commander) who is responsible to the Chief of Joint Operations (CJO) at PJHQ. JTF Commander is supported by the Joint Force Operations Staff at PJHQ who provide a fully resourced Joint Task Force Headquarters (JTFHQ) at 48 hours notice to move anywhere in the world.

Joint Force Logistics Component
The Joint Force Logistics Component (JFLogC) provides a joint logistic headquarters for operations with force logistics under the command of PJHQ. It delivers coordinated logistic support to the deployed Joint Force in accordance with the commander's priorities. The composition of the JFLogC will be determined by PJHQ during the mission planning stage. If necessary, 2 x logistic brigades can be assigned to JFLogC.

SPECIAL FORCES

Although the exact detail is highly classified, the UK Special Forces Group (UKSF) is under the command of the Director Special Forces (DSF). DSF's department is within the JFC but DSF reports directly to the Chief of the Defence Staff.

Units known to be part of the UK Special Forces Group include:

22nd Special Air Service Regiment (Army)	22 SAS
Special Boat Service (Royal Marines)	SBS
Special Forces Support Group	SFSG
Special Reconnaissance Regiment	SRR
18th (UKSF) Signal Regiment	18 SIG REGT
Special Forces Aviation Wing	
Reserve Components	

Special Forces Support Group
Based around a core group from the 1st Battalion The Parachute Regiment, the Special Forces Support Group (SFSG) is a unit within the UK Special Forces, that was established in April 2006. SFSG directly supports Special Forces operations worldwide and also provides an additional counter-terrorist capability. Personnel for the SGSG also come from the Royal Marines, and the Royal Air Force Regiment. Members of the Special Forces Support Group (SFSG) retain the cap badges of their parent units but also wear the SFSG insignia.

All SFSG personnel have passed either the Royal Marines Commando course, the Airborne Forces Selection course run by the Parachute Regiment or the RAF Pre-Parachute Selection course. Qualified personnel are then equipped and provided with additional training to fit their specific specialist role on joining the SFSG.

The UK MoD has described the main role of the SFSG as "Providing direct support to UK Special Forces intervention operations around the world. They will be prepared to operate in war-fighting, counter-insurgency and counter-terrorism operations at short notice. Their roles may include provision of supporting or diversionary attacks, cordons, fire support, force protection and supporting training tasks. Prior to the creation of the SFSG, these tasks have been carried out by other units on an ad hoc basis".

SFSG consists of four strike companies and a support company with specialist units such as a CBRN detection troop and tactical air control parties. The group is believed to be equipped with Jackal vehicles.

It is possible that the operational requirements of the next decade will result in a situation where the SFSG its current form will have difficulty in coping with the longer term demands of the operational tempo, especially during operations where 'on the ground' support to a friendly government might take place over a number of years. It might be worth examining the merit of equipping and training 3 x companies from infantry battalions in the Adaptable Force (1 UK Division) to a similar standard to that currently achieved by 1st Battalion, The Parachute Regiment.

Special Reconnaissance Regiment
The Special Reconnaissance Regiment (SRR) was formed in April 2005 to meet a growing worldwide demand a for special reconnaissance capability. The term 'special reconnaissance' covers a wide range of highly classified specialist skills and activities related to covert surveillance.

The SRR draws its personnel from existing units and can recruit new volunteers from serving members of the Armed Forces where necessary.

Other sub-units provide combat and combat service support.

18 (UKSF) Signal Regiment
This regiment provides communications and electronic warfare support to the whole of the UK Special Forces Group. Squadrons under command include:

264 (SAS) Signals Squadron
SBS Signals Squadron
267 (SRR) Signals Squadron
268 (SFSG) Signals Squadron

Special Forces Aviation Wing
This organisation supports UK SF operations with the following aircraft:

7 Squadron RAF with Chinook HC4.
47 Squadron RAF with C-130 Hercules
657 Squadron AAC with Lynx
658 Squadron AAC with AS365 Dauphin 2 and Gazelle AH1,

Special Forces Reserve (SF-R)
The two reserve SAS Regiments (21 and 23 SAS) together with 63 SAS Signal Squadron and the SBS Reserve have evolved into the Reserve Component of the UKSF Group.

JOINT HELICOPTER COMMAND (JHC)

The majority of UK service helicopters are assigned to the Joint Helicopter Command, a formation under the command of Commander Land Forces. The primary role of the JHC is to deliver and sustain effective Battlefield Helicopter and Air Assault assets, operationally capable under all environmental conditions, in order to support the UK's defence missions and tasks. Major formations under JHC command are as follows:

◆ All Army Aviation Units
◆ RAF Support Helicopter Force
◆ Commando Helicopter Force
◆ 16 Air Assault Brigade
◆ Combat Support Units
◆ Combat Service Support Units
◆ Joint Helicopter Command and Standards Wing

Our estimate for the JHC service personnel total is approximately 12,000 from all three services. During operations elements of the JHC would probably be assigned to formations/units under the command of PJHQ's Chief of Joint Operations.

Our figures suggest that the JHC appears to have over 160 aircraft (forward fleet) available for operations as follows:

Possible UK Helicopter types available during late 2015

	Forward Fleet	Depth Fleet
Royal Navy (Commando Helicopter Force)		
Sea King HAR3/A (being replaced by 20 x Merlin from end 2015)	9	1
Lynx/Wildcat	6	0
Army Air Corps		
Apache	32	18
Gazelle	19	7
Wildcat	27	7
Lynx AH9A	12	9
Defender/Islander (fixed wing)	9/4	9/4
Royal Air Force (Support Helicopter Force)		
Chinook HC4	23	14
Chinook HC5	6	1
Puma Mk 2	10	13
Merlin HC3/3A	20	7

Note: These figures suggest numbers of aircraft available for operations and not the total inventory which includes aircraft being used for training, being upgraded or in storage.

In a normal non-operational environment (with the exception of Lynx), each individual aircraft is resourced to fly approximately 400 hours per year.

Helicopters not under the command of the JHC include the Royal Navy's fleet helicopters (in support of ships at sea), and the Royal Air Force and Royal Navy's search and rescue aircraft.

Outside of operational deployments 16 Air Assault Brigade is under the command of the JHC.

DEFENCE MEDICAL SERVICES (DMS)

The Defence Medical Services include the whole of the medical, dental, nursing, health professional, paramedical, veterinary and support personnel (about 7,000 uniformed personnel) including civilian staff, employed by the three Armed Services. These elements are responsible for providing healthcare to service personnel serving in the UK, overseas and on operations. In addition and where appropriate, the families of service personnel and entitled civilians (possibly about 260,000 people). DMS also provides some aspects of healthcare to other countries' personnel overseas, in both permanent military bases and in areas of conflict and war zones.

The range of services provided by the Defence Medical Services includes:

♦ Primary healthcare
♦ Dental care
♦ Hospital care
♦ Rehabilitation
♦ Occupational medicine
♦ Community mental healthcare
♦ Specialist medical care

Defence Medical Services also provide healthcare in a range of facilities, including medical and dental centres, regional rehabilitation units and in field hospitals.

The Deputy Chief of Defence Staff – Health (DCDS(H) is accountable for the overall outputs of the Defence Medical Services.

The Surgeon General is the professional head of the Defence Medical Services and responsible for the healthcare and medical operational capability. His responsibilities include defining the standard and quality of healthcare needed in both operational and non-operational environments and assuring its delivery. He is also responsible for setting the strategy and the associated (non-clinical) policies for the Defence Medical Services.

These two senior officers oversee the work of three separate organisations:

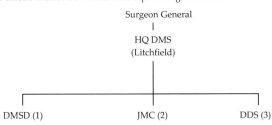

Surgeon General

HQ DMS
(Litchfield)

DMSD (1)   JMC (2)   DDS (3)

Notes:

(1) The Defence Medical Services Department (DMSD) is the headquarters for the Defence Medical Services providing strategic direction to ensure delivery of defence medical outputs. The DMSD operates through the following four directorates: Medical Operations; Medical Policy; Healthcare; Finance and Secretariat.

(2) Joint Medical Command (JMC) – This is a joint service agency providing secondary care personnel to meet requirements for operational deployments. It also supports the front line units by educating and training medical personnel through the Defence Medical and Training Agency (DEMTA). DMETA runs about 2,000 clinical courses (providing about 300,000 training days) to all three services. JMC has responsibility for the following:

- ◆ MDHUs (Ministry of Defence Hospital Units)
- ◆ RCDM (The Royal Centre for Defence Medicine)
- ◆ DMRC (The Defence Medical Rehabilitation Centre at Headley Court
- ◆ DMSTC (The Defence Medical Services Training Centre in Aldershot
- ◆ The Defence Medical Postgraduate Deanery

The JMC provides a single headquarters responsible for healthcare delivery.

(3) Defence Dental Services (DDS) – this is a joint service organisation employing both Armed Forces and civilian personnel that provides dental services in the UK at service establishments and to personnel on operations overseas. The DDS came under the 'umbrella' of the JMC from mid 2009.

Single Service Medical Care
The three armed services are responsible for delivering primary healthcare to their respective services and for providing the required medical support on operations.

Royal Naval Medical Service (RNMS)
Army Medical Services (AMS)
Royal Air Forces Medical Services (RAF MS)

Late 2014 regular and reserve personnel figures are as follows:

DMS Regular personnel	7,990
DMS Reserve personnel	2,910

Defence Nursing Staff
On operations, nursing staff and medical officers from all three services deliver primary and emergency care at the front line and secondary and critical care in field hospitals. Aeromed evacuation of casualties is supported by defence nurses who deliver intensive care nursing during patient transfers both in theatre and on return to the UK working within the Critical Care Air Support Teams.

When not deployed on operations, defence nurses work within Ministry of Defence Hospital Units within NHS Trusts across the UK to maintain their clinical skills and care for the general public. In particular, Defence Nurses working at the Royal Centre for Defence Medicine in Birmingham and at the Defence Medical Rehabilitation Centre at Headley Court contribute directly to the health care provision of military personnel.

Nursing staff for the three services (with approximate personnel figures) are found from the following organisations:

Queen Alexandra's Royal Naval Nursing Service (QARNNS)	–	300
Queen Alexandra's Royal Army Nursing Corps (QARANC)	–	800
Princess Mary's Royal Air Force Nursing Service (PMRAFNS)	–	430

Hospital Care
In the UK hospital care is provided at Ministry of Defence Hospital Units (MDHU).

The Defence Medical Services Department (DMSD) has contracts with the NHS for provision of care in MDHUs, which are run as military units embedded within selected NHS hospitals. There are MDHUs at Derriford (Plymouth), Frimley Park (Aldershot), Northallerton (near Catterick), Peterborough and Portsmouth.

In addition, the Defence Medical Services runs a number of other units which include the Royal Centre for Defence Medicine (Birmingham), Defence Services Medical Rehabilitation Centre (Headley Court) and the Duchess of Kent's Psychiatric Unit (Catterick). There are also about 245 DMS medical and dental primary care facilities mostly located in the UK. Outside of the UK primary healthcare, and some secondary healthcare, is provided on board Royal Navy ships and in overseas bases and theatres of military operations.

The Military Ward at the Queen Elizabeth Hospital in Birmingham started taking patients in 2010 and service personnel are cared for in single rooms or four-bedded bays that have additional features for the exclusive use of military patients. The ward has more staff than a normal NHS ward, a quiet room for relatives as well as a communal space for military patients to gather. A dedicated physiotherapy area has also been provided close to the ward for service patients.

On operations overseas locations Field Hospitals provide medical support that includes primary surgery, an intensive care unit, medium and low dependency nursing care beds and diagnostic support, as well as emergency medical care. These Field Hospital may be staffed by medical personnel from all three services.

Service personnel serving in Germany who require hospital care are treated in one of the five German Provider Hospitals. As the withdrawal from Germany gathers pace these services will be reduced.

Royal Centre for Defence Medicine (RCDM)
The RCDM in Birmingham provides a centre for military personnel requiring specialised care, and incorporates a facility for the treatment of service personnel who have been evacuated from an overseas deployment area after becoming ill or wounded/injured. RCDM also acts as a centre for the training of Defence Medical Service personnel.

In operation since 2001 the RCDM operates on a contract between the DMSD and the University Hospitals Birmingham (UHB) NHS Trust.

The RCDM is a Joint Service establishment with medical personnel from all three of the armed services wearing their respective Naval, Army, or Air Force uniforms.

Midlands Medical Accommodation Project
From 2010 Whittington Barracks in Lichfield became the home of military medicine. The Midlands Medical Accommodation project (MMA) will ensure that the area becomes the central focus for military medical expertise and assets. About 2,000 military and civilian staff are believed to be working at the barracks following completion of the MMA project in 2015.

The first phase – MMA Increment 1 – delivered a modern headquarters office building for the DMS at Whittington Barracks that incorporates both the Surgeon General's strategic Headquarters and those of the Joint Medical Command, both of which are fully operational.

The second phase – MMA Increment 2 – saw the DMS elements relocated from Keogh Barracks near Aldershot to a new modern training centre at Whittington Barracks. The new complex includes training facilities, a learning centre; lecture theatre, messes for Officers, Warrant Officers and Senior Non Commissioned Officers, living accommodation for permanent staff and a new Junior Ranks' dining and leisure facility.

About £200 million was invested in MMA1 and 2.

DEFENCE EQUIPMENT AND SUPPORT

In parallel with the establishment of PJHQ at Northwood it became important to combine the separate logistics functions of the three Armed Services. As a result, in 2000 the three distinct separate service logistic functions were fused into one and the Defence Logistic Organisation was formed.

From 1 April 2007 the Defence Procurement Agency (DPA) and the Defence Logistic Organisation (DLO) were merged to form Defence Equipment and Support (DE&S – a bespoke trading entity).

DE&S has been described as 'the engine' that delivers 'Through Life' equipment and logistic support, and making sure the whole factory to front line process is seamless and properly integrated.

The Headquarters of DE&S is at Abbey Wood (Bristol) a site that is the largest MoD facility in the UK. DE&S is a Top Level Budget Holder and employs over 12,000 personnel (about 75 per cent civilian). The annual DE&S budget is in the region of £14 billion and a 10 year departmental plan for the purchase and support for equipment and systems is worth around £165 billion.

The Chief of Defence Materiel leads DE&S and has overall responsibility acquiring and supporting the equipment, systems and commodities needed to generate the UK's military capability.

Chief of Defence Materiel (CDM)

During late 2015 Mr Tony Douglas will take over as the Chief Executive of DE&S.

As the UK's National Armaments Director Tony Douglas (CDM) is responsible for:

♦ Providing equipment and logistic support to current operations, including delivery against urgent operational requirements.
♦ Delivering funded equipment acquisition and support outputs, as agreed with Front Line Commands and the MoD Head Office.
♦ Delivering projects to performance, time and cost targets, in accordance with agreed asset delivery plans.
♦ Managing safety, risk and environmental issues in accordance with mandated requirements and appropriate best practice.
♦ Representing UK interests in international military and political areas, including NATO and the EU

DE&S Structure

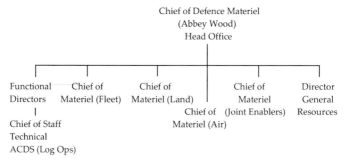

In a normal year expect the MoD to spend about 40 per cent of its budget on equipment and equipment support.

Finances already allocated to equipment and equipment support over the period 2013 to 2017 are as follows:

Financial year	15/16	16/17	17/18	18/19	19/20
£ Billions	14.5	14.3	15.4	15.9	16.9

Expenditure by programme sectors over the next ten years is shown under the following headings:

Ships	– £18.2 billion
Submarines	– £40 billion
Combat Air	– £17.9 billion

Air Support	– £13.8 billion
Helicopters	– £11.0 billion
Information Systems and Services	– £16.9 billion
ISTAR	– £4.9 billion
Land Equipment	– £15.4 billion
Weapons	– £12.6 billion

Major elements of the Land Equipment programme include:

◆ Warrior Capability Sustainment Programme, delivering capability enhancements and an extended service life.
◆ Challenger 2 Life Extension Programme.
◆ Scout Specialist Vehicle and Utility Vehicle programmes which will replace a range of ageing tracked armoured vehicles. (1)
◆ Modifications to equipment purchased as Urgent Operational Requirements for Afghanistan in order to ensure their continued utility.

Note:

(1) The contract, worth £3.5 billion to deliver 589 Scout specialist vehicles was announced in late 2014.

An important element of the Weapons Equipment programme includes:

Development of the Future Local Area Air Defence (FLAADS) System for Land and Naval forces.

Some of the DE&S responsibilities to Joint Operations include:

Logistics planning, resource management, contractual support and policy
Global fleet management and land-based equipment
Support of the naval fleet and all naval systems
Communication and Information Systems
Transport and movements
Food and ration packs
Ammunition
Fuel, Oil and Lubricants
Postal Services
Clothing and tentage
Storage for all equipment and materiel

DEFENCE INFRASTRUCTURE ORGANISATION (DIO)

Formed on 1 April 2011 and with a headquarters in Sutton Coldfield the DIO replaced the former Defence Estates organisation and brings together the majority of property and infrastructure functions from across the Ministry of Defence.

The DIO, a Top Level Budget Holder (TLB) has an annual expenditure of approximately £3 billion and assets worth over £20 billion. The overall area of the Defence Estate is estimated at being in the region of 2,400 sq kms.

The Defence Estate includes docks, airfields, barracks, training areas, schools and colleges, married quarters and roads owned and managed by the MoD.

There are five operating divisions:

◆ Major Projects – Responsible for the management of high value corporate projects.
    Land Management Services – Responsible for managing the entire estate portfolio.
◆ Defence Training Estate – responsible for all MoD Training Areas.
◆ Hard Facilities Management – Responsible for routine construction projects, mechanical and electrical support to the estate.

- ◆ Security Services Group – Responsible for the provision of security at all levels.
- ◆ Soft Facilities Management – Responsible for providing cleaning and catering type support across the MoD.

JOINT CHEMICAL, BIOLOGICAL, RADIOLOGICAL AND NUCLEAR DEFENCE

During July 2011 the MoD announced the specialist Chemical, Biological, Radiological and Nuclear (CBRN) capabilities of the 1st Royal Tank Regiment were to be transferred to the RAF Regiment's Defence CBRN Wing (20 Wing RAF Regiment) by December 2011.

No 20 Wing at RAF Honnington is now responsible for the Defence CBRN Wing .This organisation provides the CBRN reconnaissance, monitoring, detection and decontamination support required by the three armed services, and where necessary the civilian authorities.

20 Wing has three squadrons:

No 26 Squadron RAF Regiment	RAF Honington
No 27 Squadron RAF Regiment	RAF Honington
No 2623 Squadron RAuxAF Regt	RAF Honington

20 Wing possesses extremely sophisticated detection, monitoring and decontamination capabilities, including systems related to the Sampling and Identification of Biological Chemical and Radiological Agents (SIBCRA) task. 20 Wing personnel also provide support to the civil authorities as part of the UK Nuclear Event Response Organisation (NERO). In one example an RAF Regiment monitoring team was deployed to an overseas British Embassy where there was a potential contamination threat.

Winterbourne Gunner (Wiltshire) is the location of the Defence Chemical Biological Radiological and Nuclear Centre (DCBRNC). The Centre designs and runs courses that qualify individuals of all three services for CBRN defence operational and training appointments.

Porton Down (Wiltshire) houses the Defence Science and Technology Laboratory (Dstl) and the Health Agency's Centre for Emergency Preparedness and Response. Both of these organisations have important inputs relating to the defence of the UK and its population against CBRN events.

JOINT SERVICES SIGNAL ORGANISATION (JSSO)

With its headquarters at RAF Digby the JSSO is a joint service organisation providing specialist communications support to military operations in both the UK and overseas. At times this support can also provide for allied nations during multi-national operations.

Commanded by either an Army Colonel or an RAF Group Captain on rotation the JSSO also researches new systems and techniques to provide enhanced support to units of all three armed forces.

SKYNET

Astrium Services operates the Skynet military satellite constellation on a concession basis and provides the three armed services with the ground terminals to provide all Beyond Line of Sight (BLOS) communications to the MoD.

Under a £4 billion Private Finance Initiative (PFI) Astrium is contracted to provide this service until 2022.

A number of Skynet satellites have been launched over the past decade and the fourth of the Skynet 5 series, Skynet 5D was launched from French Guiana (South America) in December 2012.. Skynet 5A and Skynet 5B entered service in April 2007 and January 2008 respectively. Skynet 5C was launched in June 2008. Skynet 5D will travel at speeds of around 6,200 miles per hour when in orbit.

The Land, Air and maritime environments utilise different equipment for their principal terminal capabilities. The Land and Air environments primarily use Reacher. The maritime environment uses the Satellite Communications Terminal (SCOT).

MINISTRY OF DEFENCE POLICE AND GUARDING AGENCY

This agency has three major elements, The Ministry of Defence Police, the Ministry of Defence Guarding Agency and the Defence School of Policing and Guarding.

Ministry of Defence Police (MDP)

The MDP has its headquartered at Wethersfield, in Essex, and is deployed across the British Isles at over 80 MoD sites from Culdrose in Cornwall to the Clyde in Scotland. Organised into five divisional commands, with headquarters at York, Aldershot, Aldermaston, Foxhill and the Clyde Naval Base, the personnel total is approximately 2,600 (including about 100 in the Defence Police Criminal Investigation Department).

The majority of MDP tasks are security orientated and include the security of military bases, protecting against the sabotage of assets and the threat of terrorist incursion. At the same time the MDP has a role as a civilian police force creating a safe crime free environment. The MDP is supported by a number of specialist units that include the largest fraud squad in the UK, marine units that are equipped with a large number of amphibious craft, over 400 police dogs, a special escort group and a multi-capability operational support unit.

During early 2011 it was announced that the MDP had established a Defence Crime Board, to provide strategic direction to the defence-wide effort to reduce the harm done to the defence budget, safety, security and military operational capability by crime and fraud.

All MDP officers are trained in the use of firearms and at any one time about 70 per cent of MDP officers on duty will be armed.

The annual budget is in the region of £170 million.

Ministry of Defence Guard Service (MGS)

The Ministry of Defence Guard Service is the uniformed, unarmed element forming part of the larger Ministry of Defence Police and Guarding Agency. The Ministry of Defence Guard Service was formed into a corporate structure as part of the Ministry of Defence Police and Guarding Agency in April 2004. The MGS has a personnel total of around 2,500 personnel who are located at over 100 locations across the UK. There are six regional headquarters locations at Aldershot, Bath, Clyde Naval Base, London, Shrewsbury and York. Primary duties of the MGS include:

◆ Control of entry and exit
◆ Issue of entry passes
◆ Searching of vehicles and personnel
◆ Perimeter patrolling
◆ Key control

We would expect the annual cost of the MGS and to be in the region of £100 million.

Defence School of Policing and Guarding (DSPG)

The DSPG is a Joint Service training centre located in Southwick Park, near Fareham in Hampshire and delivers intermediate and advanced service police and guarding training. The DSPG is accountable to the Army Recruiting and Training Division but receives considerable input from the three single-service Provost Marshals and respective training requirements authorities. Courses at the DSPG range from one day to 25 weeks.

The school trains around 2,000 individuals each year.

MILITARY CORRECTIVE TRAINING CENTRE (MCTC)

The MCTC takes servicemen and women who have been sentenced to periods of detention from 14 days to two years. The vast majority are serving periods of detention to which they have been sentenced by court martial or after summary hearing by their commanding officers. Most detainees have offended against Armed Forces law rather than criminal law, and few are committed for offences that would have resulted in custody had they been in civilian life.

All detainees are held in accordance with rules determining committal to custody within the Armed Forces Act 2006.

Staff at the MCTC are drawn mainly from the Military Provost Staff Corps (MPSC) with representatives from the other services.

Numbers of detainees held during the period 2011–2013 is given below:

MCTC Detainees 2011–2013

Sentence length	FY 2011–12	FY 2012–13
Under 60 days	490	320
61 to 112 days	130	80
113 days to 6 months	110	60
6 months to 1 year	50	40
1 year to 18 months	10	10
18 months to 24 months	10	10
Total detainees	800	520

Latest figures identified

CHAPTER 5 – UNITS OF THE REGULAR ARMY (DURING 2015)

The Cavalry
The cavalry consists of 9 armoured regiments and one mounted ceremonial regiment as follows:

The Household Cavalry
The Household Cavalry Regiment	HCR
The Household Cavalry Mounted Regiment	HCMRD

The Royal Armoured Corps
1st The Queen's Dragoon Guards	QDG
The Royal Scots Dragoon Guards	SCOTS DG
The Royal Dragoon Guards	RDG
The Queen's Royal Hussars	QRH
The Royal Lancers	RL
The King's Royal Hussars	KRH
The Light Dragoons	LD
1st Royal Tank Regiment	1 RTR

The Infantry
Comprised of 31 battalions available for operations (including two Guards Battalions on public duties in London).

The Guards Division
1st Bn Grenadier Guards	1 GREN GDS
1st Bn Coldstream Guards	1 COLM GDS
1st Bn Scots Guards	1 SG
1st Bn Irish Guards	1 IG
1st Bn Welsh Guards	1 WG

Note: There are generally two battalions from the Guards Division on public duties in London at any one time. When a Regiment is stationed in London on public duties it is given an extra company to ensure the additional manpower required for ceremonial events is available.

The Scottish Division
The Royal Scots Borderers, 1st Bn The Royal Regiment of Scotland	1 SCOTS
The Royal Highland Fusiliers, 2nd Bn The Royal Regiment of Scotland	2 SCOTS
The Black Watch, 3rd Bn The Royal Regiment of Scotland	3 SCOTS
The Highlanders, 4th Bn The Royal Regiment of Scotland	4 SCOTS
The Argyll and Sutherland Highlanders, 5th Bn The Royal Regiment of Scotland	5 SCOTS

Note: The Argyll and Sutherland Highlanders, 5th Bn The Royal Regiment of Scotland is a company sized unit that undertakes ceremonial duties in Scotland.

The Queen's Division
1st Bn The Princess of Wales's Royal Regiment (Queen's and Royal Hampshire)	1 PWRR
2nd Bn The Princess of Wales's Royal Regiment (Queen's and Royal Hampshire)	2 PWRR
1st Bn The Royal Regiment of Fusiliers	1 RRF
1st Bn The Royal Anglian Regiment	1 R ANGLIAN
2nd Bn The Royal Anglian Regiment	2 R ANGLIAN

The King's Division
1st Bn The Duke of Lancaster's Regiment (King's, Lancashire and Border)	1 LANCS
2nd Bn The Duke of Lancaster's Regiment (King's, Lancashire and Border)	2 LANCS
1st Bn The Yorkshire Regiment (14th/15th, 19th and 33rd/76th Foot)	1 YORKS
2nd Bn The Yorkshire Regiment (14th/15th, 19th and 33rd/76th Foot)	2 YORKS

The Prince of Wales's Division
1st Bn The Mercian Regiment (Cheshire)	1 MERCIAN
2nd Bn The Mercian Regiment (Worcesters and Foresters)	2 MERCIAN
1st Bn The Royal Welsh	1 R WELSH
1st Bn The Royal Irish Regiment	1 R IRISH

The Rifles
1st Bn The Rifles	1 RIFLES
2nd Bn The Rifles	2 RIFLES
3rd Bn The Rifles	3 RIFLES
4th Bn The Rifles	4 RIFLES
5th Bn The Rifles	5 RIFLES

The Brigade of Gurkhas
1st Bn The Royal Gurkha Rifles	1 RGR
2nd Bn The Royal Gurkha Rifles	2 RGR

The Parachute Regiment
1st Bn The Parachute Regiment	1 PARA
2nd Bn The Parachute Regiment	2 PARA
3rd Bn The Parachute Regiment	3 PARA

Note: 1st Bn The Parachute Regiment forms the core element of the Special Forces Support Group and is not generally included in the infantry order of battle.

Since 2002 there have been four infantry training battalions at the Infantry Training Centre located at Catterick in North Yorkshire.

Under Director Special Forces
The 22nd Special Air Service Regiment	22 SAS
Special Reconnaissance Regiment	SRR

Although the SAS cannot be classed as a traditional infantry unit, for brevity the SAS are listed here. Members of the regiment are found from all arms and services of the Army after exhaustive selection tests.

The Royal Regiment of Artillery (RA)
1st Regiment Royal Horse Artillery	1 RHA
3rd Regiment Royal Horse Artillery	3 RHA
4th Regiment Royal horse Artillery	4 RHA
5th Regiment	5 REGT
7th (Parachute) Regiment Royal Horse Artillery	7 RHA
12th Regiment	12 REGT
14th Regiment	14 REGT
16th Regiment	16 REGT
19th Regiment	19 REGT
26th Regiment	26 REGT

29th Commando Regiment	29 REGT
32nd Regiment	32 REGT
47th Regiment	47 REGT

Note: The King's Troop Royal Horse Artillery is a ceremonial unit and 14th Regiment is a training unit.

The Corps of Royal Engineers (RE)

21st Engineer Regiment	21 ENGR REGT
22nd Engineer Regiment	22 ENGR REGT
23rd Engineer Regiment (Air Assault)	23 ENGR REGT
24th Commando Regiment	24 CDO REGT
26th Engineer Regiment	26 ENGR REGT
32nd Engineer Regiment	32 ENGR REGT
33rd Engineer Regiment (EOD)	33 ENGR REGT
35th Engineer Regiment	35 ENGR REGT
36th Engineer Regiment	36 ENGR REGT
39th Engineer Regiment (Air Support)	39 ENGR REGT
42nd Engineer Regiment (Geographic)	42 ENGR REGT

The Royal Corps of Signals (R SIGNALS)

1st Signal Regiment	1 SIG REGT
2nd Signal Regiment	2 SIG REGT
3rd Signal Regiment	3 SIG REGT
10th Signal Regiment	10 SIG REGT
14th Signal Regiment (Electronic Warfare)	14 SIG REGT
15th Signal Regiment (Information Systems)	15 SIG REGT
16th Signal Regiment	16 SIG REGT
18th (UKSF) Signal Regiment	18 SIG REGT
21st Signal Regiment (Air Support)	21 SIG REGT
22nd Signal Regiment	22 SIG REGT
30th Signal Regiment	30 SIG REGT

The Army Air Corps (AAC)

1st Regiment	1 REGT AAC
3rd Regiment	3 REGT AAC
4th Regiment	4 REGT AAC
5th Regiment	5 REGT AAC

THE SERVICES

The Royal Logistic Corps (RLC)

1st Close Support Regiment	1 REGT RLC
3rd Close Support Regiment	3 REGT RLC
4th Close Support Regiment	4 REGT RLC
6th Force Logistic Regiment	6 REGT RLC
7th Force Logistic Regiment	7 REGT RLC
9th Theatre Logistic Regiment	9 REGT RLC
10th Queens Own Gurkha Logistic Regiment	10 REGT RLC
11th Explosive Ordnance Disposal Regiment	11 REGT RLC
13th Air Assault Regiment	13 REGT RLC
17th Port and Maritime Regiment	17 REGT RLC
27th Theatre Logistic Regiment	27 REGT RLC
29th Postal, Courier & Movements Regiment	29 REGT RLC

Royal Electrical and Mechanical Engineers (REME)

1st Close Support Battalion REME	1 BN REME
2nd Close Support Battalion REME	2 BN REME
3rd Armoured Close Support Battalion REME	3 BN REME
4th Armoured Close Support Battalion REME	4 BN REME
5th Force Support Battalion REME	5 BN REME
7th (Air Assault) Battalion REME	7 BN REME

Royal Army Medical Corps (RAMC)

1st Armoured Medical Regiment	1 MED REGT
2nd Medical Regiment	2 MED REGT
3rd Medical Regiment	3 MED REGT
4th Armoured Medical Regiment	4 MED REGT
5th Armoured Medical Regiment	5 MED REGT
16th Close Support Medical Regiment	16 MED REGT
22nd Field Hospital	22 FD HOSP
33rd Field Hospital	33 FD HOSP
34th Field Hospital	34 FD HOSP

Intelligence Corps (I Corps)

1st Military Intelligence Battalion	1 MI BN
2nd Military Intelligence Battalion	2 MI BN
4rd Military Intelligence Battalion	3 MI BN

Royal Military Police (RMP)

1st Regiment Royal Military Police	1 RMP
3rd Regiment Royal Military Police	3 RMP
4th Regiment Royal Military Police	4 RMP
Special Investigation Branch Regiment	SIB
Special Operations Unit	SOU
Military Provost Staff Unit	MPSC

Military Bands

Following the 2007 re-organisation of military bands the Regular Army (Corps of Army Music) has 24 bands as follows:

Household Cavalry	–	70 musicians	–	2 bands
Grenadier Guards	–	49 musicians	–	1 band
Coldstream Guards	–	49 musicians	–	1 band
Scots Guards	–	49 musicians	–	1 band
Welsh Guards	–	49 musicians	–	1 band
Irish Guards	–	49 musicians	–	1 band
Royal Artillery	–	49 musicians	–	1 band
Royal Engineers	–	35 musicians	–	1 band
Royal Signals	–	35 musicians	–	1 band
Royal Logistic Corps	–	35 musicians	–	1 band
REME	–	35 musicians	–	1 band
Adjutant General's Corps	–	35 musicians	–	1 band
Army Air Corps	–	35 musicians	–	1 band
Royal Armoured Corps	–	70 musicians	–	2 bands
Royal Regiment of Scotland	–	35 musicians	–	1 band
Queens Division	–	35 musicians	–	1 band

Kings Division	– 35 musicians	– 1 band
Prince of Wales's Division	– 35 musicians	– 1 band
The Rifles	– 35 musicians	– 1 band
Parachute Regiment	– 35 musicians	– 1 band
Royal Irish Regiment	– 35 musicians	– 1 band
Royal Gurkha Rifles	– 35 musicians	– 1 band

During 2014 the Corps of Army Music had 799 personnel and requires an annual intake of some 66 recruits.

CHAPTER 6 – RESERVE FORCES

OVERVIEW

There have been reserve land forces in Britain since medieval times. Over time, the titles and structures of these reserve forces have changed, but until World War Two essentially comprised four separate elements: Volunteers, Militia, and Yeomanry provided the part-time, voluntary territorial forces; while retired Regular Army personnel made up the Army Regular Reserve on a compulsory basis, subject to diminishing obligations with age. Today the Army Reserve is formed from the same components – both Regular and Volunteers, with the difference that the erstwhile Volunteers, Militia, and Yeomanry are now incorporated into a single volunteer force as the Army Reserve (previously Territorial Army).

There are three reserve elements:

♦ The Army Regular Reserve
♦ The Long Term Reserve
♦ Volunteer Reserves

The Army Regular Reserve
Comprises ex-regular other ranks and officers who retain a liability to be called up for military service after they leave service. Other ranks who have voluntarily left the Army with less than 18 years service retain a reserve liability for up to six years or until they reach the 18-year point. The Army Regular Reserve also includes personnel who have applied to return to military service on fixed term reserve contracts. These include some mobilised and High Readiness Reserves, Full Time Reserve Service and Additional Duties Commitments. Officers retain a reserve liability until they are in receipt of their pension.

During late 2014 there were about 35,000 Army Regular Reserves.

The Long Term Reserve
Consists of ex-regular other ranks who have completed their reserve liability or have no reserve liability on discharge but who can be recalled for service under section 68 of the Reserve Forces Act. This would only happen under circumstances where national danger is imminent, an emergency has arisen or in the event of an attack on the United Kingdom. The Long Term Reserve liability includes the Regular Reserve liability and remains to age 55 or up to 18 years after leaving service, whichever is earlier.

During late 2014 there were about 36,000 Long Term Reserves.

The Army Reserve (Volunteers)
The Army Reserve provides highly trained soldiers who can work alongside the Regulars on missions in the UK and overseas. Personnel are essentially civilians who accept an annual training commitment and a liability to call-out for permanent service (which is time-limited, depending on the type of call-out order). They typically attend training on a part-time basis throughout the year, including an Annual Camp which runs for around two weeks. When they are serving or training they are paid at the same rates as regular personnel and if they complete a specified amount of training per year they then become eligible for an annual Bounty payment.

Future Reserve 2020 (FR20) – Volunteer Reserves
The 2010 Strategic Defence and Security Review (SDSR) stated that the Reserve Forces should be an integral part of this Future Force; providing additional capacity as well as certain specialists whom it would not be practical or cost effective to maintain in the regular forces. The 2011 Reserve Forces Review recommended a Maritime Reserves of 3,100 trained personnel, an Army Reserve of 30,000 trained personnel, and the Royal Auxiliary Air Force (RAuxAF) personnel strength of 1,800.

Current plans call for the Army Reserve to recruit up to 30,000 trained soldiers plus another 8,000 soldiers in training, to provide an integrated and trained Army by 2018. The Army Reserve will be manned, trained and equipped as part of the Whole Force.

Formed Army Reserve units are paired with Regular Units.

As of early 2015 there were an estimated 20,480 trained personnel in the Army Reserve.

Officers	–	4,160
Soldiers	–	16,310

As of late 2015 there are 70 major units in the Army Reserve Order of Battle:

Army Reserve Order of Battle, as identified in Mid 2015

Arm or Corps	Number of regiments or battalions
Infantry	14
Armour	4
Royal Artillery	7
Royal Engineers	4
Special Air Service	2
Royal Signals	4
Equipment Support	2
Logistics	12
Intelligence Corps	4
Army Air Corps	1
Medical	15 (1)
Total	70

(1) Total includes Medical Regiments and Field Hospitals.

ARMY RESERVE MAJOR UNITS AND SUB-UNIT LOCATIONS FROM 2016.

Major Unit	Headquarters Location	Sub-unit locations
Royal Armoured Corps		
The Royal Yeomanry	Fulham and Croydon	Croydon, Nottingham, Leicester, Dudley, Telford
The Royal Wessex Yeomanry	Bovington	Salisbury, Swindon, Cirencester, Hereford, Paignton, Exeter
The Scottish and North Irish Yeomanry	Edinburgh	Ayr, Belfast, Cupar
The Queen's Own Yeomanry	Newcastle	Newcastle, York, Chester, Wigan
Royal Artillery		
The Honourable Artillery Company	City of London	City of London
101 (Northumbrian) Regiment Royal Artillery	Gateshead	Blyth, Newcastle, South Shields, Leeds
103 (Lancashire) Regiment Royal Artillery	St Helens	Liverpool, Manchester Wolverhampton, Bolton

104 Regiment Royal Artillery	Newport	Bristol, Abertillery, Cardiff, Worcester, Newport
105 Regiment Royal Artillery	Edinburgh	Newtonards, Coleraine, Glasgow, Arbroath, Shetland, Edinburgh
106 (Yeomanry) Regiment Royal Artillery	Lewisham	Grove Park, Portsmouth, Southampton
Central Volunteer HQ Royal Artillery	Woolwich	Woolwich, Larkhill, Bath

Royal Engineers

The Royal Monmouthshire Royal Engineers (Militia)	Monmouth	Jersey, Cwmbran, Swansea, Oldbury, Stoke-on-Trent
71 Engineer Regiment	RAF Leuchars	Paisley, Inchinnan, Cumbernauld, Orkney, Bangor
75 Engineer Regiment	Warrington	Birkenhead, Manchester, Holton
Reserve engineer units attached to regular units	At various UK locations	See Note (1)

Royal Signals

32 Signal Regiment	Glasgow	Belfast, Londonderry, Darlington, Leeds, Edinburgh, East Kilbride
37 Signal Regiment	Redditch	Birmingham, Coventry, Liverpool, Manchester Darlington, Leeds, Sheffield, Nottingham
39 Signal Regiment	Bristol	Bath, Windsor, Cardiff, Gloucester
71 (City of London) Signal Regiment	Bexleyheath	Lincoln's Inn, Whipps Cross, Colchester, Chelmsford, Uxbridge, Coulsdon

Infantry

6th Battalion Royal Regiment of Scotland	Glasgow	Edinburgh, Bathgate, Galashiels, Ayr, Dumfries, Kilmarnock, Glasgow, Motherwell
7th Battalion Royal Regiment of Scotland	Perth	Dumbarton, Stirling, Dundee, Inverness, Stornoway, Aberdeen, Elgin, Peterhead
3rd Battalion Princess of Wales Royal Regiment	Canterbury	Farnham, Brighton, Eastbourne, Rochester, Canterbury
4th Battalion The Duke of Lancaster's Regiment	Preston	Blackburn, Workington, Carlisle, Barrow in Furness
5th Battalion The Royal Regiment of Fusiliers	Newcastle	Durham, Doncaster, Newcastle, Hexham, Cramlington, Alnwick
3rd Battalion The Royal Anglian Regiment	Bury St Edmunds	Norwich, Lowestoft, Leicester, Lincoln, Chelmsford, Hertford
4th Battalion The Yorkshire Regiment	York	Hull, Beverley, Scarborough, Huddersfield, Barnsley

4th Battalion the Mercian Regiment	Wolverhampton	Birmingham, Nottingham, Mansfield, Stoke-on-Trent,
3rd Battalion the Royal Welsh	Cardiff	Swansea, Pontypridd, Colwyn Bay
2nd Battalion the Royal Irish Regiment	Lisburn	Belfast, Newtonabbey, Bellarmine, Portadown, Enniskillen
4th Battalion the Parachute Regiment	Pudsey	Glasgow, Edinburgh, White City, St Helens, Pudsey, Hebburn
The London Regiment	Westminster (Rochester Row)	Westminster (Horseferry Road), Edgware Balham, Blackheath, Camberwell
6th Bn The Rifles	Exeter	Gloucester, Bristol, Dorchester, Poole, Plymouth, Barnstaple, Shrewsbury
7th Bn The Rifles	Reading	Abingdon, London (Davies Street), West Ham

Army Air Corps

6 Regiment Army Air Corps	Bury St Edmunds	Taunton, Yeovil, Bury St Edmunds, Milton Keynes, Luton, Portsmouth, Middle Wallop
Aviation Specialist Group	Middle Wallop	Middle Wallop

Royal Logistic Corps

150 Transport Regiment	Hull	Leeds, Hull, Doncaster
151 Transport Regiment	Croydon	Brentwood, Maidstone, Sutton, Barnett, Southall
152 Fuel Support Regiment	Belfast	Londonderry, Coleraine, Belfast,
154 (Scottish) Transport Regiment	Dunfermline	Dunfermline, Glasgow, Edinburgh, Irvine
156 Supply Regiment	Liverpool	Birkenhead, Salford, Bootle, Lancaster
157 (Welsh) Transport Regiment	Cardiff	Queensferry, Swansea, Haverfordwest, Carmarthen, Cardiff
158 Transport Regiment	Peterborough	Bedford, Ipswich, Colchester, Loughborough, Lincoln
159 Supply Regiment	Canley	Telford, Tynemouth, West Bromwich, Coventry
162 Postal Courier & Movements Regiment	Nottingham	Swindon, Nottingham, Coulby Newham,
165 (Wessex) Port & Enabling Regiment	Plymouth	Plymouth, Southampton,
166 Supply Regiment	Grantham	Banbury, Grantham, Aylesbury
167 Catering Support Regiment	Grantham	Grantham
2 Operational Support Group	Grantham	Grantham

Royal Army Medical Corps

225 (Scottish) Medical Regiment	Dundee	Stirling, Glenrothes, Dundee
253 (North Irish) Medical Regiment	Belfast	Limavady, Enniskillen, Belfast
254 (East of England) Medical Regiment	Cambridge	Ditton, Colchester, Norwich, Hitchin, Brentwood
201 (Northern) Field Hospital	Newcastle	Newton Aycliffe, Stockton on Tees, Newcastle
202 (Midlands) Field Hospital	Birmingham	Coventry, Stoke-on-Trent, Shrewsbury, Abingdon
203 (Welsh) Field Hospital	Cardiff	Swansea, Crickhowell, Colwyn Bay, Cardiff
204 (North Irish) Field Hospital	Belfast	Portadown, Belfast
205 (Scottish) Field Hospital	Glasgow	Aberdeen, Dundee, Edinburgh, Inverness, Glasgow
207 (Manchester) Field Hospital	Manchester	Stockport, Bury, Chorley, Manchester
208 (Liverpool) Field Hospital	Liverpool	Liverpool, Chester, Blackpool, Lancaster
212 (Yorkshire) Field Hospital	Sheffield	Leeds, York, Nottingham, Lincoln, Hull
243 (Wessex) Field Hospital	Keynsham	Gloucester, Exeter, Plymouth, Truro, Portsmouth
256 (City of London) Field Hospital	Walworth	Kensington, Kingston upon Thames, Brighton
306 Hospital Support Regiment	Strensall	Strensall
335 Medical Evacuation Regiment	Strensall	Strensall
Army Medical Services Operational Support Group	Strensall	Strensall

Royal Electrical and Mechanical Engineers

101 Battalion REME	Wrexham	Prestatyn, Liverpool, Manchester, West Bromwich, Telford
102 Battalion REME	Newton Aycliffe	Newcastle upon Tyne, Scunthorpe, Rotherham, Sheffield, Newton Aycliffe
103 Battalion REME	Crawley	Croydon, Portsmouth, Ashford, Bexleyheath, Barnett, Brentwood
104 Battalion REME	Northampton	Corby, Coventry, Redditch, Swindon, Nottingham, Derby
105 Battalion REME	Bristol	Yeovil, Taunton, Gloucester, Bristol, Bridgend, Cwmbran
106 Battalion REME	East Kilbride	Belfast, Lisburn, Dunfermline, Edinburgh, Grangemouth

Royal Military Police

1 Regiment Royal Military Police	Livingston and Stockton on Tees	Livingston and Stockton on Tees
3 Regiment Royal Military Police	Cannock and Manchester	Cannock and Manchester
4 Regiment Royal Military Police	Tulse Hill	Tulse Hill
Special Investigation Branch Regiment	Bulford	Bulford
1 Company Military Provost Staff Corps	Colchester	Colchester

These RMP Reserve units are attached to the regular regiments shown.

Royal Army Veterinary Corps

1 Military Working Dog Regiment RAVC	North Luffenham	North Luffenham

Intelligence Corps

3 Military Intelligence Battalion	London (Worship Street)	Cambridge, Hampstead, Worship Street)
5 Military Intelligence Battalion	Edinburgh	Glasgow, Newcastle, Leeds, Edinburgh
6 Military Intelligence Battalion	Manchester	Lisburn, Stourbridge, Bletchley, Manchester
7 Military Intelligence Battalion	Bristol	Cardiff, Southampton, Exeter, Hermitage, Bristol
Specialist Group of Military Intelligence	Hermitage	Hermitage
Media Operations Group	Kingston Upon Thames	

Note:

(1) There are Reserve Engineer units attached to regular units at the following locations: Bangor, Newcastle, Sheffield, Batley, Chilwell, Chesterfield, Plymouth, London, Bath, Reading, Wyton, Ewell, Wakefield, Hull, Ilford, Southend, Wimbish, Catford, Bexleyheath, Westminster, Reigate, Rochester, Royal Tunbridge Wells.

ORGANISATION

Army Reserve units are widely dispersed across the country – much more so than the Regular Forces, and in many areas they are the visible face of the Armed Forces. They help to keep society informed about the Armed Forces, and of the importance of defence to the nation, and have an active role supporting the Cadet organisations. They provide a means by which the community as a whole can contribute to the security of the United Kingdom.

The basic command structure and organisation of the Army Reserve is the same as for Regular units, by way of regiments, battalions and companies. In addition, the Directors of the various Arms and Services have the same responsibilities for the Army Reserve as their Regular units.

Recruits need to be at least 17 years old in order to join the Army Reserve. The upper age limit depends on what an individual has to offer, but it is normally 30 for those joining as an officer and 32 as a soldier. There are exceptions to the upper age limit for those with certain specialist skills or previous military experience.

Unless recruits have previous military experience, when they join the Army Reserve they will have to undergo basic recruit training. Basic training (Phase 1 Alpha) takes place over four weekends at Regional Army Training Units (ATU) or an eight day course at similar training units. Following successful completion of Phase 1 Alpha training recruits then go on to undertake a consolidated 15 day course (Phase 1 Bravo) at the Army Training Centre (Pirbright). This establishment is the Army's largest single Phase 1 recruit training establishment and is comprised of two Army training regiments, 1 ATR and 2 ATR plus a headquarters support unit.

Both courses use training modules from the common military syllabus for standard entry recruits. During this basic training stage, recruits will learn basic soldiering skills according to the Army Reserve Common Military Syllabus. This covers areas as diverse as how to wear uniform, physical fitness, weapon handling, first aid, fieldcraft, map reading and military terminology.

ATR (Pirbright) has an average annual throughput of approximately 4,700 recruits. In addition, there are nine regional ATUs.

Personnel who have qualified through TSC A and B form the main part of the active, Army Reserve. They train regularly, and are paid at the same rates as the regular forces on a pro-rata basis.

Most volunteers commit to around some 40 days training a year, comprised of drill nights and weekends plus 14 days annual training. Some reservists exceed these commitments.

The Reserve Forces Act 1996 provided for other categories of reservists, such as:

♦ Full Time Reserve Service (FTRS) – reservists who wish to serve full time with regulars for a predetermined period in a specific posting.
♦ Additional Duties Commitment – part-time service for a specified period in a particular post.

The Act also provided a category of service:

♦ Sponsored Reserves, are contractor staff who have agreed to join the Reserves and have a liability to be called up when required to continue their civilian work on operations alongside the Service personnel who depend upon them. Some 3,000 sponsored reservists have served in Iraq and Afghanistan.

TYPES OF ARMY RESERVE UNITS

The most familiar type of unit is the 'Independent'. This will be found at the local Army Reserve Centre (formerly called the Drill Hall). One or more Army Reserve units will be accommodated at the centre, varying in size from a platoon or troop (about 30 Volunteers) to a Battalion or Regiment (about 600 Volunteers). These units will have their place in the Order of Battle, and as with Regular Army units, are equipped for their role. Most of the personnel will be part-time. Volunteers parade one evening each week and perhaps one weekend each month in addition to the annual two-week unit training period.

Some staff with Army Reserve units will be regular soldiers. Many units have regular Commanding Officers, Regimental Sergeant Majors, Training Majors, Adjutants and Instructors. The Permanent Staff Instructors (PSI) who are regular Senior Non-Commissioned Officers, are key personnel who help organise the training and administration of the Volunteers.

In the main, Army Reserve units have a General Purpose structure which will give them flexibility of employment across the spectrum of military operations. All Infantry Battalions, including Parachute Battalions, have a common establishment of three Rifle Companies and a Headquarters Company. Each rifle company sometimes has a support platoon with mortar, anti-tank, reconnaissance, Medium Machine Gun (MMG) and assault pioneer sections under command.

The other type of unit is the 'Specialist'. These are located centrally, usually at the Headquarters or Training Centre of the Arm or Corps. Their members, spread across the country, are mainly civilians who already have the necessary skills or specialities, and require a minimum of military training.

An example of these can be found in the Army Medical Services Specialist Units whose doctors, surgeons, nurses and technicians from all over the country meet at regular intervals on a training area at home or abroad. They are on the lowest commitment for training, which is the equivalent of just two weekends and a two week camp each year, or it can be even less for some medical categories.

OFFICERS

Officer recruiting and training may take one of two forms. Officers can be recruited from the ranks, and appointed officer cadets by their unit commander, before taking the Army Reserve Commissioning Course at the Royal Military Academy, Sandhurst. Alternatively, the direct entry officer training scheme allows potential officers to enter officer training right from the very start of their time in the Army Reserve. Initial Officer Training is designed to produce officers with the generic qualities to lead soldiers both on and off operations and includes three weeks spent on the Army Reserve Commissioning Course at the Royal Military Academy, Sandhurst.

MOBILISATION AND CALL OUT

Before reservists can be mobilised and sent on operations, a 'Call Out Order' has to be signed by the Secretary of State for Defence. He has the power to authorise the use of reserves in situations of war or on humanitarian and peacekeeping operations.

Before they are sent to their operational postings, reservists must undergo a period of induction where they are issued with equipment, given medical examinations and receive any specialist training relevant to their operations. For the Army Reserve and the RMR (Royal Marines Reserve), this takes place at the Reinforcements Training and Mobilisation Centre (RTMC) near Nottingham.

Under the Reserve Forces Act 1996, principal call out powers would be brought into effect in a crisis by the issue of a call out order. Members of the Reserve Forces are then liable for service anywhere in the world, unless the terms of service applicable in individual cases restrict liability to service within the UK.

Call out powers are vested in and authorised by Her Majesty the Queen who may make an order authorising call-out:

♦ If it appears to her that national danger is imminent
♦ Or that a great emergency has arisen
♦ Or in the event of an actual or apprehended attack on the United Kingdom.

The Secretary of State for Defence may make an order authorising call out:

♦ If it appears to him that warlike preparations are in preparation or progress.
♦ Or it appears to him that it is necessary or desirable to use armed forces on operations outside the UK for the protection of life or property.
♦ And for operations anywhere in the world for the alleviation of distress or the preservation of life or property in time of disaster or apprehended disaster.

Reservists and employers may apply for deferral of, or exemption from call out. It is recognised that those called out may not find the outcomes of their initial applications to their satisfaction. Therefore a system of arbitration has been set up.

Call Out Procedure

Army Reserve soldiers and officers are called out using a Call Out Notice specifying the time, date and place to which they are to report. If Army Reserve Units or Sub-Units are called out, they form up with their vehicles and equipment at their Army Reserve Centres or other designated locations. They would then be deployed by land, sea and air to their operational locations in the UK or overseas. However, if Army Reserve personnel are called out as individuals, they would report to a Temporary Mobilisation Centre where they would be processed before posting to reinforce a unit or HQ.

REIMBURSEMENT

The Reserve Forces Act (RFA) 1996 enables reimbursement to be made to Employers and Reservists for some of the additional costs of employees being called out. Some reservists will have financial commitments commensurate with their civilian salary and so provisions are in place to minimise financial hardship.

The MoD is also able to offset the indirect costs of employees being called out incurred by an employer, for example, the need to recruit and train temporary replacements. If employers or reservists are dissatisfied with the financial assistance awarded they may appeal to tribunals set up for this.

Pay

Army Reserve personnel are paid for every hour of training. They also receive an annual bonus, known as a bounty, subject to achieving a minimum time commitment. Travel costs for training are refunded.

As of 2015, daily rates of pay are the same for Army Reserve personnel and their Regular Army equivalents (See Pay Scales in the Miscellaneous Chapter). The exact pay rate also varies according to particular trade and type of commitment.

Hourly income is taxable, but the Annual Training Bounty is a tax-free lump sum. The value of the bounty depends on the specific unit and individual training requirement but, on a higher commitment. There is an annual training commitment to qualify for a bounty.

MANAGEMENT

Two structures have been set up within the Army Reserve in order to improve management of reserves:

♦ Reserves Manning and Career Management Division
♦ Reinforcement, Training and Mobilisation Centre (RTMC)

The role of the first is to centralise the coordination of all personnel management for the Army Reserve, bringing it more into line with the regular Army and also providing a single focus for identifying and notifying individuals for mobilisation, while the second is in charge of administrative preparation, individual training and provision of human resources requirements of individual reservists.

There are current major efforts to improve Army Reserve recruiting but getting to a total of 30,000 trained personnel is going to be a challenge. The drop-out rate among volunteers can be as high as 30 per cent in the three first years of their engagement and unless figures like these can be turned around it will be difficult to make any meaningful increase in the numbers available.

The RTMC is based at Chilwell near Nottingham and prepares all branches of the Reserve Forces and Civilians for service with the Regular Forces (in addition to Regular Individual Reinforcements). Service can range from deployment into an operational area or for a humanitarian mission.

The RTMC also assists in welcoming the troops back into the UK on return from operations and helping them return to their civilian lives.

Reserve Forces' and Cadets' Association (RFCA)

At local level, administration and support of the major elements of the Reserve Forces are carried out through the Reserve Forces' and Cadets' Association, working within the context described in the 1996

Reserve Forces Act. This is a tri-Service role which has been carried out by the Reserve Forces' and Cadets' Association and their predecessor organisations for many years. It is an unusual arrangement, but has been found to be a successful one. The Reserve Forces' and Cadets' Association system ensures that people from the local communities in which the Reserve Forces and Cadets are based, are involved in the running of Reserve and Cadet units. It also provides Reserve Forces and Cadets representatives with the right of direct access to Ministers, so that they can make representation about Reserves issues. This provides an important balance and ensures that the case for the Reserves is clearly articulated at a high level.

Reserve Forces' and Cadets' Association have a second role as administrators and suppliers of services to the Reserve and cadet forces organisations.

SaBRE (Supporting Britain's Reservists and Employees)
Formerly the National Employers' Liaison Committee (NELC)

SaBRE has grown out of the National Employers' Liaison Committee (NELC) which was formed in 1986 with a brief to provide independent advice to Ministers on the measures needed to win and maintain the support of employers, in both the public and private sectors, for those of their employees who are in the Volunteer Reserve Forces (VRF). The committee is made up of prominent businessmen and is supported by the secretariat. SaBRE provides advice on:

- The ways of educating employers on the role of the Reserve Forces in national defence, the vital role employers have to play in giving their support, and the benefits to employers and their employees of Reserve Forces training and experience.
- The current problems and attitudes of employers in relation to service by their employees in the Reserve Forces.
- Methods and inducements needed to encourage and retain the support of employers.
- Appropriate means of recognising and publicising support given by employers to the Reserve Forces.

CADETS

The Army Cadet Force is one of four cadet forces sponsored and supported by the MoD. Other Cadet Forces are the Combined Cadet Force, the Sea Cadet Corps, and the Air Training Corps. Although the cadet forces are sponsored by the MoD they are not a part of our Armed Forces.

During 2012, the Government announced a new Schools Cadet Expansion Programme to enable up to 100 more state-funded schools in England to develop cadet units by the end of 2015. The Government's goal is to significantly increase the number of young people who are able to access the cadet experience – a development that is likely to deliver significant benefits to schools and young people.

Army Cadets can be found in two separate organisations, The Combined Cadet Forces and the Army Cadet Force:

Combined Cadet Force
The Combined Cadet Force (CCF) is a tri-Service military cadet organisation based in schools and colleges throughout the UK. Although it is administered and funded by the Services it is a part of the national youth movement.

The CCF receives assistance and support for its training programme from the Regular and Reserve Forces, but the bulk of adult support is provided by members of school staffs who are responsible to head teachers for the conduct of cadet activities. CCF officers wear uniform but they are not part of the Armed Forces and carry no liability for service or compulsory training.

There are some 240 CCF contingents with as many as 45,000 cadets, of whom about 28,000 are Army Cadets with about 1,700 instructors. The role of the CCF is to help boys and girls to develop powers of leadership through training which promotes qualities of responsibility, self-reliance, resourcefulness, endurance, perseverance and a sense of service to the community. Military training is also designed to demonstrate why defence forces are needed, how they function and to stimulate an interest in a career as an officer in the Services.

The CCF is believed to receive about £10 million in funding each year.

Army Cadet Force

The role of the Army Cadet Force (ACF) is to inspire young people to achieve success with a spirit of service to the Queen, country and their local community, and to develop the qualities of good citizenship, responsibility and leadership.

Some reports suggest that Army cadets make up between 25 per cent to 30 per cent of regular army recruits. Many cadets move on to join the Army Reserve. There are about 1,600 ACF detachments based in communities around the UK with a strength of around 44,000 cadets. The ACF is run by over 8,000 adults drawn from the local community who manage a broad programme of military and adventurous training activities designed to develop character and leadership. The Army Cadets are administered by the MoD. The total budget provided to the Army Cadets is believed to have been in the region of £40 million during 2010–2011.

Mid 2015 figures suggest a total of 41,000 Army Cadets with about 9,000 adult instructors.

Cadet Training Centre

The UK Cadet Training Centre (CTC) Frimley Park in Surrey trains adult volunteers in the Army Cadet Force and the Combined Cadet Force (Army), helping new recruits understand the cadet movement's ethos and teaching them to train their cadets in a safe and effective manner.

CHAPTER 7 – THE HOUSEHOLD CAVALRY AND THE ROYAL ARMOURED CORPS

The Cavalry

The cavalry consists of 9 armoured regiments and one mounted ceremonial regiment as follows:

The Household Cavalry

The Household Cavalry Regiment	HCR
The Household Cavalry Mounted Regiment	HCMR

The Royal Armoured Corps

1st The Queen's Dragoon Guards	QDG
The Royal Scots Dragoon Guards	SCOTS DG
The Royal Dragoon Guards	RDG
The Queen's Royal Hussars	QRH
The Royal Lancers	RL
The King's Royal Hussars	KRH
The Light Dragoons	LD
1st Royal Tank Regiment	1 RTR

Reserve Army Yeomanry

The Royal Yeomanry	RY
The Royal Wessex Yeomanry	RWxY
The Scottish and North Irish Yeomanry	SNIY
The Queen's Own Yeomanry	QOY

OVERVIEW

The Household Cavalry (HCav) and The Royal Armoured Corps (RAC) are grouped together as one arm and have traditionally provided the armoured (tank) forces and the armoured reconnaissance component of the British Army.

The Household Cavalry and the RAC is composed of 10 regular regiments (including the two regiments of the Household Cavalry, discussed below) and the four reserve Yeomanry Regiments with the Army Reserve. Apart from the Royal Tank Regiment, which was formed in the First World War with the specific task of fighting in armoured vehicles, the regular element of the RAC is provided by the successors of those regiments that formed the mounted units of the pre-mechanised era. The Yeomanry Regiments are tasked with providing a variety of operational reinforcement tasks in support of the regular RAC.

Although very much part of the RAC as an 'Arm', the Household Cavalry (HCav) is a distinct corps consisting of two regiments. The Household Cavalry Mounted Regiment (HCMR), which is permanently stationed in London has the task of providing mounted troops for state ceremonial functions. The Household Cavalry Regiment (HCR) is stationed in Windsor and is an Armoured Cavalry Regiment that plays a full role in operational and training activity within the Field Army. Officers and soldiers from the Household Cavalry are posted between the two regiments as needs dictate (For general purposes, in this publication, the term RAC includes the HCav).

Roles

Armoured Cavalry Regiments with a total unit strength figure of 528 personnel provide the reconnaissance and surveillance capability previously provided by Force Reconnaissance Regiments. Until the arrival into service of the Scout SV in 2020 these regiments will continue to use the Combat Vehicle Reconnaissance (Tracked).

The Light Cavalry Regiments with a total unit strength figure of figure of 402 personnel will provide a mobile tactical reconnaissance capability in both mounted and dismounted roles. In the main Light Cavalry Regiments will be equipped with Jackal and Coyote vehicles.

T56 Regiments with a total unit strength figure of 587 personnel will continue to be equipped with Challenger 2 Main Battle Tanks.

Regiments and Roles

Unit	Role	Location	Affiliated reserve unit
Household Cavalry Regiment	Armoured Cavalry	Windsor	
Royal Dragoon Guards	Armoured Cavalry	Catterick	
Royal Lancers	Armoured Cavalry	Catterick	
Light Dragoons	Light Cavalry	Catterick	The Queens Own Yeomanry (R) (Newcastle)
1st Queen's Dragoon Guards	Light Cavalry	Swanton Morley	The Royal Yeomanry (R) (London)
The Royal Scots Dragoon Guards	Light Cavalry	Leuchars	The Scottish and North Irish Yeomanry
1st Royal Tank Regiment	Armour (T56)	Tidworth	Royal Wessex Yeomanry (R)
Kings Royal Hussars	Armour (T56)	Tidworth	Royal Wessex Yeomanry (R)
Queen's Royal Hussars	Armour (T56)	Tidworth	Royal Wessex Yeomanry (R)

Under the Army 2020 plans the overall establishment of the Royal Armoured Corps will be around 6,000 personnel.

Training

AFV Training Group	Bovington

THE ARMOURED CAVALRY REGIMENT

Each of the three brigades in 3 (United Kingdom) Division will have its own Armoured Cavalry Regiment structured and equipped to conduct a range of enabling and reconnaissance tasks in all environments. Squadrons will either work in their own Regimental Battle Group or be detached as squadrons to support other Battle Groups in their brigade.

The basic task of Reconnaissance is to obtain accurate information about the enemy and develop an intelligence picture in their areas of responsibility. Commanders rely on this up-to-the minute real time intelligence to ensure effective counters are launched.

In a defensive scenario the Armoured Cavalry Regiment's task is to identify the direction and strength of the enemy thrusts, impose maximum delay and damage to the enemy's reconnaissance forces, while allowing main forces to manoeuvre to combat the threat. They would be assisted in such a task by using their own organic long range anti-tank guided weapons and other assets that might be attached such as anti-tank helicopters (Lynx with TOW and perhaps Apache Longbow (WAH64D). In support would be longer range artillery assets of the Brigade Artillery inside an air defended area (ADA) maintained by Rapier and Stormer HVM air defence missiles.

An Armoured Cavalry regiment will be structured around three Sabre squadrons, a Command and Support squadron and a Headquarters squadron. The Sabre squadrons will each have three Reconnaissance troops, each with four vehicles, and a Support troop. The Command and Support squadron will contain three Guided Weapons troops and a Surveillance troop.

Possible Regimental Structure

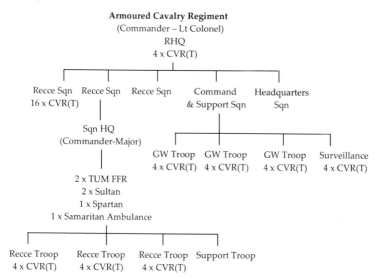

Armoured Cavalry Regiment
(Commander – Lt Colonel)
RHQ
4 x CVR(T)

Recce Sqn — Recce Sqn — Recce Sqn — Command & Support Sqn — Headquarters Sqn
16 x CVR(T)

Sqn HQ
(Commander-Major)

GW Troop   GW Troop   GW Troop   Surveillance
4 x CVR(T)   4 x CVR(T)   4 x CVR(T)   4 x CVR(T)

2 x TUM FFR
2 x Sultan
1 x Spartan
1 x Samaritan Ambulance

Recce Troop   Recce Troop   Recce Troop   Support Troop
4 x CVR(T)   4 x CVR(T)   4 x CVR(T)

A regiment usually operates with 66 x CVR(T). Total unit strength will be 528 personnel.

The majority of CVR(T) in Recce Troops are Scimitars that will be replaced by the Scout SV from 2020.

Armoured Cavalry Regiments will take part in a three year readiness cycle. The Training year will include live firing and include some simulated training such as CATT and CAST. The Regiment will take part in a major battle Group in Canada (BATUS) with live firing and tactical engagement simulation.

LIGHT CAVALRY REGIMENT

Expect the Light Cavalry Regiments to have a similar structure to the Armoured Cavalry Regiments based around 3 x Sabre Squadrons (each with 16 x Jackal) with a total unit strength figure of 402 personnel. These regiments will provide a mobile tactical reconnaissance capability in both mounted and dismounted roles and maintain a close relationship with their partnered Army Reserve Yeomanry Regiment. In the main Light Cavalry Regiments will be equipped with Jackal and Coyote vehicles while the majority of vehicles in the Yeomanry Regiments will be WMIK (Protected Patrol Vehicles) with possibly some Foxhound.

ARMOURED REGIMENT (TYPE 56)

The UK operates 227 x Challenger 2 main battle tanks with 168 in three operational regiments. The remaining 59 are used for training or are held in reserve. All three Challenger 2 Regiments are located side by side at Tidworth in Hampshire sharing common support and training facilities.

Main battle tanks will continue to provide a crucial combat capability in all armies of the future. The Armoured Regiment provides fire support to other arms (especially infantry on the objective) and the destruction of opposing armour.

The following diagram shows the current outline structure of an Armoured Regiment equipped with Challenger 2 main battle tanks. A Challenger 2 Regiment with three Squadrons of main battle tanks would have an all up total of 56 tanks when deployed for war.

Possible Regimental Structure

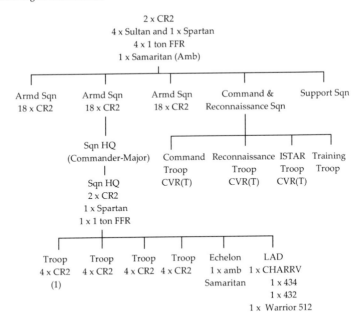

2 x CR2
4 x Sultan and 1 x Spartan
4 x 1 ton FFR
1 x Samaritan (Amb)

Armd Sqn	Armd Sqn	Armd Sqn	Command &	Support Sqn
18 x CR2	18 x CR2	18 x CR2	Reconnaissance Sqn	

Sqn HQ
(Commander-Major)

Sqn HQ
2 x CR2
1 x Spartan
1 x 1 ton FFR

Command Troop CVR(T) — Reconnaissance Troop CVR(T) — ISTAR Troop CVR(T) — Training Troop

Troop	Troop	Troop	Troop	Echelon	LAD
4 x CR2	4 x CR2	4 x CR2	4 x CR2	1 x amb	1 x CHARRV
(1)				Samaritan	1 x 434
					1 x 432
					1 x Warrior 512

Notes:

(1) Tank Troop commanded by 2Lt/Lt with Troop Sergeant as 2ic in own tank. The third tank is commanded by a Corporal.

(2) Totals: 56 x CR2, 8 x SCIMITAR, 4 x CHARRV. Total unit strength for war is approx 587.

(3) A Challenger 2 has a crew of 4 – Commander, Driver, Gunner and Loader/Operator.

(4) After extensive upgrades Challenger 2 will probably stay in service for another 20 years.

Armoured Regiments (Type 56) will also take part in a three year readiness cycle with a training year that will include live firing and include some simulated training such as CATT and CAST. The Regiment will take in a major battle Group in Canada (BATUS) with live firing and tactical engagement simulation.

The Royal Wessex Yeomanry has five squadrons, is equipped with Challenger 2 and provides trained tank crews to support the three T56 Regiments in 3 (United Kingdom) Division.

ARMOUR IN THE 21ST CENTURY

Armour has provided battle winning shock action and firepower since the earliest tanks helped to break the stalemate of the Western Front during the First World War. In the same way, armoured reconnaissance, with the ability to penetrate the enemy's forward defences and gain information by using stealth and firepower, has shaped the way in which armour has been used to its best advantage.

Defence represents the best use of ground features in conjunction with engineering and concealed firepower. The ability of armour to overwhelm all but the heaviest defences and deliver a group of highly capable armoured fighting platforms into the combat area remains a battle winning capability embraced by all major armies.

The modern main battle tank weighs between 50 and 70 tonnes, can move at up to 60 kph and can virtually always guarantee a first round hit with its main armament out to 2000 m. Last tested in combat in the Gulf War of 2003, UK armoured forces demonstrated the advantages of armour in a desert landscape. Amongst these was the ability to cover rough terrain quickly and by the use of superior concentrated firepower, create operational level, rather than simple local tactical, advantage. These tanks used the most up to date information systems and state of the art imaging and sighting systems to locate, close with and destroy the enemy. The 2003 Gulf War experience underlined the need for all elements of manoeuvre forces to be able to move swiftly and securely with protection and firepower to maintain a high 'operational tempo'. This includes infantry, artillery and of course the massive logistic supply required.

The argument that 'the days of the tank are over' has been around for many years and certainly since the appearance of the man-portable guided missile in large numbers such as during the Yom Kippur war almost 30 years ago. The advent of the highly capable Attack Helicopter and long-range, smart top-attack precision munitions has only added to this debate. However, tanks remain in the world in large numbers – at least 50,000 by current estimates – and in a surprisingly large number of countries. Whilst the supremacy of armour on the modern battlefield will continue to be challenged by ever more sophisticated anti-armour systems, the requirement for highly mobile, protected direct firepower that can operate in all conditions and climates will remain an enduring requirement to support the infantry. It is this 'endurance' characteristic and the ability to operate in all circumstances which is unique and is not shared by helicopters and aircraft. Ever military man will agree that the firepower and flexibility of the main battle tank provides a capability on the battlefield that no other system can match.

It would appear that the UK has decided to retain 227 MBT in service. However, other countries appear to have placed a very high priority on the numbers to be retained in their MBT fleets:

International Comparison – Major Army Formations and Equipment Available (Estimate)

Serial	Country	Main Battle Tanks
1	United States	1,500
2	China	3,000
3	Japan	600
4	Russia	2,000
5	European Union	4,000

Note:
Numbers in this table are our estimates of the numbers of modern main battle tanks available after analysis of a number of sources such as HIS/Jane's, the International Institute for Strategic Studies (IISS) and the Stockholm Institute for Peace Research (SIPRI).

What is certain to change in the future is the shape and size of future tanks. The key is that new technology will allow protection to be delivered in quite different ways. Traditionally, protection has been provided through ballistic armour which, because of its weight, has to be optimised over a relatively narrow frontal arc, with reduced protection on the sides, top rear and belly. Thus full protection is only possible on a small proportion of the total surface area. In the future a more holistic approach is likely to incorporate a wide range of 'survivability' characteristics in view of the three-dimensional and all round threat. These measures include: signature reduction in all aspects – acoustic, visual, thermal, radar cross-section etc; suites of active and passive defensive aids and electro-optic countermeasures; and inherent redundancy in vehicle design and crew i.e. the ability to sustain considerable damage yet be able to continue fighting. The concept is based on a theory of 'don't be detected – if detected, don't be acquired – if acquired, don't be hit – if hit, don't be penetrated – if penetrated, don't be killed'. Such an approach is likely to see future tanks of much smaller design and of significantly lesser weight. In turn, reduced weight and size will improve mobility and enable armour to be deployed more rapidly, strategically if necessary, whilst also reducing the very considerable mobility and logistic support that the heavy 60–70 tonne MBTs of today require.

In terms of firepower, smart, extended range munitions such as fire and forget Gun Launched Anti-tank Guided Missiles, pre-programmable ammunition and other novel natures are all likely to increase the potency of armour. In coming to a balanced view on the future of the tank, the heavy modern tank of today has as much in common with the Mark V tank of 1916 as it will have with its successor in 2030.

Digitisation of the future battlefield has been identified as essential, but base architecture programmes essential for the target data transmission through battlefield management systems is currently running some ten to fifteen years behind schedule. This time lag may enable the tank in its present form to survive for much longer than many analysts had previously predicted.

In the next decade of the 21st Century, we see the major defence orientated countries of the world undergoing a major doctrinal and conceptual rethink based on the information age, embracing new IT and digital technology capabilities. The future, however, always has its roots in the present and while the large fleets of tanks we now have may be more visible from space, and more difficult to protect from remotely fired missiles and guns, the armies who have them will continue to explore and exploit armoured 'stretch' technologies to ensure their armoured capability is credible.

We have no doubt that in both limited and general war the main battle tank is one of the essential systems that will determine the outcome of any battle, and there is also a sound argument to be made regarding the utility of the main battle tank in some counter insurgency operations. Of special interest is the successful use of Leopard MBT in Afghanistan by Canadian, Danish and German forces.

It is impossible to know where the British Army will be and what it will be doing 10 years from now. Experience has taught us that the only thing that we can be sure of is that the current operational requirement, which generally calls for lighter armour will almost certainly be totally different from what it is today. We firmly believe that the main battle tank will continue to have a major effect on military operations in this difficult and dangerous world for many years to come.

"The man who looks 10 years out and says he knows what the strategic situation will look like, is quite frankly the Court Jester".

General Sir Richard Dannet KCB CBE MC ADC Gen

CHAPTER 8 – ARMOURED AND PROTECTED VEHICLES

ARMOURED VEHICLES

Challenger 2

(227 available – mid 1015) Crew 4; Length Gun Forward 11.55 m; Height 2.5 m; Width 4.2 m with appliqué armour; Ground Clearance 0.51 m; Combat Weight 62.5 tonnes; Main Armament 1 x 120 mm L30 CHARM Gun; Ammunition Carried max 50 rounds stowed – APFSDS, HESH and Smoke; Secondary Armament Co-axial 7.62 mm Chain Gun; Loaders pintle mounted 7.62 mm GPMG; Ammunition Carried 4000 rounds 7.62 mm; Engine CV12 12 cylinder – Auxiliary Power Unit 4 – stroke diesel; Gearbox TN54 epicyclic – 6 forward gears and 2 reverse; Road Speed 59 kph; Cross-Country Speed 40 kph; Fuel Capacity 1,592 litres usable internal plus 2 x 175 litre external fuel drums.

Challenger 2 was manufactured by Vickers Defence Systems and production was undertaken at their factories in Newcastle-Upon-Tyne and Leeds. The British Army officially took delivery of its last Challenger 2 MBT during April 2002. At 1999 prices Challenger 2 is believed to cost £4 million per vehicle.

Challenger 2. (Copyright BAe Systems)

Although the hull and automotive parts of the Challenger 2 are based upon that of its predecessor Challenger 1, Challenger 2 incorporates over 150 improvements which have achieved substantially increased reliability and ease of maintenance. The Challenger 2 turret is, however, of a totally new design. The vehicle has a crew of four – commander, gunner, loader/signaller and driver and is equipped with a 120 mm rifled Royal Ordnance L30 gun firing all current tank ammunition natures.

The design of the turret incorporates several of the significant features that Vickers had developed for its Mk 7 MBT (a Vickers turret on a Leopard 2 chassis). The central feature is an entirely new fire control system based on the Ballistic Control System developed by Computing Devices Company (Canada) for the US Army's M1A1 MBT. This second generation computer incorporates dual 32-bit processors with a MIL STD1553B databus and has sufficient growth potential to accept Battlefield Information Control System (BICS) functions and navigation aids (a GPS satnav system). The armour is an uprated version of Challenger 1's Chobham armour.

Following the 2010 SDSR the majority of the UK' Challenger 2's are stationed in the UK following the return of British Forces from Germany. There are 3 x Regiments in the UK with a vehicle fleet of around 168 vehicles with the remaining 59 vehicles being used for training or being kept in reserve.(some of which will be stationed at an overseas training area – possibly Suffield in Canada).

Challenger Repair and Recovery Vehicle (CRARRV)

(80 available – mid 2015) Crew 3; Length 9.59 m; Operating Width 3.62 m; Height 3.005 m; Ground Clearance 0.5 m; Combat Weight 62,000 kg; Max Road Speed 59 kph; Cross Country Speed 35 kph; Fording 1.07 m; Trench Crossing 2.3 m; Crane – Max Lift 6,500 kg at 4.9 m reach; Engine Perkins CV12 TCA 1200 26.1 V-12 direct injection 4-stroke diesel.

Between 1988 and 1990 the British Army ordered 80 Challenger CRARRV in two batches and the contract was completed with the last vehicles accepted into service during 1983. A 'Type 56' tank Challenger 2 Regiment has 4 x CHARRV, one with each sabre squadron and one with the REME Light Aid Detachment (LAD).

The vehicle has a crew of three plus additional space in a separate compartment for another two REME fitters. The vehicle is fitted with two winches (main and auxiliary) plus an Atlas hydraulically operated crane capable of lifting a complete Challenger 2 powerpack. The front dozer blade can be used as a stabiliser blade for the crane or as a simple earth anchor.

Warrior (MCV – 80 Fv 510)

(400 available – mid 2015) Weight loaded 24,500 kg; length 6.34 m; Height to turret top 2.78 m; Width 3.0 m; Ground Clearance 0.5 m; Max Road

CRARRV on display at the Land Warfare Centre. (Image Bthebest)

Speed 75 kph; Road Range 500 km; Engine Rolls Royce CV8 diesel; Horsepower 550 hp; Crew 2 (carries 8 infantry soldiers); Armament L21 30 mm Rarden Cannon; Coaxial EX-34 7.62 mm Hughes Helicopter Chain Gun; Smoke Dischargers Royal Ordnance Visual and Infra Red Screening Smoke (VIRSS).

Warrior is an Armoured Infantry Fighting Vehicle (AIFV) in service with armoured infantry battalions. The original purchase of Warrior was for 789 units and the vehicle is in service with six armoured infantry battalions serving in the UK with 3 (UK) Division.

Warrior armed with the 30 mm Rarden cannon gives the crew a good chance of destroying enemy APCs at ranges of up to 1,500 m and the vehicle carries a crew of three and seven dismounted infantry.

The vehicle is CBRN proof, and a full range of night vision equipment is included as standard. Warrior variants include an Artillery Observation Vehicle and a Repair and Recovery version.

Warrior has seen successful operational service in the Gulf (1991), with British troops serving in the Balkans and more recently in Iraq. The vehicle has proven protection against mines, and there is dramatic BBC TV footage of a Warrior running over a Serbian anti-tank mine during the conflict in the Balkans with little or no serious damage to the vehicle or crew.

The hull and mechanical components of Warrior are exceptional and few other vehicles in the world can match it for reliability and performance. The Warrior armament fire control system and electronics require upgrading if the vehicle is to remain in service to 2025 as intended.

Warrior AIFV. (Copyright BAe Systems)

During October 2011, the UK awarded a £1 billion contract to Lockheed Martin for upgrades to the British Army's Warrior fleet under the Warrior Capability Sustainment Programme (WCSP).

The mid-life WCSP consists of three key upgrades:

◆ Warrior Fightability & Lethality Improvement Programme (WFLIP), which modifies the existing turret and the weapons systems.
◆ Warrior Enhanced Electronic Architecture (WEEA), which adds an integrated set of modern, expandable electronics and communications equipment.
◆ Warrior Modular Protection System (WMPS), which will enable the vehicle to be fitted with different armour solutions to meet different requirements.

The first WCSP vehicles will enter production in 2016 with deliveries starting in 2018.

Following a period of training and integration, an armoured infantry company equipped with the upgraded Warriors is planned to be fully operational by 2020 with a total number of 380 Warrior IFVs to reach a full operational capability. Deliveries are set to conclude in 2022.

AFV 432 and Bulldog
(Approx 800 in service of which about 750 are base line vehicles – models include command vehicles, ambulances, and 81 mm mortar carriers). Crew 2 (Commander and Driver); Weight loaded 15,280kg; Length 5.25 m; Width 2.8 m; Height 2.28 m; Ground Pressure 0.78 kg km squared; Armament 1 x 7.62 Machine Gun; 2 x 3 barrel smoke dischargers; Engine Rolls Royce K60 No 4 Mark 1-4; Engine Power 240 bhp; Fuel Capacity 454 litres; Max Road Speed 52 kph; Road Range 580 km; Vertical Obstacle 0.9 m; Trench Crossing 2.05 m; Gradient 60 degrees; Carries up to 10 men; Armour 12.7 mm max.

In service since the early 1960s the basic 432 armoured personnel carrier is NBC proof and when necessary can be converted for swimming when it has a water speed of 6 kph (if required). Properly maintained it is a rugged and reliable vehicle with a good cross-country performance.

All in-service Bulldog vehicles are currently being upgraded to the Bulldog Mk 3 standard. The Mk 3 Bulldog features a Cummins 6BT 250 engine (also fitted to Scimitar) with Allison X200-4C automatic transmission, along with an enhanced breaking, electrical, and cooling systems.

For counter-insurgency operations the up-armoured FV430 provides a similar level of protection to Warrior and the vehicle is able to carry out many of the same tasks, thereby relieving the pressure on heavily committed Warrior vehicles in armoured infantry battlegroups.

Bulldog. (Copyright BAe Systems)

AFV 103 Spartan
(about 300 available) Crew 3; Weight 8,172 kg; Length 5.12 m; Height 2.26 m; Width 2.26 m; Ground Clearance 0.35 m; Max Road Speed 80 kph; Road Range 483 kms; Engine Jaguar J60 No.1 Mark 100B; Engine Power 190 bhp; Fuel Capacity 386 litres; Ammunition Carried 3,000 rounds of 7.62 mm; Armament 1 x 7.62 Machine Gun.

Spartan is the APC of the Combat Vehicle Reconnaissance Tracked (CVRT) series of vehicles, which included Fv 101 Scorpion, Fv 102 Striker, Fv 104 Samaritan, Fv 105 Sultan, Fv 106 Sampson and Fv 107 Scimitar. Spartan is a very small APC that can only carry four men in addition to the crew of three. It is therefore used to carry small specialised groups such as the reconnaissance teams, air defence sections, mortar fire controllers and ambush parties.

Spartan. (MoD Crown Copyright 2015)

Samaritan, Sultan and Sampson are also APC type vehicles, Samaritan is the CVRT ambulance vehicle, Sultan is the armoured command vehicle and Sampson is an armoured recovery vehicle. FV 433 Stormer (60 available) is an air defence vehicle based on a CVR(T) type chassis.

The MoD recently announced that CVRT vehicles would be taken out of service in 2020, with the exception of those vehicles fitted with an environmental mitigation upgrade These vehicles would remain in service until 2026.

Fv 107 Scimitar
(Approx 220 available) Armament 1 x 30 mm Rarden L21 Gun; 1 x 7.62 mm Machine Gun; 2 x 4 barrel smoke dischargers; Engine BTA 5.9 Cummins diesel; Fuel Capacity 423 litres; Max Road Speed 80 kph; Combat Weight 8,000 kg; Length 4.9 m; Height 2.096 m; Width 2.2 m; Ground Clearance 0.35 m; Road Range 644 km; Crew 3; Ammunition Capacity 30 mm – 160 rounds; 7.62 mm – 3,000 rounds; Main Armament Elevation – 10 degrees to + 35 degrees.

CVR(T) Scimitar is the mainstay reconnaissance vehicle with which all Armoured Cavalry are equipped as well as some reconnaissance platoons of armoured battlegroups. The Scimitar is an ideal reconnaissance vehicle, mobile and fast with good communications and excellent viewing equipment. The vehicle's small size and low ground pressure make it extremely useful where the terrain is hostile and movement difficult.

Scimitar in Afghanistan. (MoD Crown Copyright 2015)

Scimitar is due to be replaced by the Scout Reconnaissance vehicle in 2020.

PROTECTED VEHICLES

Panther Command and Liaison Vehicle (Panther CLV)
(Approximately 400 available); Weight 7 tonnes; Armament 1 x 7.62 mm GPMG with Remote Weapon Station.

The UK MoD announced in July 2003 that the BAE Systems Land Systems (formerly Alvis) Multi-role Light Vehicle (MLV) had been selected as the British Army's Future Command and Liaison Vehicle (FCLV). The first procurement contract was signed in November 2003 for an initial 401 vehicles, with an option for up to 400 more. The vehicle has been named the Panther Command and Liaison Vehicle (CLV).

Panther CLV is based on a design by Iveco Defence Vehicles Division of Italy and the vehicles were manufactured during the period 2006 to 2010. Acquisition cost for some 400

Panther CLV. (Attributed to Simon Q)

vehicles is £193 million spread over five years. The first batch of 50 vehicles was delivered in late 2007.

The vehicle is air transportable, underslung beneath a Chinook helicopter or carried inside C130, C17 and A400M aircraft and is capable of operations in all weathers, day and night using thermal imaging equipment. The vehicles are protected against a range of threats and are fitted with a 7.62 mm weapon system (capable of upgrade to 12.7 mm) which allows the user to operate the machine guns with a camera and joystick from inside the vehicle.

Panther will replace a range of vehicles which are reaching the end of their operational lives, for example some types of Land Rover, some FV432 and a number of CVR(T) vehicles. Panther is also entering service with the Royal Air Force Regiment.

Jackal (4 x 4 Patrol Vehicle)

(Approximately 200 in service – mid 2015; Length 5.39 m; Width 2.0 m; Height 1.97 m; Weight 6,650 kg.

During June 2007 the UK MoD announced the purchase of 130 new weapons-mounted patrol vehicles under an Urgent Operational Requirement for troops in Iraq and Afghanistan. The Jackal high mobility weapons platform delivers a new level of power to the WMIK fleet, with more firepower and a better range and mobility. The vehicle will have a top speed of around 80 mph. Further announcements since 2007 suggest that the Jackal fleet will reach 300 vehicles by early 2015.

The vehicle can be fitted with a range of firepower including a .50 calibre machine gun or an automatic grenade launcher and a general purpose machine gun, as well as carrying a crew of four soldiers with their personal weapons.

First deployed on operations in 2008 Jackal was designed by Supacat Ltd and manufactured by Devonport Management Ltd (DML) at their facility in Plymouth.

Jackal. (MoD Crown Copyright 2015)

Under Army 2020 plans, in the main Jackal vehicles will be in service with the light cavalry regiments serving under the command of 1 (UK) Division. The retained Jackal fleet should number about 150 vehicles.

Coyote

The Coyote is a larger version of the jackal (with six wheels) and mainly used to provide combat support and logistics. Coyote is an element in the Tactical Support Vehicle (TSV) programme, the other vehicles being Husky and Wolfhound.

Mastiff 2 Force Protection Vehicle (FPV)

(400 available) Height 2.64 m; Width 2,53 m; Length 7.08 m; Top speed 90 kph; All up weight 23,500 kg; Payload 6,350 kg.

Mastiff 2 which replaced the earlier Mastiff 1 (Ridgeback) is a heavily armoured, wheeled, troop carrying vehicle suitable for road patrols and convoys and is the newest delivery in a range of protected patrol vehicles being used for operations. Manufactured by the US Company Force Protection Inc (where it is named Cougar) Mastiff 2 is a 6 x 6 wheel-drive patrol vehicle which carries six people, plus two crew. It has a maximum speed of 90 kph and can be armed with a machine gun, 50 mm cannon or 40 mm automatic grenade launcher

Mastiff vehicles. (MoD Crown Copyright 2015)

The UK MoD purchased some 108 vehicles in an original order worth approximately US$70.1 million (£35 million) and these vehicles were first deployed in Iraq during December 2006. During October 2007 the MoD announced the purchase of another 140 Mastiff in a contract worth around £100 million.

A total of approximately 400 Mastiff of all types are in service during mid-2015. Approximately 60 of the Mastiff fleet are the troop carrying variant, with the rest split between battlefield ambulance, interim electronic countermeasures, interim EOD, and the enhanced communications variant. Mastiff is in service with the protected mobility battalions under command of the three brigades in 3 (UK) Division.

Ridgeback

(approximately100 available) During 2013 it was announced that Ridgeback (Mastiff 1) would be reintroduced into service to cater for requirements in the army's 2020 force structure. The vehicle would probably be used to support roles within infantry and cavalry units after refurbishment.

Wolfhound

(125 available) This is a variant of the highly successful Mastiff which is generally used for carrying logistic items including extremely heavy loads to the forward troops. The vehicle can also be used by the Royal Artillery to tow the 105 mm Light Gun and carry ammunition. Wolfhound is an element in the Tactical Support Vehicle programme, the other vehicles being Husky and Coyote.

A first batch of 97 Wolfhounds were ordered in April 2009 and in February 2010 an additional 28 Wolfhounds were procured under a £20 million contract with manufacturer Integrated Survivability Technologies. Two versions were supplied: a utility vehicle and a military working dog/EOD vehicle.

Husky

(350 available) Length; 6.86 m; Width 2.43 m; Height 2.36 m.

Husky is a protected logistic support vehicle designed for a range of missions in Afghanistan that include transporting combat supplies to troops in areas where high-intensity operations are taking place. An ambulance version of the vehicle is also available.

Husky is an element in the Tactical Support Vehicle programme, the other vehicles being Wolfhound and Coyote.

Husky. (Attriibuted to Mattias Kabel)

Warthog

(115 available) Length 8.9 m; Front Compartment 2.9 m – crew 3; Rear Compartment 2.3 m – crew 8; Maximum Speed 60 kph; Armament – heavy machine gun.

Capable of operating in a range of operational environments and particularly suited to some of the operational areas in Afghanistan. Warthog is blast protected, armed with a heavy machine gun and provides an excellent platform for infantry operating in a close combat environment.
There are four vehicle variants – troop carrier, command vehicle, repair and recovery vehicle and ambulance.

115 vehicles were purchased from Singapore Technologies Kinetics in a contract worth around £150 million. Warthog entered service in 2010.

Warthog. (MoD Crown Copyright 2015)

Warthog replaces the earlier Viking vehicles which have now been withdrawn to the UK to be used for training.

During October 2013 the MoD announced that the two Royal Artillery UAV regiments, 32 and 47, would be equipped with the Warthog system following modifications and decisions regarding numbers to remain in service. The vehicles are likely to be used to transport Desert Hawk mini UAVs. Currently (mid 2015) the Royal Artillery is considering the ability of Warthog to support other battlefield artillery support roles. The total retained Warthog fleet will probably consist of about 100 vehicles.

Foxhound

(400 on order) Height; 2.35 m; Length 5.2 m; Width 2.1 m; Weight 7,500 kg; Top speed 110 kph.

Foxhound is a light protected patrol vehicle that was procured under a £180 million contract for 200 vehicles signed in November 2010. Other contracts in 2011 and 2012 increased the number being ordered to around 400.

Manufactured by Force Protection Europe Foxhound will replace many of the Snatch Land Rovers that have proved vulnerable on recent operations. Light and agile, Foxhound allows for options in operational scenarios that are not available when only heavier armoured is available.

The vehicle has a 'V' shaped hull to protect against blast and its engine can be removed and replaced in around 30 minutes. Crew and passengers sit inside a protective pod, which can be quickly adapted to transform the patrol vehicle into an ambulance or supply truck. It is claimed that Foxhound can drive away from an ambush on only three wheels.

First vehicles were in-service during 2011 with initial operational use in the Spring of 2012. Foxhound will be in service with the regular infantry battalions under the command of the brigades assigned to 1 (United Kingdom) Division.

Foxhound. (MoD Crown Copyright 2015)

Future armoured vehicles

Development of the previously named Future Rapid Effects System (FRES) has been recast as three separate medium weight armoured vehicle projects as follows:

Specialist Vehicle
Utility Vehicle
Terrier Engineer Vehicle

Specialist Vehicle (SV):

During September 2014 General Dynamics UK was awarded a £3.5 billion contract by the UK MoD to deliver 589 Scout (SV) armoured vehicles to the British Army.

The contract directly safeguards or creates up to 1,300 jobs across the programme's UK supply chain, with 300 of these at General Dynamics UK's Oakdale site.

The SCOUT Specialist Vehicle (SV) consists of six variants and will be delivered between 2017 and 2024, alongside the provision of initial in-service support and training. This is the biggest single order placed by the MoD for armoured vehicles for around 30 years.

The Scout vehicle will provide improved protection against a wide range of threats and bring significant benefits, including greater firepower, improved situational awareness, more protection and enhanced mobility. It will carry three crew and mount both a new type of 40mm cannon and a machine gun. It will replace the Scimitar armoured fighting vehicle.

The Scout design is derived from modifying the ASCOD vehicle, which is already in service with

Scout SV. (MoD Crown Copyright 2015)

some NATO nations, is well-proven and is suitable for export sales. Work will continue alongside this programme to update existing armoured reconnaissance vehicles in service in Afghanistan, such as the Scimitar, to maintain their operational capabilities.

Utility Vehicle (UV): The Ministry of Defence decided to restructure this programme in early 2009. In the longer term it is expected that the Utility Vehicle will become the core element of the Army's armoured vehicle fleet.

A major UV requirement is that it should be able to be transported in a C-130 Hercules aircraft which will place severe constraints on the platform weight and eventual design. However, experience in Iraq and Afghanistan has underlined the vulnerability of existing vehicles to attack by roadside bombs and rocket-propelled grenades, causing analysts to believe that the UV will be better armoured. As a result, planned weight of the vehicles has risen from about 17 tons to between 20 tons and 27 tons which raises questions over whether they will be too heavy for the RAF's new A400M transport aircraft. It appears likely that the UV will be wheeled.

It would appear that the 2010 SDSR revived the future of the FRES UV, stating that it "will be the core of the army's armoured manoeuvre fleet" and a crucial medium capability for the army's future multirole brigades. Some efforts are being made to bring the in-service date of FRES UV forward although budget pressures make the 2020 date most likely.

Following Anglo-French bilateral defence talks at Brize Norton in late January 2014, the MoD confirmed it would accept the offer of a loan of a company of Nexter VBCI (Véhicule Blindé de Combat d'Infanterie) 8x8 infantry combat vehicles to see if the vehicle could meet requirements of the army. The VBCI had previously lost during the FRES UV competition before the programme was shelved. Further details on the programme were revealed in June 2014 with the name of Project Brittany. In September 2014 a company from 4 Rifles travelled to France to be trained by the French Army on the VBCI and to then test the vehicle alongside French troops.

VBCI. (Attributed to Daniel Steger (Lausanne, Switzerland)

The Utility vehicle is expected to replace the FV 432 APC and many variants of the CVR(T) vehicle family.

CHAPTER 9 – INFANTRY

The role of the infantry

"To seek out and close with the enemy, to kill or capture him, to seize or hold ground, to repel attack, by day or night, regardless of season, weather or terrain".

REGIMENTS AND BATTALIONS

The British Infantry is based on the well tried and tested Regimental System, which has proved to be repeatedly successful on operations over the years. It is based on Regiments, most of which have one or more regular Battalion and all have associated Army Reserve Battalions. The esprit de corps of the Regimental system is maintained in the names and titles of British Infantry Regiments handed down through history with a tradition of courage in battle. The repeated changing size of the British Army, dictated by history and politics, is reflected in the fact that many of the most illustrious Regiments still have a number of Regular and Territorial Reserve Battalions. For manning purposes, in a number of cases Infantry Regiments are grouped within administrative 'Divisions'. These 'Divisions' are no longer field formations but represent original historical groupings based on recruiting geography.

The 'Division' of Infantry is an organisation that is responsible for all aspects of military administration, from recruiting, manning and promotions for individuals in the Regiments under its wing, to the longer term planning required to ensure continuity and cohesion. Divisions of Infantry have no operational command over their regiments, and should not be confused with the remaining operational divisions, such as 3rd (United Kingdom) Division and 'the adaptable force' 1st (United Kingdom) Division.

There are currently 31 Regular Infantry Battalions available. This figure excludes 5th Battalion The Royal Regiment of Scotland, a public duties company sized unit, and 1st Battalion The Parachute Regiment a major unit forming the core of the Special Forces Support Group.

The majority of these battalions are now situated in permanent locations.

During early 2016 we believe that infantry battalions are located as follows:

United Kingdom	26 battalions (2 Resident in Northern Ireland)
Germany	2 battalions (in the process of returning to the UK)
Cyprus	2 battalions
Falkland Islands	1 company group on detachment
Brunei	1 battalion (Gurkha)

INFANTRY STRUCTURE

The 2016 administrative 'Divisions of Infantry' are structured as follows:

The Guards Division	– 5 regular battalions
The Scottish Division	– 5 regular battalions (1)
The Queen's Division	– 5 regular battalions
The King's Division	– 4 regular battalions
The Prince of Wales Division	– 4 regular battalions

Not administered by 'Divisions' of Infantry but operating under their own similar administrative arrangements are the following:

The Rifles	– 5 regular battalions
The Parachute Regiment	– 3 regular battalions (2)
The Brigade of Gurkhas	– 2 regular battalions

Notes:
(1) The 5th Battalion of the Royal Regiment of Scotland (public duties – ceremonial) is included in this total.
(2) 1st Bn The Parachute Regiment forms the core element of the Special Forces Support Group and are not counted in the infantry battalion total.

Reserve battalions were under the administrative command of the following:

The Guards Division	– 1 reserve battalion
The Scottish Division	– 2 reserve battalions
The Queen's Division	– 3 reserve battalion
The King's Division	– 2 reserve battalions
The Prince of Wales Division	– 3 reserve battalions
The Rifles	– 2 reserve battalions
The Parachute Regiment	– 1 reserve battalion
The Royal Gibraltar Regiment	– 1 composite battalion

In total the British Army has 31 regular battalions available for service and this total combined with the 14 TA battalions (excluding the Royal Gibraltar Regiment) could provide mobilisation strength of 45 infantry battalions.

Outside the above listed Regiments are three companies of guardsmen each of approximately 90 men, who provide a supplement to the Household Division Regiments while on public duties in London. This allows Regiments of the Foot Guards to continue to carry out normal training on roulement from guard duties.

The 5th Battalion The Royal Regiment of Scotland (a company sized unit with about 110 personnel) carries out public duties in Edinburgh.

Gibraltar also has its own single battalion of the Royal Gibraltar Regiment comprising one regular and two volunteer companies.

The following listing shows the 2015 infantry structure.

Infantry Structure 2015

	Army 2020 Role	*Army 2020 establishment (1)*	*Army 2020 Location*
1st Battalion, Grenadier Guards	Light Role Infantry	501	Aldershot
1st Battalion, Coldstream Guards	Public Duties	501	Windsor
1st Battalion, Scots Guards	Heavy Protected Mobility	605	Aldershot
1st Battalion, Irish Guards	Public Duties	501	Hounslow
1st Battalion, Welsh Guards	Light Protected Mobility	505	Pirbright
1st Battalion, Royal Regiment of Scotland	Light Role Infantry	501	Belfast
2nd Battalion, Royal Regiment of Scotland	Light Role Infantry	501	Edinburgh
3rd Battalion, Royal Regiment of Scotland	Light Protected Mobility	505	Fort George
4th Battalion, Royal Regiment of Scotland	Heavy Protected Mobility	605	Catterick
5th Battalion, Royal Regiment of Scotland	Public Duties	110	Edinburgh

1st Battalion, Princess of Wales's Royal Regiment	Armoured Infantry	612	Bulford
2nd Battalion, Princess of Wales's Royal Regiment	Light Role Infantry	612	Cyprus
1st Battalion, Duke of Lancaster's Regiment	Light Role Infantry	505	Cyprus
2nd Battalion, Duke of Lancaster's Regiment	Light Role Infantry	501	Weeton
1st Battalion, Royal Regiment of Fusiliers	Armoured Infantry	612	Tidworth
1st Battalion, Yorkshire Regiment	Armoured Infantry	612	Tidworth
2nd Battalion, Yorkshire Regiment	Light Protected Mobility	501	Catterick
1st Battalion, Royal Welsh	Armoured Infantry	612	Tidworth
1st Battalion, Mercian Regiment	Armoured Infantry	612	Bulford
2nd Battalion, Mercian Regiment	Light Role Infantry	501	Chester
1st Battalion, Royal Irish Regiment	Light Protected Mobility	505	Tern Hill
1st Battalion, Royal Anglian Regiment	Light Role Infantry	501	Woolwich
2nd Battalion, Royal Anglian Regiment	Light Protected Mobility	505	Cottesmore
2nd Battalion, Parachute Regiment	Parachute	593	Colchester
3rd Battalion, Parachute Regiment (2)	Parachute	593	Colchester
1st Battalion, Royal Gurkha Rifles	Light Role Infantry	563	Shorncliffe
2nd Battalion, Royal Gurkha Rifles	Light Role Infantry	499	Brunei
1st Battalion, The Rifles	Light Role Infantry	501	Chepstow
2nd Battalion, The Rifles	Light Role Infantry	501	Ballykinler
3rd Battalion, The Rifles	Light Protected Mobility	505	Edinburgh
4th Battalion, The Rifles	Heavy Protected Mobility	605	Aldershot
5th Battalion, The Rifles	Armoured Infantry	612	Tidworth

(1) The Army 2020 establishment figure reflects only those officers and soldiers from that unit's specific battalion. This figure does not include attached personnel from other arms.
(2) As a part of the Parachute Regiment, 1st Battalion, Parachute Regiment does not appear in the above listing because the battalion provides the core element of the Special Forces Support Regiment (see Joint Forces Chapter).

PROVISIONAL INFANTRY BATTALION STRENGTHS (ARMY 2020)

Battalion role	Unit strength
Armoured Infantry	729
Heavy Protected Mobility Infantry	709
Light Protected Mobility Infantry	581
Light Role Infantry	561
Royal Gurkha Rifles	567
Parachute Regiment	660

The above table shows battalion strengths that include attached personnel from other arms such as the Royal Electrical and Mechanical Engineers, Royal Army Medical Corps, Adjutant General's Corps (Staff and Personnel Support) etc. The REME LAD for an armoured infantry battalion could number 80 personnel

INFANTRY BATTALIONS (LISTED BY ROLE)

Armoured Infantry (6)

	Army 2020 Role	Army 2020 personnel	Army 2020 Location
1st Battalion, Princess of Wales's Royal Regiment	Armoured Infantry	729	Bulford
1st Battalion, Royal Regiment of Fusiliers	Armoured Infantry	729	Tidworth
1st Battalion, Yorkshire Regiment	Armoured Infantry	729	Tidworth
1st Battalion, Royal Welsh	Armoured Infantry	729	Tidworth
1st Battalion, Mercian Regiment	Armoured Infantry	729	Bulford
5th Battalion, The Rifles	Armoured Infantry	729	Tidworth

NB: This table includes personnel attached from other arms.

Heavy Protected Mobility (3)

	Army 2020 Role	Army 2020 personnel	Army 2020 Location
1st Battalion, Scots Guards	Heavy Protected Mobility	709	Aldershot
4th Battalion, Royal Regiment of Scotland	Heavy Protected Mobility	709	Catterick
4th Battalion, The Rifles	Heavy Protected Mobility	709	Aldershot

NB: This table includes personnel attached from other arms.

Infantry – Light Protected Mobility (6)

	Army 2020 Role	Army 2020 personnel	Army 2020 Location
1st Battalion, Welsh Guards	Light Protected Mobility	581	Pirbright
3rd Battalion, Royal Regiment of Scotland	Light Protected Mobility	581	Fort George
2nd Battalion, Yorkshire Regiment	Light Protected Mobility	581	Catterick
1st Battalion, Royal Irish Regiment	Light Protected Mobility	581	Tern Hill
2nd Battalion, Royal Anglian Regiment	Light Protected Mobility	581	Cottesmore
3rd Battalion, The Rifles	Light Protected Mobility	581	Edinburgh

NB: This table includes personnel attached from other arms.

Infantry – Light Role (12)

	Army 2020 Role	Army 2020 personnel	Army 2020 Location
1st Battalion, Grenadier Guards	Light Role Infantry	561	Aldershot
1st Battalion, Royal Regiment of Scotland	Light Role Infantry	561	Belfast
2nd Battalion, Royal Regiment of Scotland	Light Role Infantry	561	Edinburgh
2nd Battalion, Princess of Wales's Royal Regiment	Light Role Infantry	561	Cyprus
1st Battalion, Duke of Lancaster's Regiment	Light Role Infantry	561	Cyprus
2nd Battalion, Duke of Lancaster's Regiment	Light Role Infantry	561	Weeton
2nd Battalion, Mercian Regiment	Light Role Infantry	561	Chester
1st Battalion, Royal Anglian Regiment	Light Role Infantry	561	Woolwich
1st Battalion, Royal Gurkha Rifles	Light Role Infantry	567	Shorncliffe
2nd Battalion, Royal Gurkha Rifles	Light Role Infantry	567	Brunei
1st Battalion, The Rifles	Light Role Infantry	561	Chepstow
2nd Battalion, The Rifles	Light Role Infantry	561	Ballykinler

NB: This table includes personnel attached from other arms.

Infantry – Other Roles (5)

	Army 2020 Role	Army 2020 personnel	Army 2020 Location
1st Battalion, Coldstream Guards	Public Duties	594	Windsor
1st Battalion, Irish Guards	Public Duties	594	Hounslow
5th Battalion, Royal Regiment of Scotland	Public Duties	110	Edinburgh
2nd Battalion, Parachute Regiment	Parachute	660	Colchester
3rd Battalion, Parachute Regiment	Parachute	660	Colchester

NB: Personnel figures reflect total unit strength and include personnel attached from other arms.

In addition to the above there are 3 x Guards Division Public Duties Companies who supplement the Guards Battalions on public duties in London:

Company	Establishment
Nijmegen Coy Grenadier Guards	106
7 Coy Coldstream Guards	106
F Coy Scots Guards	106

Infantry Battalion Rotation
Brunei: 1 RGR and 2 RGR will continue to rotate through Brunei with battalion changes happening at roughly 30–36 month intervals.

Cyprus: Battalions will be drawn from across the Adaptable Force to fulfil the standing commitments in Cyprus.

State Ceremonial and Public Duties: Continues to be provided by two of the five Foot Guards battalions and the incremental companies in London and Scotland.

INFANTRY – ARMY RESERVE BATTALIONS

There are 14 x Army Reserve Battalions and all of them are affiliated to Regular Battalions. We believe that the eventual aim is for all of these battalions to have a personnel strength of around 500 by 2020 and there are longer term plans for whole sub-unit deployments on some low intensity missions. In the short term it would appear that the emphasis is on deploying platoons that are properly trained and equipped alongside their regular counterparts.

Battalion	Headquarters Location	Administrative Division
6th Battalion Royal Regiment of Scotland (R)	Glasgow	Scottish
7th Battalion Royal Regiment of Scotland (R)	Perth	Scottish
3rd Battalion Princess of Wales Royal Regiment (R)	Canterbury	Queens
5th Battalion The Royal Regiment of Fusiliers (R)	Newcastle	Queens
3rd Battalion The Royal Anglian Regiment (R)	Bury St Edmunds	Queens
4th Battalion The Duke of Lancaster's Regiment (R)	Preston	Kings
4th Battalion The Yorkshire Regiment (R)	York	Kings
4th Battalion the Mercian Regiment (R)	Wolverhampton	Prince of Wales
3rd Battalion the Royal Welsh (R)	Cardiff	Prince of Wales
2nd Battalion the Royal Irish Regiment (R)	Lisbon	Prince of Wales
4th Battalion the Parachute Regiment (R)	Pudsey	Parachute Regiment
The London Regiment (R)	Westminster	Guards
6th Bn The Rifles (R)	Exeter	Rifles
7th Bn The Rifles (R)	Reading	Rifles

INFANTRY STRENGTH

During early 2016 the total infantry personnel figure will probably be in the region of 24,000 (our estimate). In general, about 90 per cent of infantry personnel are classified as deployable or 'Fit for Task' at any one time.

During an average year we would expect to see about 2,400 recruits joining the infantry. About 400 recruits would join the Guards Division, 1,800 joining the Line Regiments and about 200 joining the Parachute Regiment. In addition we would expect to see about 200 infantry officers leaving Sandhurst following commissioning.

OPERATIONAL UNITS

As explained in Chapter 2, it would be unusual for the Infantry to fight as battalion units especially in armoured or mechanised formations. If the task is appropriate, the HQ of an infantry battalion will become the HQ of a 'battle group', and be provided with armour, artillery, engineers and possibly aviation to enable it to become a balanced Battle Group. Similarly Infantry Companies can be detached to HQs of Armoured Regiments to make up Armoured Battle Groups.

In the pages that follow, the groupings are based on Unit Establishment figures for peace support operations. For Warfighting (High Intensity) a pairing mechanism operates which provides augmentation which allows a unit to meet its role. For example, an Armoured Infantry Regiment will receive additional Manoeuvre Support assets and another Rifle Company to reach its Warfighting Establishment (WFE) of 4 x Companies, 9 x Mortars and 18 x Medium Range Anti-Tank Guided Weapons (ATGW).

It should be noted that the organisations listed next are under a state of change as the demand of the Army 2020 structure become more apparent. This is especially true of the organisations for the manoeuvre support companies.

Types of Infantry Battalions

Armoured Infantry Battalion	- Equipped with Warrior AFV.
Heavy Protected Mobility Battalion	- Equipped with Mastiff APC.
Light Protected Mobility Battalion	- Equipped for General Service with Foxhound PPV.
Light Role Battalion	- Equipped for General Service.
Infantry Battalion Air Assault	- Equipped for Air Assault Operations.

ARMOURED INFANTRY BATTALION (PROVISIONAL OUTLINE ARMY 2020)

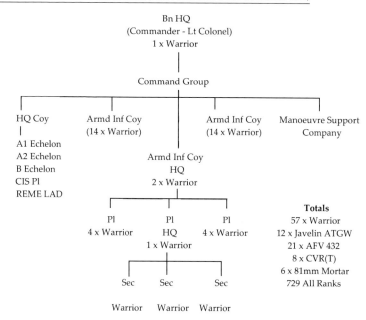

Armoured Infantry Battalion – Manoeuvre Support Company

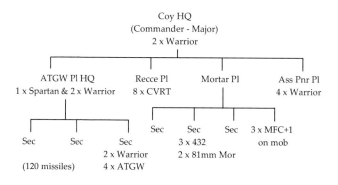

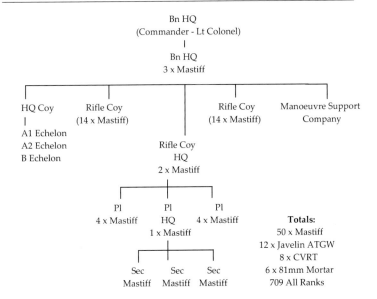

Heavy Protected Mobility Battalion – Manoeuvre Support Company

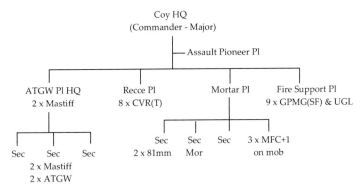

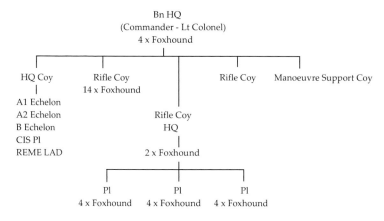

Totals
12 x Javelin ATGW
6 x 81mm Mortars
50 x Foxhound
581 All Ranks

Light Protected Mobility Battalion – Manoeuvre Support Company

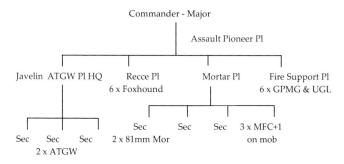

Many battalions now have sniper sections equipped with the Long Range Rifle that has an effective range of up to 1,100 m plus.

Current plans appear to include considerable Army Reserve reinforcements during training and if necessary for operations when battalions operating in this role are deployed. Affiliated battalions are shown in the next table.

Light Protected Mobility Battalion – Army Reserve Affiliations

Unit	Role	Location	Affiliated reserve unit
2nd Bn the Yorkshire Regiment	Light Protected Mobility	Catterick	4th Bn The Yorkshire Regiment (R) (York)
2nd Bn the Royal Anglian Regiment	Light Protected Mobility	Cottesmore	3rd Bn the Royal Anglian Regiment (R) (Bury St Edmunds)
1st Bn the Royal Irish Regiment	Light Protected Mobility	Tern Hill	2nd Bn the Royal Irish Regiment (R) (Lisburn)
1st Bn The Welsh Guards	Light Protected Mobility	Pirbright	3rd Bn The Royal Welsh (R) (Cardiff)
3rd Bn The Rifles	Light Protected Mobility	Edinburgh	5th Bn The Royal Regiment of Fusiliers (R) (Newcastle)
3rd Bn The Royal Regiment of Scotland	Light Protected Mobility	Fort George	7th Bn The Royal Regiment of Scotland (R) (Perth)

LIGHT ROLE INFANTRY BATTALION (PROVISIONAL OUTLINE ARMY 2020)

The Light Role Infantry Battalion (561 personnel) continues to evolve and the resultant structure appears to be based around the usual three Rifle Companies each with three platoons. Two of these platoons are from the Regular Battalion and the third from the affiliated Army Reserve Battalion (eg 6 Rifles is affiliated to 1 Rifles).

The third regular rifle platoon in each company has now be re-roled as a GPMG SG platoon resulting in a rifle company that will probably look like this:

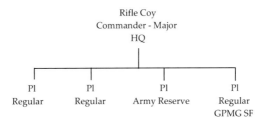

The evolving Manoeuvre Support Company will probably resemble the following:

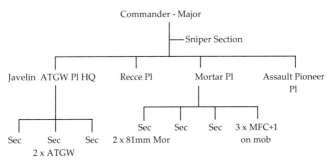

Many battalions now have sniper sections equipped with the Long Range Rifle that has an effective range of up to 1,100 m plus.

HQ Coy has the usual mix of support elements that includes REME LAD, QM's Department, MT Platoon, Medical and CIS Platoon.

Light Role Infantry Battalion – Army Reserve Affiliations

Unit	Role	Location	Affiliated reserve unit
1st Bn The Royal Anglian Regiment	Light Role Infantry	Woolwich	3rd Bn the Princess of Wales's Royal Regiment (R) (Canterbury)
1st Bn the Grenadier Guards	Light Role Infantry	Aldershot	The London Regiment (R) (Westminster)
2nd Bn The Rifles	Light Role Infantry	Ballykinler	7th Bn The Rifles (R) (Reading)
2nd Bn The Mercian Regiment	Light Role Infantry	Chester	4th Bn The Mercian Regiment (R) (Wolverhampton)
2nd Bn The Duke of Lancaster's Regiment	Light Role Infantry	Weeton	4th Bn the Duke of Lancaster's Regiment (R) (Preston)
2nd Bn The Royal Regiment of Scotland	Light Role Infantry	Edinburgh	6th Bn The Royal Regiment of Scotland (R) (Glasgow)
1st Bn The Rifles	Light Role Infantry	Chepstow	6th Bn The Rifles (R) (Exeter
2nd Bn The Parachute Regiment	Air Assault	Colchester	4th Bn The Parachute Regiment (R) (Pudsey)
2nd Bn The Parachute Regiment	Air Assault	Colchester	

PLATOON ORGANISATION

The basic building bricks of the Infantry Battalion are the platoon and the section.

Under normal circumstances, the whole platoon with the exception of the LMG (Light Machine Gun) gunners are armed with IW – SA80 (Individual Weapon).

In an armoured or mechanised battalion, the platoon vehicles could be either Warrior or AFV 432.

Under normal circumstances expect a British infantry platoon to resemble the organisation in the following diagram:

Armoured or Heavy Protected Infantry Platoon
Platoon Commander (2/Lt or Lt)
Platoon Sergeant
Radio Operator

Mounted in Warrior or Mastiff

Section Warrior/Mastiff	Section Warrior/Mastiff	Section Warrior/Mastiff
Fire Team	Fire Team	Fire Team
Sec Comd (Cpl) Rifleman Rifleman LMG Gunner	Sec Comd Rifleman Rifleman LMG Gunner	Sec Comd Rifleman Rifleman LMG Gunner
Fire Team	Fire Team	Fire Team
Sec 2i/c Rifleman Rifleman LMG Gunner	Sec 2i/c Rifleman Rifleman LMG Gunner	Sec 2i/c (Lcpl) Rifleman Rifleman LMG Gunner

Note: In addition to the above, infantry platoons deploying on operations could have a range of other weapons and systems available to them.

INFANTRY WEAPONS AND SYSTEMS

Javelin LF ATGW

Launch Unit: Weight 6.4 kg; Sight magnification x 4; Missile: Range 2,500 m; Weight 11.8 kg; Length 1.08 m; Seeker – Imaging infra-red; Guidance – Lock on before launch, automatic self-guidance; Missile – Two stage solid propellant with a tandem shaped charge; Weight of Launch unit and missile 22 kg.

The UK version of the US Javelin ATGW system, is a more sophisticated guided weapon with a range of some 2,500 m and a production contract was signed in early 2003 worth over £300 million. Industry sources suggest that up to 5,000 missiles and 300 firing posts were ordered. First deliveries to the UK were made in 2004 and the system has replaced Milan. In UK service Javelin has a number of modifications which include an enhanced Command Launch Unit (CLU) with a wider field of view, and the ability to recognise targets at longer ranges.

Javelin. (Copyright Eros Hoagland)

Although Javelin has been developed mainly to engage armoured fighting vehicles, the system can also be used to neutralise bunkers, buildings, and low-flying helicopters. Javelin's top-attack tandem warhead is claimed to defeat all known armour systems.

The US Army and Marine Corps have been using Javelin for some years and the system is either in service, or has been selected by Australia, Ireland, Jordan, Lithuania, New Zealand, and Taiwan. Over 7,000 Javelin launchers have been manufactured since 1995. Javelin is planned to be in UK service until 2025.

Figures suggest that in the 12 months to November 2009 some 580 missiles were fired. The cost of each missile is approximately £49,000.

MBT LAW

Max Range: 600 m; Weight 12.5 kg; Calibre 150 mm (warhead – top attack); Length 1016 mm; Guidance Predicted Line of Sight (PLOS).

MBT LAW (formerly NLAW) is a man-portable, short-range anti-armour weapon. It will provide a capability out to a range of 600 m, against main battle tanks and light armoured vehicles; have the ability to be fired from enclosed spaces and defensive positions and be a means of attack against personnel in structures.

The MBT LAW prime contractor is SAAB Bofors Dynamics of Sweden, with Thales Air Defence Ltd as the main UK sub-contractor. Deliveries began in December 2008 and the system replaces LAW 80 and the interim ILAW (Bofors AT-4). The final cost of the MBT LAW contract is in the order of £400M.

The MBT LAW system has been developed in a collaborative programme with Sweden. Entry into service began in mid-2009, although it had been subject to some delays as a result of qualification problems.

81 mm L16 Mortar

(400 in service including 100 SP) Max Range HE 5,650 m; Elevation 45 degrees to 80 degrees; Muzzle Velocity 255 m/s; Length of barrel 1280 mm; Weight of barrel 12.7 kg; Weight of base plate 11.6 kg; In action Weight 35.3 kg; Bomb Weight HE L3682 4.2 kg; Rate of Fire 15 rpm; Calibre 81 mm.

The 81mm Mortar is on issue to all infantry battalions, with each battalion having a mortar platoon with three or four sections; and each section deploying two mortars. These mortars are the battalion's organic Manoeuvre Support Firepower and can be used to put a heavy weight of fire down on an objective in an extremely short period. Mortar fire is particularly lethal to infantry in the open and in addition is very useful for neutralising dug-in strong points or forcing armour to close down.

The fire of each mortar section is controlled by the MFC (Mortar Fire Controller) who is usually an NCO and generally positioned well forward with the troops being supported. Most MFCs will find themselves either very close to or co-located with a Task Group Commander. The MFC informs the base plate (mortar position) by radio of the location of the target and then corrects the fall of the bombs, directing them onto the target.

Mortar fire can be used to suppress enemy positions until assaulting troops arrive within 200-300 m of the position. The mortar fire then lifts onto enemy counter attack and supporting positions while the assault goes in. The 81 mm Mortar can also assist with smoke and illuminating rounds.

The mortar is carried in an AFV432 or a Truck (Utility Light or Medium) and if necessary can be carried in two, man portable loads of 11.35 kg and one 12.28 kg respectively. In the past, infantry companies working in close country have carried one 81 mm round per man when operating in areas such as Borneo or Aden where wheeled or tracked transport was not available. For Air Mobile and Air Assault operations mortar rounds are issued in twin packs of two rounds per man on initial deployment. These are used as initial ammunition resources until further ammunition loads can be flown in.

The L16A2 81 mm Mortar has undergone a mid life upgrade (MLU) to embrace recent technological developments. The inclusion of the new SPGR (Specialised Personal GPS Receiver) and the LH40C (Laser) combine to make the new TLE (Target Locating Equipment). This generates a significant enhancement in first round accuracy and the ease, and speed with which accurate fire missions can be executed. Additionally, the equipment reduces the number of adjustment rounds which will be used and lead to greater dispersal of mortar barrels, thus increasing protection for the mortar crew soldiers. Plans continue to develop further synergies with The Royal Artillery to improve the existing levels of co-ordination between Artillery and Mortars in fighting the indirect fire battle.

81 mm Mortar firing illuminating rounds. (MoD Crown Copyright 2015)

Official figures suggest that in the 12 months to November 2009 some 145,600 81 mm mortar rounds were fired on operations and training. The cost of an 81 mm mortar round varies from between £190–£890 dependent upon the type of round that is fired. In the main various types of high explosive (HE) and illuminating are used.

51 mm Light Mortar
(About 1,000 available) Range 750 m; Bomb Weight 800 gms (illum), 900 gms (smk), 920 gms (HE); Rapid Rate of Fire 8 rpm; Length of barrel 750 mm; Weight Complete 6.275 kg; Calibre 51.25 mm.

The 51 mm Light Mortar is a weapon that can be carried and fired by one man, and is found in the HQ of an infantry platoon. The mortar is used to fire smoke, illuminating and HE rounds out to a range of approximately 750 m; a short range insert device enables the weapon to be used in close quarter battle situations with some accuracy. The 51 mm Light Mortar has replaced the older 1940s 2 inch mortar.

Although the weapon remains available it is approaching its planned out of service date. The capability provided by the 51 mm mortar is being replaced by a combination of systems including the 40 mm Underslung Grenade Launcher and rocket hand-fired illumination and smoke rounds. In Afghanistan, the 51 mm capability is being augmented by a purchase of a more modern 60 mm mortar.

5.56 mm Individual Weapon (IW) (SA 80 and SA 80A2)
Effective Range 400m; Muzzle Velocity 940 m/s; Rate of Fire from 610-775 rpm; Weight 4.98 kg (with 30 round magazine); Length Overall 785 mm; Barrel Length 518 mm; Trigger Pull 3.12-4.5 kg.

Designed to fire the standard NATO 5.56 mm x 45 mm round, the SA 80 was fitted with an x4 telescopic (SUSAT) sight as standard. The total buy for SA 80 was for 332,092 weapons:

At 1991/92 prices the total cost of the SA80 contract was in the order of £384.16 million. By late 1994 some 10,000 SA 80 Night Sights and 3rd Generation Image Intensifier Tubes for use with SA80 had been delivered.

The SA 80 had a mixed press and following some severe criticism of the weapons mechanical reliability the improved SA 80A2 was introduced into service during late 2001.

SA 80A2: Some 13 changes were made to the weapon's breech block, gas regulation, firing-pin, cartridge extractor, recoil springs, cylinder and gas plug, hammer, magazine and barrel. Since modification the weapon has been extensively trialled.

Mean time before failure (MTBF) figures from the firing trials for stoppages, following rounds fired are as follow:

	SA 80A2	LSW
UK (temperate)	31,500	16,000
Brunei (hot/wet)	31,500	9,600
Kuwait (hot/dry)	7,875	8,728
Alaska (cold/dry)	31,500	43,200

The first SA 80A2 were in operational service during early 2002 and these weapons were in service across the army by late 2004. The cost of the programme was £92 million and some 200,000 weapons were modified by the time the programme ended in May 2006.

The SA80 A2 can be fitted with the Heckler and Koch 40 mm Underslung Grenade Launcher (UGL) which is generally issued on the scale of two per infantry section (or one per four man fire team). This allows an infantry section to lay down HE fragmentation munitions up 350 m in front of their position. With six UGL available to an infantry platoon there is a major enhancement to their operational effectiveness.

During 2013 the UK MoD issued a request to industry for tenders relating to a 30,000 Modular Assault Rifle Systems (MARS) with a projected 10 year in-service life. The tender stated that MARS would be in service with "certain military units".

As yet we have no indication of any further progress relating to this tender. Industry sources suggest that a MARS system could about £2,500 per rifle.

SA 80 being used on exercise. (MoD Crown Copyright 2015)

5.56mm Light Machine Gun (Minimi)
Effective range 800 m; Calibre 5.56 mm; Weight 7.1 kg; Length 914 mm; Feed 100-round disintegrating belt; Cyclic rate of fire 700 to 1000 rounds per minute.

FN Herstal's Minimi belt fed 5.56mm Light Machine Gun (LMG), has entered service on a scale of one per four-man fire team. The Minimi has been used operationally by British troops in Afghanistan and Iraq and the UK MoD has bought 2,472 weapons. The contract which will boost the firepower within infantry sections was believed to have been completed in late 2007.

The Minimi is in service with the Australian, Canadian and New Zealand Armies as well as the US Armed Forces.

7.62 mm General Purpose Machine Gun (GPMG)
(9,000 in service – our estimate) Range 800 m (Light Role) l,800 m (Sustained Fire Role); Muzzle Velocity 538 m/s; Length 1.23 m; Weight loaded 13.85 kg (gun + 50 rounds); Belt Fed; Rate of Fire up to 750 rpm; Rate of Fire Light Role 100 rpm; Rate of Fire Sustained Fire Role 200 rpm.

An infantry machine gun which has been in service since the early 1960s, the GPMG can be used in the light role fired from a bipod or can be fitted to a tripod for use in the sustained fire role. The gun is also found pintle-mounted on many armoured vehicles. Used on a tripod the gun is

General Purpose Machine Gun. (Copyright Eros Hoagland)

effective out to 1,800 m although it is difficult to spot strike at this range because the tracer rounds in the ammunition belt burns out at 1,100 m.

Machine Gun platoons in air assault battalions remain equipped with the GPMG in the sustained fire role. GPMG performance has recently been enhanced by the issue of a Maxi Kite night image intensification sight giving excellent visibility out to 600 m. The GPMG is due to be withdrawn from service in 2015.

12.7 mm Heavy Machine Gun (HMG)
Effective range – up to 2000 m; Calibre 12.7 mm; Weight 38.15 kg (gun only); Length: 1,656 mm; Barrel Length 1,143 mm; Muzzle Velocity 915 m/s; Cyclic rate of fire – 485–635 rounds per minute.

The 12.7 mm Heavy Machine Gun (HMG) is an updated version of the Browning M2 'Fifty-cal' – generally recognised as one of the best heavy machine guns ever developed. Currently, the HMG provides integral close-range support from a ground mount tripod or fitted to a Land Rover TUM or protected patrol vehicle using a Weapon Mount Installation Kit (WMIK) and a variety of sighting systems. The performance of the HMG has recently been enhanced with a new 'soft mount' (to limit recoil and improve accuracy) and a quick change barrel.

HMG mounted on a tripod. (Copyright John Pearson)

Long Range Rifle (LRR)
(580 available) Effective range 1,100 m plus;
Weight 6.8 kg; Calibre 8.59 mm; Muzzle velocity 936 m/s; Length 1,300 mm; Feed 5-round box.

The SA 80A2 is designed to shoot accurately out to 300 m and be easily handled in combat situations. With the disappearance of the Enfield .303 during the early 1960s the skill of shooting accurately above 400 m has largely died away. The 7.62 Sniper Rifle filled the gap for a while but the vulnerability of the round to wind deflection over longer ranges made it desirable to come up with a weapon which could be fired with some precision in all phases of modern warfare.

L115 Long Range Rifle. (Copyright John Pearson)

The result has been the development by Accuracy International UK of the 8.59 mm (.338) Long Range Large Calibre Rifle L115A3 capable of shooting accurately out to 1100 m and beyond depending on atmospheric conditions. The weapon has been issued to JRRF (Joint Rapid Reaction Force) units on the basis of 14 per battalion, with one per platoon and a small pool for snipers in the battalion reconnaisance platoons. The LRR came into service in early 2000.

Reports suggest that in November 2009 a British Army sniper operating near Musa Qala in Afghanistan using a L115A3 rifle shot two Taliban machine gunners at a range of 2,475 m.

Grenade Machine Gun (GMG)

This is a 40 mm high explosive grenade weapon that has a range of up to 1.5 km for point targets and about 2 kms for neutralising/suppressing area targets. Capable of firing up to 340 rounds per minute it is usually mounted on TUM/Land Rover type or Protected Vehicles because of the problems associated with carrying large amounts of ammunition.

9 mm Pistols

The UK MoD has ordered more than 25,000 9 mm Glock 17 Gen4 pistols to replace the Browning L9A1s currently in service. The Glock 17 is lighter, more accurate, and has a higher capacity magazine (17 rounds compared to 13). Announced in January 2013 the contract with Viking Arms Ltd also includes more than 25,000 holsters.

Future Infantry Soldier Technology (FIST)

The UK MoD's FIST programme covers the development of all areas of technology applicable to the dismounted infantry soldier and concentrates on the integration of systems. FIST will provide infantry soldiers with improved situational awareness, lethality and survivability.

The five main areas of capability to be enhanced are C4I (command, control, communications, computers and intelligence), lethality (weapons and sights), mobility (navigation, size and weight of equipment), survivability (clothing, stealth, body armour) and sustainability (logistical considerations).

For operations the unit commander will specify the FIST systems tailored to the operational and mission requirements.

It is expected that 35,000 sets of FIST equipment will be ordered for issue to the Army, Royal Air Force Regiment and Royal Marines. FIST will enter service in stages between 2015 and 2020.

THE RIGHT STUFF

Sydney Jary led 18 Platoon of the 4th Battalion The Somerset Light Infantry in Normandy, the Netherlands and Germany during 1944 and 1945.

"Had I been asked at any time before August 1944 to list the personal characteristics which go to make a good infantry soldier, my reply would have been wide of the mark.

Like most I would no doubt have suggested that only masculine ones like, aggression, physical stamina, a hunting instinct and the competitive nature. How wrong I would have been. I would now suggest the following.

Firstly sufferance, without which one could not survive. Secondly, a quiet mind which enables the soldier to live in harmony with his fellows through all sorts of difficulties and sometimes under dreadful conditions. As in a closed monastic existence, there is simply no room for the assertive or acrimonious. Thirdly, but not less important, a sense of the ridiculous which helps soldier surmount the unacceptable. Add to these a reasonable standard of physical fitness and a dedicated professional competence, and you have a soldier for all seasons. None of the NCOs or soldiers, who made 18 Platoon what it was, resembled the characters portrayed in the most books and films about war. All were quiet, sensible and unassuming men and some, by any standard, were heroes.

If I now have to select a team for a dangerous mission and my choice was restricted to stars of the sports field or poets, I would unhesitatingly recruit from the latter."

CHAPTER 10 – ARMY AVIATION AND AVIATION SUPPORT

ARMY AIR CORPS

The Army obtains the major element of its aviation support from Army Air Corps (AAC), an organisation with four separate operational regiments, two training regiments, one reserve regiment and a number of independent squadrons and flights. Other aviation support is provided by the RAF.

The Army Air Corps battlefield helicopter fleet has accumulated a vast amount of operational experience in recent years, and is arguably a more capable force than that possessed by any other European nation.

The flexibility of battlefield helicopters has been demonstrated in Iraq during 2003 and during recent operations in Afghanistan and Libya. For example, In Iraq 3 Regiment, Army Air Corps, with two Pumas from the RAF Support Helicopter Force attached, was deployed forward as a combined-arms battle group, initially within 16 Air Assault Brigade and later in conjunction with 7 Armoured Brigade. The battle group had responsibility for an area that extended over 6,000 square kilometres, and provided a versatile combat arm during the warfighting phase. In both Iraq and Afghanistan helicopters proved to be the most efficient means of covering the vast operational area, providing offensive support and also in distributing humanitarian aid to isolated communities.

FORCE STRUCTURE

AAC manpower is believed to number about 2,000 personnel, including about 500 officers. Unlike the all-officer Navy and Air Force helicopter pilot establishments, almost two-thirds of AAC aircrew are non-commissioned officers. The AAC is supported by REME and RLC personnel numbering some 2,200 all ranks. Total AAC-related manpower is believed to be around 4,200 personnel of all ranks.

With certain exceptions, during peace, all battlefield helicopters come under the authority of the Joint Helicopter Command (JHC – see Joint Forces Chapter).

The introduction into AAC service of the WAH-64D Apache Longbow attack helicopter has transforming AAC doctrine, organisation, and order of battle. The British Army designation of the type is Apache AH Mk1 and approximately 48 aircraft are concentrated in two Attack Regiments. Theses are 3 and 4 Regiments at Wattisham in Suffolk.

Each attack regiment is believed to have 3 x attack squadrons equipped with 8 x Apache AH Mk1.

Current (2015) AAC Regimental and Squadron locations are shown below.

Army Air Corps force structure and helicopters during late 2015.

Regiment	Squadron	Location	Helicopter/aircraft	Fleet (estimate)
1 Regiment	652,661,659,669,672	Yeovilton	Wildcat	24
2 (Trg) Regiment	676,668	Middle Wallop	Ground training and support	-
3 Attack Regiment	653, 662 & 663 (1)	Wattisham	Apache	24
4 Attack Regiment	654, 664 & 656 (1)	Wattisham	Apache	24
5 Regiment	651, 665	Aldergrove	Gazelle, Lynx, Islander, Defender	8,8,4,9
6 Regiment (R)	666,675,677,678.679	Bury St Edmunds	Support	n/a

7 (Training) Regiment	670,671,673	Middle Wallop	Squirrel, Gazelle, Lynx, Bell 212, Apache	20
Independent units				
Joint Special Forces Aviation Wing	657	Odiham	Lynx, Wildcat	12
Development & Trials	667	Middle Wallop	All types	Variable
Initial Training	660	Shawbury	Squirrel HT 1	12

Flights include 7 Flight (Brunei), 8 Flight (Hereford), 12 Flight (Germany), 25 Flight (UK Trg Support), 29 BATUS Flight – Canada

Note: There appear to be future plans for the two attack regiments to be structured around 2 x squadrons each. Aircraft numbers are believed to be remain at 24 for each regiment.

The AAC Centre at Middle Wallop in Hampshire acts as a focal point for all Army Aviation, and it is here that the majority of corps training is carried out at the School of Army Aviation.

Although the AAC operates some fixed-wing aircraft for training and liaison flying, the main effort goes into providing helicopter support for the land forces. About 140 AAC helicopters are believed to be in operational service in late 2015.

9 x Britten-Norman Defender and 4 x Islander (fixed wing aircraft) are used for reconnaissance and airborne command. The Defender has a top speed of about 320 km/h (200 mph) and a range of around 1,500 kms (990 miles). These aircraft are currently flown by 651 Squadron.

THE AVIATION MISSION

Combat Aviation: To find, fix and strike, either independently, or as the lead element, or as a constituent of combined arms groupings, throughout the depth of the battlefield and the 24 hour battle, and throughout the full spectrum of operations.

Combat Support Aviation: To provide enabling capabilities for combined arms operations, throughout the depth of the battlefield and the 24 hour battle, and throughout the full spectrum of operations.

Roles of Army Aviation

In a Combat Role: To conduct air manoeuvre using direct fire and manoeuvre, as part of the land battle component.

In a Combat Support Role: To provide ISTAR (intelligence, surveillance, target acquisition and reconnaissance) as a collection asset in its own right or potentially as a platform for other sensors, including ECM (electronic countermeasures): NBC (nuclear, chemical and biological) reconnaissance: ESM (electronic support measures): radar and other electronic systems.

Other tasks may include:

◆ To provide direction of fire support (ground/air/maritime/special forces).
◆ To provide mobility for combat forces.
◆ To assist in command and control, including acting as airborne command posts.
◆ To provide a limited extraction capability.

In a Combat Service Support Role: To provide movement for personnel and materiel including casualty evacuation (CASEVAC).

AAC ATTACK REGIMENT ORGANISATION

We would expect an AAC Attack Regiment to be organised on the lines shown in the diagrams below.

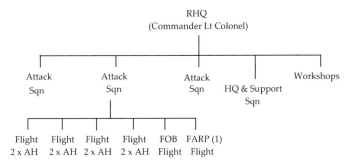

Total: 24 x AH (Attack Helicopters)

Notes:

(1) FOB – Forward Operating Base: FARP- Forward Arming and Refuelling Point.

(2) There appear to be future plans for an attack regiments to be structured around 2 x squadrons each.

ARMY AVIATION TRAINING

The School of Army Aviation at Middle Wallop in Hampshire trains Army pilots using the Army's front line aircraft, the Gazelle, the Lynx and the Apache AH Mk 1 (Wildcat training takes place at Yeovilton). It also trains soldiers to support these aircraft on the ground, to protect their operating bases, to provide communications between the ground and aircraft, and to arm and refuel them. The training activity conducted by SAAvn is divided into ground training and flying training.

Ground training is conducted by 2 Regiment AAC and consists of:

Phase 2 training to provide special to arm training for recruits on completion of their basic training at Winchester Army Training Regiment, and,

Phase 3 training to provide career progress courses for trained soldiers.

Flying training is conducted by 7 Regiment and consists of:

Army Flying Grading
Operational Training Phase of the Army Pilots Course
Conversion to the Army Air Corps operational aircraft

The AAC Centre at Middle Wallop is under the ownership of the Army Training and Recruitment Agency (ATRA). There is also a detachment of 132 Aviation Support Squadron, Royal Logistics Corps, which comes under the Joint Helicopter Command, based at the AAC Centre. The Headquarters of the Director of Army Aviation is also based at Middle Wallop. There may be up to 12 Attack Helicopters allocated to the School of Army Aviation for training purposes at any one time.

HQ DAAvn (Director Army Aviation) is responsible for providing advice and support on Army Aviation and AAC training matters. In this regard HQ DAAvn is responsible for the training policy for both aircrew and ground crew. The School of Army Aviation (SAAvn) undertakes AAC Special-to-Arm training. AAC Soldier Basic Training takes place at ATR Winchester.

The AAC recruits pilots from three main sources:

Direct Entry (Officers only)
The ranks of the AAC (Corporals and above)
Officers and soldiers from other arms and branches of the Service (Corporal and above)

Officers join the Corps after completing the Commissioning course at the Royal Military Academy Sandhurst. Unlike the all-officer Navy and Air Force helicopter pilot establishments, almost two-thirds of AAC aircrew are non-commissioned officers. Within the Army, NCOs, of at least LCpl rank with a recommendation for promotion, from within the AAC and from the remainder of the Army may also apply for pilot training. NCO pilots spend the majority of their service flying and many go on to be commissioned as Officers, normally to fill specialist flying appointments such as flying instructors.

There are three phases to selection for Army pilot training:

Aircrew Selection tests are conducted at RAF College Cranwell. These tests are common to the three Services and last two days. Army candidates require a minimum aircrew aptitude score of 80/180 to progress onto the next phase. RAF/RN require higher scores, but the Army is able to accept a lower score at this point, as Army candidates also have to pass Army Flying Grading which the AAC considers a far more accurate indicator of potential to be an Army pilot.

Army Flying Grading (AFG) is conducted at Middle Wallop. This consists of 13 hours, over a three week period, in a Slingsby Firefly 160. The aim of this course is to test aptitude in a live flying environment and to identify whether students have the capability to become an Army pilot.

Students who have successfully demonstrated the necessary flying potential at AFG will progress onto the final phase at the Pilot Selection Centre. This is run by HQ SAAvn and selection includes aptitude tests, a medical, and finally a selection interview.

Flying training

There are several stages in AAC flying training.

Groundschool

The Army Flying Course starts with four weeks of groundschool instruction at RAF College Cranwell. Students learn the basic building blocks of aviation – such as Meteorology, Principles of Flight, Aircraft Operations, Navigation and Technical instruction.

Elementary Flying Training (EFT)

EFT is the first element of Army Flying Training at RAF Barkston Heath. This phase consists of 40 flying hours of elementary fixed- wing flying training over 14 weeks on the Slingsby Firefly.

Aeromedical and Survival Training

After EFT, students complete a week of aeromedical and survival training at RNAS Yeovilton, Lee-on-Solent and Plymouth.

Defence Helicopter Flying School

The Defence Helicopter Flying School (DHFS) at RAF Shawbury provides basic single-engine helicopter training for the three Services and some overseas countries. The DHFS also provides advanced twin-engine helicopter training for RAF aircrew and other special courses for the three Services.

At the DHFS, much of the training effort is contracted out to FBS Ltd – a consortium of Flight Refuelling Aviation, Bristow Helicopters Ltd and Serco Defence. All DHFS military and civilian instructors are trained by the Central Flying School (Helicopter) Squadron. The single-engine basic flying course incorporates some 36 flying hours over nine weeks on the Squirrel helicopter with the instructors of No 660 Squadron. Army students complete nine weeks training before they leave to start their Operational Training Phase at Middle Wallop.

Operational Training Phase (OTP)

The penultimate phase is conducted at the School of Army Aviation at Middle Wallop. Training is focused on converting helicopter pilots into Army pilots. It starts with a week of tactics training, preparing students for the military part of the course. The OTP phase involves 82 flying hours in 18 weeks, and is conducted on the Squirrel helicopter.

Conversion to Type (CTT)

The final phase is conducted at the School of Army Aviation at Middle Wallop. Before being posted to a regiment, students have to convert onto an operational helicopter type. The Conversion to Type (CTT) course takes around nine weeks. At Middle Wallop, Apache aircrew and ground crew training is conducted by Aviation Training International Limited (ATIL).

Conversion to Role (CTR)

Once a pilot has been converted onto type at Middle Wallop, he or she will proceed to a Regiment. At the Regiment a special CTR course will be held to bring the pilot up to combat ready status.

Expect 3 and 4 Attack Regiments to have approximately 60 trained helicopter crew for each regiment. This figure includes qualified helicopter instructors and regimental headquarters personnel, whose primary role is not as helicopter crew. The figures do not include aviation crewmen, such as air door gunners and winch operators.

AAC AIRCRAFT

In late 2015, the AAC aircraft fleet comprises the following types: Apache AH Mk1, Lynx AH7/9, Wildcat and Gazelle helicopters, and the fixed-wing Islanders and Defenders. Contractor-owned Bell 212s are also used by the Army flights in some areas for utility and transport tasks.

Apache (AH Mk1)

(67 ordered and delivered) Gross Mission Weight 7,746 kgs (17,077 lb); Cruise Speed at 500 m 272 kph; Maximum Range (Internal Fuel with 20 minute reserve) 462 kms; General Service Ceiling 3,505 metres (11,500 ft); Crew 2; Carries – 16 x Hellfire II missiles (range 6,000 metres approx); 76 x 2.75" CRV-7 rockets; 1,200 30mm cannon rounds; 4 x Air-to-Air Missiles; Engines 2 x Rolls Royce RTM-332.

The UK MoD ordered 67 Apache based on the US Army AH-64D manufactured by Boeing in 1995. Boeing built the first eight aircraft, and partially assembled the other 59. The UK Westland helicopter company undertook final

Apache. (Copyright Agustawestland)

assembly, flight testing and programme support at their Yeovil factory. Full operating capability for all three Apache Attack Regiments was achieved in mid 2007 and in UK service the aircraft is known as the AH Mk1.

We believe that there are 48 in-service aircraft in two regiments (each of 24 aircraft). The remaining 19 aircraft are used for trials, training and a war maintenance reserve (WMR). The Apache is flown on operations by 3 and 4 Regiments Army Air Corps, based at Wattisham in Suffolk. The two regiments provided a continuous presence in Afghanistan on rotation from 2006 until 2014. During operations in Libya in 2011 AAC Apache helicopters operated against ground targets from HMS Ocean on station in the Mediterranean.

The Apache can operate in all weathers, day or night, and can detect, classify and prioritise up to 256 potential targets at a time. Apart from the 'Longbow' mast-mounted fire control radar, the aircraft is equipped with a 127 x magnification TV system, 36 x magnification thermal imaging, and 18 x magnification direct view optics. The missile system incorporates Semi-Active Laser and Radio Frequency versions of the Hellfire missile, whose range is at least 6 kms. Apart from the Rolls-Royce engines, specific British Army requirements include a secure communications suite and a Helicopter Integrated Defensive Aids System (HIDAS). Programme cost was some £3 billion.

During July 2012 the MoD announced a project worth over £800 million to sustain the Apache AH Mk 1 fleet out to 2040.

Rather dated figures showed the estimated cost (full funded – including forward and depth servicing, fuel costs, crew costs, training costs etc) for an Apache flying hour is £42,000. The marginal cost or direct running cost for one hour (most of which are fuel costs) is £5,000.

Hellfire Missile

Weight 46 kg; Diameter 17.8 cm; Wingspan 33 cm; Length 1163 cm; Warhead HEAT (High explosive ant-tank); Guidance Semi-active laser homing with millimetre wave radar seeker.

The Hellfire missile has shown itself to be a remarkably successful weapon system for Apache attack helicopter operations, proving to be accurate and reliable and providing airborne fire support to ground forces.

During May 2013 the MoD signed a £15 million contract to replenish the stock of Hellfire missiles used by Apache helicopters. Successful use of the missile in both Afghanistan and Libya (from the deck of HMS Ocean) had reduced UK stocks of the missiles and a replenishment was required. Current estimates suggest that the cost of each missile is in the region of £50,000.

Some estimates suggest that over 700 Hellfire missiles were fired from AAC Apache aircraft between 2008 and the end of 2014.

Wildcat (AW159)

(34 being delivered) Crew 2 pilots and a door gunner; 6 x passengers at light scales; Length 15.2 m; Height 3.7 m; Main rotor diameter 12.8 m; Max take off weight 6,000 kg; Engine 2 x LHTEC CTS800-4N turboshaft, 1,015 kW (1,361 hp); Max speed 290 km/h (180 mph); Range: 770 km (480 miles).

The MoD has ordered 62 x Wildcat helicopters, 28 in the naval version (to replace Lynx Mk 8) and 34 in the army version (to replace Lynx AH Mark 7/9).

The prime contractor for the Wildcat contract is AgustaWestland who have subcontracted elements of the project to other companies. The most recent estimate of the cost of the project is £1.644 billion.

Wildcat. (Copyright Agustawestland)

Essentially a Battlefield Reconnaissance Helicopter (BRH) the Wildcat is a development of the older Lynx. Composed of around 95 per cent new components, the Wildcat is the first AgustaWestland helicopter to be designed inside an entirely digital environment. The aircraft also has greater durability and stealth qualities. Both army and navy versions are based on a common airframe.

During late 2011 a further four helicopters were ordered and these four plus four from the army total of 34 were reconfigured as Wildcat Light Assault Helicopters.

Wildcat will be flown by 1 Regiment Army Air Corps operating from Yeovilton. The in-service date for the army variant was 2014.

In the longer term arming the Wildcat with the Lightweight Multirole Missile is one of the options being considered to meet the Future Anti Surface Guided Weapon (Light) (FASGW(L)) requirement.

Lynx AH – Mark 9A

(Approximately 21 x AH9A available) Length Fuselage 12.06 m; Height 3.4 m; Rotor Diameter 12.8 m; Max Speed 330 kph; Cruising Speed 232 kph; Range 885 km; Engines 2 Rolls-Royce Gem 41; Power 2 x 850 bhp; Fuel Capacity 918 litres (internal); Weight (max take off) 4,763 kg; Crew one pilot, one air-gunner/observer; Armament 8 x TOW Anti-Tank Missiles; 2-4 7.62 mm machine guns; Passengers-able to carry 10 PAX; Combat radius approximately 100 kms with 2 hour loiter.

AAC Lynx operating in Afghanistan. (MoD Crown Copyright 2015)

Until the introduction of Apache, Lynx was the helicopter used by the British Army to counter the threat posed by enemy armoured formations. Armed with 8 x TOW missiles the Lynx was the mainstay of the British armed helicopter fleet.

The Lynx AH9A is the only remaining Lynx type in service with the AAC. This aircraft has been upgraded to Light Assault Helicopter (LAH) status, which comprises the fitting of the Night Enhancement Package (NEP) and a range of specialist equipment. The LAH upgrade includes the Digital Night Vision Goggle (D-NVG) system, which allows flight, navigation and instrumentation data to be seen through NVGs; the Sen Pax ARC231 secure airborne communications system; four-man troop seating; provision for door-mounted FN Herstal M-3M (GAU-21) 12.7 mm machine guns; and the L-3 Wescam MX-10 EO/infrared (IR) system. Some aircraft will also be equipped with a fast-roping frame. The majority of upgrade work was completed by late 2012 and we believe that the aircraft will remain in service until 2018.

Gazelle AH1

(Approx 32 available) Fuselage Length 9.53 m; Height 3.18 m; Rotor Diameter 10.5 m; Maximum Speed 265 kph; Cruising Speed 233 kph; Range 670 km; Engine Turbomeca/Rolls-Royce Astazou 111N; Power 592 shp; Fuel Capacity 445 litres; Weight 1,800 kg (max take off); Armament 2 x 7.62 mm machine guns (not a standard fitting).

Gazelle is the general purpose helicopter in use by the AAC, and it is capable of carrying out a variety of battlefield roles. Gazelle is a French design built under licence by Westland Aircraft. It is equipped with a Ferranti AF 532 stabilised, magnifying observation aid. The fleet is now some 30 years old and due to be withdrawn progressively by 2018 – being replaced by the Wildcat Lynx and possibly some leased aircraft.

RAF SUPPORT

The second agency that provides aviation support for the Army is the Royal Air Force. In general terms, the RAF provides helicopters that are capable of moving troops and equipment around the battlefield, and fixed-wing fighter ground attack (FGA) aircraft that provide close air support to the troops in the vicinity of the Forward Edge of the Battlefield Area (FEBA). The RAF also provides the heavy air transport aircraft that will move men and material from one theatre of operations to another. RAF rotary support available is as follows:

RAF Support Helicopters

7 Squadron	11 x Chinook HC4/HC4A/HC5/HC6	Odiham
18 Squadron	10 x Chinook HC4/HC4A/HC5/HC6	Odiham
27 Squadron	9 x Chinook HC4/HC4A/HC5/HC6	Odiham
33 Squadron	12 x Puma HC2	Benson
230 Squadron	12 x Puma HC2	Benson
28 Squadron	12 x Merlin HC3/3A	Benson
78 Squadron	12 x Merlin HC3/3A	Benson

All the above aircraft are under the control of the Joint Helicopter Command (JHC).

Chinook HC4/HC4A/HC5
In service with:

7 Squadron	11 x Chinook HC4/HC4A/HC5/HC6	Odiham
18 Squadron	10 x Chinook HC4/HC4A/HC5/HC6	Odiham
27 Squadron	9 x Chinook HC4/HC4A/HC5/HC6	Odiham

Crew 3/4; Fuselage Length 15.54m; Width 3.78m; Height 5.68m; Weight (empty) 10,814kg; Internal Payload 8,164kg; Rotor Diameter 18.29m; Cruising Speed 158mph/270 kph; Service Ceiling 4,270m; Mission Radius (with internal and external load of 20,000kgs including fuel and crew) 55kms; Rear Loading Ramp Height 1.98m; Rear Loading Ramp Width 2.31m; Engines 2 x Avco Lycoming T55-712 turboshafts.

The Chinook is a tandem-rotored, twin-engined medium-lift helicopter and the first aircraft of this type entered service with the RAF in 1982. It has a crew of four (pilot, navigator and 2 x crewmen) and is capable of carrying 54 fully equipped troops or a variety of heavy loads up to approximately 10 tons. The triple hook system allows greater flexibility in load carrying and enables some loads to be carried faster and with greater stability. In the ferry configuration with internally mounted fuel tanks, the Chinook's range is over 1,600 km (1,000 miles). In the medical evacuation role the aircraft can carry 24 stretchers.

Chinook HC 2. (Copyright Alasdair Taylor)

RAF Chinook aircraft were upgraded to the HC2 standard between 1993 and 1996 for some £145m. The HC2 upgrade modified the RAF Chinooks to the US CH-47D standard. New equipment included infra-red jammers, missile approach warning indicators, chaff and flare dispensers, a long-range fuel system, and machine gun mountings. In 1995, the UK MoD purchased a further 14 x Chinooks (6 x HC2 and 8 x HC2a – now Mk3) for £240 million.

During 2003 the Chinook Night Enhancement Package (NEP) was installed in the HC2 fleet. The NEP was based upon experience gained during operations in Afghanistan and allows Chinook aircraft to operate at night and in very low-light conditions, often at the limit of their capabilities.

A £62 million contract with Boeing to convert eight Chinook Mk3 helicopters to a support helicopter role was announced by the Ministry of Defence in December 2007. The first helicopters were operational in Afghanistan in 2010.

The RAF currently has a fleet of 53 Chinook (late 2015) delivered between 1981 and 2015 of which we believe around 30 are available to the Forward Fleet at any one time. There appears to be plans to procure another 14 Mk 6 aircraft. The purchase cost for 14 x Mk 6 aircraft is £841 million and the first of these aircraft entered service in May 2014. All 14 aircraft should be fully operational by early 2017.

The most recent upgrade and currently underway is Project Julius. This enhancement introduces an integrated digital 'glass' cockpit, moving map tablet and new crewman's workstation across the whole of the fleet of Chinook helicopters. Pilots will now be able to determine what flight and tactical information is displayed to them at any given time, improving the ergonomics of the cockpit. Under Project Julius HC2/HC2A's are being upgraded to the HC4/HC4A standard, and the HC3's to the HC5 standard. Following the upgrade these aircraft will be better positioned for the switch between Special Forces and Support Helicopter tasks.

Puma HC2

In service with:

33 Squadron	12 x Puma HC2	Benson
230 Squadron	12 x Puma HC2	Benson

Crew 2 or 3; Capacity up to 20 troops or 7,055lb underslung; Fuselage Length 14.06m rotors turning 18.15m; Width 3.50m; Height 4.38m; Weight (empty) 3,615kg; Maximum Take Off Weight 7,400kg; Max Speed 163mph/261 kph; Service Ceiling 4,800m; Range 550kms; 2 x Turbomeca Turmo 111C4 turbines.

Following the retirement of the last Wessex in 2003, the Puma is now the oldest helicopter in RAF service. The "package deal" between the UK and France on helicopter collaboration dates back to February 1967. The programme covered the development of three helicopter types – the Puma, Gazelle and Lynx. Production of the aircraft was shared between the two countries, the UK making about 20 per cent by value of the airframe, slightly less for the engine, as well as assembling the aircraft procured for the RAF. Deliveries of the RAF Pumas started in 1971.

Puma HC 1. (Photographed by Adrian Pingstone)

Capable of many operational roles, Puma can carry 16 fully equipped troops or 20 at light scales. In the casualty evacuation role (CASEVAC), six stretchers and six sitting cases can be carried. Underslung loads of up to 3,200 kg can be transported over short distances and an infantry battalion can be moved using about 34 Puma lifts.

The first of 24 upgraded Puma Mk2 aircraft entered service in 2012 with the entire fleet upgraded in early 2014. The entire upgrade package cost about £300 million including one-off costs associated with developing modifications, trials activity, provision of initial support and conversion training for aircrew and maintainers. The actual cost of modifying each helicopter was in the region of £10 million.

Pumas upgraded to HC2 standard should be able to remain in service until about 2025.

Merlin HC3

In service with:

28 Squadron	12 x Merlin HC3/3A	Benson
78 Squadron	12 x Merlin HC3/3A	Benson

Note: RAF Merlin aircraft will be transferred to the Royal Navy Commando Helicopter Force during late 2015/2016.

Crew 4; Capacity up to 24 combat-equipped troops, or 16 stretchers and a medical team, or 4 tonnes of cargo (2.5 tonnes as an underslung load). Length 22.81m; Rotor Diameter 18.59m; Max Speed 309k/ph (192mph); Engine 3 x Rolls Royce/Turbomeca RTM 322 turboshafts.

The RAF acquired 22 x EH101 (Merlin) support helicopters for £755m in March 1995.

Merlin is a direct replacement for the Westland Wessex, and it operates alongside the Puma and Chinook in the medium-lift role. Its ability to carry troops, artillery pieces, light vehicles and bulk loads, means that the aircraft is ideal for use with the UK Army's 16 Air Assault Brigade. Deliveries took place between 2000–2002.

The aircraft can carry a load of 24–28 troops with support weapons. The maximum payload is 4,000 kg and Merlin has a maximum range of 1,000km, which can be extended by external tanks

Merlin HC 3. (Copyright Alasdair Taylor)

or by air-to-air refuelling. The Merlin Mk 3 has sophisticated defensive aids, and the aircraft is designed to operate in extreme conditions with corrosion-proofing for maritime operations. All weather, day/ night precision delivery is possible because of GPS navigation, a forward-looking infra-red sensor and night vision goggle compatibility. In the longer term, the aircraft could be fitted with a nose turret fitted mounting a .50 calibre machine gun.

During March 2007 the UK MoD announced the acquisition of 6 x additional Merlin Mk 3a from Denmark. These aircraft were ordered to support operations in Afghanistan from 2009.

After four years of continuous front line support RAF Merlin aircraft returned from Afghanistan in June 2013. The Merlins had flown for more than 18,000 hours in the dust and heat of Helmand, moving more than 7,900 tonnes of equipment and transporting over 130,000 personnel during the period. In Afghanistan Merlin had been used mainly as a troop transporter.

Following an upgrade we would expect Merlin Mk 3/3A aircraft to remain in service until 2030.

RAF TRANSPORT AIRCRAFT

C-130 Hercules

In service with:

24 Squadron	6 x Hercules C-130J	Brize Norton
30 Squadron	6 x Hercules C-130J	Brize Norton
47 Squadron	6 x Hercules C-130J	Brize Norton
70 Squadron	6 x Hercules C-130J	Brize Norton

The squadron totals are given as a guide to what we believe are the average aircraft figures per squadron at any one time.

C-130J Hercules

Crew: 2 Pilots and 1 Loadmaster; Engines: Four Allison AE 2100D3 turboprops; Max speed; 355kts Range: 3,700 nautical miles; Max altitude: 32,000ft; Length: 34.34m; Span: 40.38m; Payload 19,958 kg; Range 5,250 kms; Take off distance 950 m at 70,300 kg gross weight.

The C-130 Hercules has been the workhorse of the RAF transport fleet since 1967 when the first aircraft entered service. Over the years it has proved to be a versatile and rugged aircraft, primarily intended for tactical operations including troop carrying, parachuting, supply dropping and aeromedical duties. The Hercules can operate from short unprepared airstrips, but also possesses the endurance to mount long range strategic lifts if required. The aircraft was a derivative of the C-130E used by the United States Air Force, but fitted with British Avionic equipment, a roller-conveyor system for heavy air-drops and with more powerful engines. The crew of five (K version) included, pilot, co-pilot, navigator, air engineer and air loadmaster.

Hercules C-130J. (MoD Crown Copyright 2015)

The K Series aircraft finally retired from RAF service in late 2013.

Hercules C-130J C4/C5

The RAF has replaced its Hercules K C1/C3 aircraft with second-generation C-130Js on a one-for-one basis. Twenty-five Hercules C4 and C5 aircraft were ordered in December 94, and the first entered service in 2000. Deliveries were completed by 2003 at a total cost of just over £1bn.The C4 is the same size as the older Hercules C3 which features a fuselage lengthened by 4.57 m (15ft 0 in) than the original C1. The Hercules C5 is the new equivalent of the shorter model. With a flight deck crew of two plus one loadmaster, the C-130J can carry up to 128 infantry, 92 paratroops, 8 pallets or 95 medical stretchers.

The C4/C5s has Allison turboprop engines, R391 6-bladed composite propellers and a Full Authority Digital Engine Control (FADEC). This propulsion system increases take-off thrust by 29 per cent and is 15 per cent more efficient. Consequently, there is no longer a requirement for the external tanks to be fitted. An entirely revised 'glass' flight deck with head-up displays (HUD) and 4 multi-function displays (MFD) replaced many of the dials of the original aircraft. These displays are compatible with night-vision goggles (NVG). MoD figures suggest that there are 24 C-130J in service.

Latest reports suggest that the C-130J will be retired in 2022.

C-17 Globemaster

In service with:

99 Squadron	6 x C-17A	Brize Norton

Crew of 2 pilots and 1 loadmaster. Capacity Maximum of 154 troops. Normal load of 102 fully-equipped troops, up to 172,200lb (78,108kg) on up to 18 standard freight pallets or 48 litters in the medevac role; Wingspan 50.29m; Length overall 53.04m; Height overall 16.8m; Loadable width 5.5m; Cruising speed 648kph (403 mph); Range (max payload) 4,444km (2,400 miles); Engines 4 x Pratt and Whitney F117 turbofans.

The C-17 meets an RAF requirement for an interim strategic airlift capability pending the introduction into service of the A400M Atlas. The decision to lease four C-17 aircraft for some £771m from Boeing was taken in 2001, and the aircraft entered service in 2001. The lease was for a period of seven years, with the option to buy or extend at the end of that period. The option to buy the leased aircraft was exercised in August 2006 together with signature of the contract to procure a fifth new C-17 aircraft which was delivered in April 2008. A sixth C-17 was ordered as a result of a £130 million contract signed in December 2007 and was delivered in July 2008. Two more were ordered in 2010 and 2012.

C-17 Globemaster at RAF Lakenheath. (Airman 1st Class Tiffany Deuel USAF)

The C-17 fleet is capable of the deployment of 1,400 tonnes of freight over 3,200 miles in a seven day period. The aircraft is able to carry one Challenger 2 MBT, or a range of smaller armoured vehicles, or up to three WAH-64 Apache aircraft at one time. Over 150 troops can be carried. In-flight refuelling increases the aircraft range.

By 2013 the unit cost of a C-17 was believed to have risen to around £200 million.

No 99 Sqn has some 180 flight crew and ground staff.

A400M Atlas (Previously Future Large Aircraft – FLA)

Crew 2 pilots and 1 loadmaster; Length 45.1 m; Wingspan 42.4 m; Height 14.7 m; Payload 37,000 kg; Cruising speed 780 km/h (485 mph); Range 3,298 km (2,049 miles) at maximum payload; Ferry range 8,710 km (5,412 miles); Take off distance 980 m; Passengers 116 fully equipped troops or 66 stretchers accompanied by 25 medical personnel.

In 2000 the MoD committed to 25 x Airbus A400M (later reduced to 22) to meet the Future Transport Aircraft (FTA) requirement for an air lift capability to replace the remaining Hercules C-130K and C-130J fleet.

The A400 is a collaborative programme involving eight European nations (Germany, France, Turkey, Spain, Portugal, Belgium, Luxembourg and United Kingdom), procuring a total of 174 aircraft. The expected UK project cost is some £3.2 billion for 22 aircraft and the first aircraft were delivered to the RAF in 2014 with an in-service date of March 2015. Full Operating

First Production A400M. (Copyright Airbus Military)

Capability (FOC) should be possible in 2018 when 12 aircraft should be in service.

The A400M will provide tactical and strategic mobility to all three Services. Atlas's capabilities will enable the aircraft to operate from well established airfields and semi-prepared rough landing areas in extreme climates and all weather by day and night; to carry a variety of vehicles and other equipment, freight, and troops over extended ranges; to be capable of air dropping paratroops and equipment; and to be capable of being unloaded with the minimum of ground handling equipment. Atlas will also meet a requirement for an airlift capability to move large single items such as attack helicopters and some Royal Engineers' equipment. In short, Atlas is capable of transporting 32 tonnes of cargo over a range of 4,500 km.

Airbus Military SL of Madrid, a subsidiary of Airbus Industrie, is responsible for management of the whole of the A400M programme. Companies involved in the programme are. BAE Systems (UK), EADS (Germany, France and Spain), Flabel (Belgium) and Tusas Aerospace Industries (Turkey).

It now looks likely that the RAF will probably retain its C-17s, and will operate a mixed transport fleet comprising the C-130J, A-400 Atlas and C-17 until at least the end of the decade.

Orders for other nations include Germany 53; France 50; Spain 27; Belgium 7; Turkey 10; Luxembourg 1 and Malaysia 4.

CHAPTER 11 – ARTILLERY AND FIRE SUPPORT

OVERVIEW

The Royal Regiment of Artillery (RA) provides the battlefield fire support and air defence for the British Army in the field. Its various regiments are equipped for conventional fire support using field guns, for area and point air defence using air defence missiles and for specialised artillery fire and locating tasks.

The RA remains one of the larger organisations in the British Army with 12 x operational regiments included in its regular Order of Battle. Mid 2015 personnel figures suggest that the RA had a personnel figure of about 7,000 officers and soldiers.

Following ongoing restructuring during early 2016 the Royal Artillery will have the following structure:

Field Regiments (AS 90 SP Guns & GMLRS))	3 (1)
Field Regiments (Light Gun)	4 (2)
Air Defence Regiments (Rapier)	1
Air Defence Regiment (HVM)	1
Surveillance & Target Acquisition Regiment	1
UAV Regiment	2
Training Regiment (School Assets Regt)	1
The Kings Troop (Ceremonial)	1

Note:

(1) These three Regiments have 2 x 155 mm AS 90 Batteries and 1 x GMLRS (Precision Fires) Battery. Expect to see 6 x AS 90 in each battery and 6 x GMLRS in each Precision Fires Battery.
(2) Of these four 105 mm Light Gun Regiments, one is a Commando Regiment (29 Cdo Regt) and another is an Air Assault Regiment (7 PARA RHA). Most Light Gun Batteries have 6 x guns.
(3) There are 3 x GMLRS Batteries in one of the Reserve Regiments (101 Regiment).
(4) The Schools Asset Regiment (14 Regiment) is not included in the totals given for artillery in Chapter 1.

Although the artillery is organised into Regiments, much of the 'Gunner's' loyalty is directed towards the battery in which they serve. The guns represent the Regimental Colours of the Artillery and it is around the batteries where the guns are held that history has gathered. A Regiment will generally have three or four gun batteries under command.

The Royal Horse Artillery (RHA) is also part of the Royal Regiment of Artillery and its Regiments have been included in the totals above. There is considerable cross posting of officers and soldiers from the RA to the RHA, and some consider service with the RHA to be a career advancement.

CURRENT ORGANISATION

In late 2015 the structure of the Regular Regiments of the Royal Artillery are as follows:

Regiment	Role	Formation
1 Regiment RHA	155 mm AS 90 & GMLRS	1 Artillery Brigade
3 Regiment RHA	105 mm Light Gun	1 Artillery Brigade
4 Regiment RA	105 mm Light Gun	1 Artillery Brigade
5 Regiment RA	STA & Special Ops (1)	1 Intelligence and Surveillance Brigade

7 (Parachute Regiment) RHA	105 mm Light Gun	16 Air Assault Brigade
12 Regiment RA	HVM	HQ Joint Ground Based Air Defence
14 Regiment RA	All School Equipments	HQ Royal Artillery
16 Regiment RA	Rapier	HQ Joint Ground Based Air Defence
19 Regiment RA	155 mm AS 90 & GMLRS	1 Artillery Brigade
26 Regiment RA	155 mm AS 90 & GMLRS	1 Artillery Brigade
29 Commando Regiment RA	105 mm Light Gun (2)	3 Commando Brigade
32 Regiment RA	UAVs	1 Intelligence and Surveillance Brigade
47 Regiment RA	UAVs	1 Intelligence and Surveillance Brigade
The King's Troop RHA	13-Pounders (Ceremonial)	London District

Notes:

(1) STA – Surveillance and target acquisition.
(2) The Regimental HQ of 29 Commando Regiment with one battery is at Plymouth. The other two batteries are at Arbroath and Poole. Those at Poole provide the amphibious warfare Naval Gunfire Support Officers (NGSFO).
(3) Regiments equipped with 155 mm AS 90 now have 2 x AS 90 batteries and 1 x GMLRS battery.

Royal Artillery Locations (early 2016)

Regiment	Location
1 Regiment Royal Horse Artillery	Larkhill, Wiltshire (2016/17)
3 Regiment Royal Horse Artillery	Albemarle Barracks, Hexham
4 Regiment Royal Horse Artillery	Alanbrooke Barracks. Topcliffe
5 Regiment Royal Artillery	Marne Barracks, Catterick
7 (Parachute) Regiment Royal Horse Artillery	Merville Barracks, Colchester
12 Regiment Royal Artillery	Baker Barracks, Thorney Island
14 Regiment Royal Artillery	Royal Artillery Barracks, Larkhill
16 Regiment Royal Artillery	Baker Barracks, Thorney Island
19 Regiment Royal Artillery	Larkhill, Wiltshire (2016/17)
26 Regiment Royal Artillery	Larkhill, Wiltshire (2016/17)
29 (Commando) Regiment Royal Artillery	RHQ 8, 23, 79 Batteries, Plymouth
32 Regiment Royal Artillery	Roberts Barracks, Larkhill, Wiltshire
47 Regiment Royal Artillery	Larkhill, Wiltshire
The King's Troop Royal Horse Artillery	Woolwich, London

RESERVE ARTILLERY

Under the 2010 SDSR restructuring plans the 6 x Royal Artillery Reserve Regiments were restructured as follows:

1 x STA and Special Operations Regiment
1 x GMLRS Regiment
1 x Unmanned Air Vehicle Regiment
1 x Ground Based Air Defence Regiment (HVM)

2 x Close Support Regiments (105 mm Light Gun)

TA Artillery Regiment	Role	Paired Regular Unit
HAC	STA and Special Ops	5 Regiment RA
101 Regiment RA	GMLRS (1)	3 Regiment RHA
103 Regiment RA	Light Gun (2)	4 Regiment RA
104 Regiment RA	UAVs	32/47 Regiment
105 Regiment RA	Light Gun	3 Regiment RHA
106 Regiment RA	HVM – Stormer and LML(3)	12 Regiment RA

Note:

(1) With 3 x GMLRS Batteries.

(2) The two Reserve light gun regiments each have four gun batteries.

(3) LML – Light Mobile Launcher.

Royal Artillery Reserve Unit Locations

Regiment	Headquarters	Battery Locations
The Honourable Artillery Company	City of London	City of London
101 (Northumbrian) Regiment Royal Artillery	Gateshead	Blyth, Newcastle, South Shields, Leeds
103 (Lancashire) Regiment Royal Artillery	St Helens	Liverpool, Manchester Wolverhampton, Bolton
104 Regiment Royal Artillery	Newport	Bristol, Abertillery, Cardiff, Worcester, Newport
105 Regiment Royal Artillery	Edinburgh	Newtonards, Coleraine, Glasgow, Arbroath, Shetland, Edinburgh
106 (Yeomanry) Regiment Royal Artillery	Lewisham	Grove Park, Portsmouth, Southampton
Central Volunteer HQ Royal Artillery	Woolwich	Woolwich, Larkhill, Bath

Training

Artillery recruits spend the first period of recruit training (Phase 1 Training, Common Military Syllabus) at the Army Training Centre (Pirbright), or the Army Foundation College – Harrogate.

Artillery training (Phase 2) is carried out at the Royal School of Artillery (RSA) at Larkhill in Wiltshire. During Phase 2 intensive training is given in gunnery, air defence, surveillance or signals. Soldiers also undergo driver training on a variety of different vehicles. After Phase 2 training officers and gunners will be posted to RA units worldwide, but almost all of them will return to the RSA for frequent career and (Phase 3) employment courses.

ARTILLERY FIRE SUPPORT

The Royal Artillery provides the modern British formation with a protective covering on the battlefield. The close air defence assets cover the immediate airspace above and around the formation, with the artillery assets reaching out to over 50 kms in front, and 60 kms across the flanks of the formation being supported. A formation that moves out of this protective covering is open to immediate destruction by an intelligent enemy.

A UK division (Reaction Force) has it own Divisional Artillery Group (DAG) assigned for operations under command. For high intensity operations this artillery might consists of a core group of three

155 mm AS90 Regiments, with a number of other specialist artillery units. Other artillery units could include reserve reinforcement units. In war the composition of the DAG will vary according to the task. The following is a reasonable example of the possible organisation for a DAG.

Armoured Divisional Artillery Group (DAG) – Organisation for War

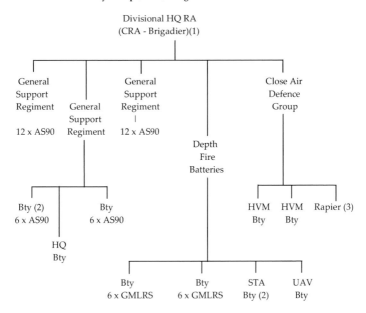

Notes:

(1) This is a diagram of the artillery support which may typically be available to a UK Division deployed with the ARRC. Expect each brigade in the division to have one Close Support Regiment with AS 90. Artillery regiments are commanded by a Lieutenant Colonel and a battery is commanded by a Major.

(2) The STA (Surveillance and Target Acquisition Battery may have a metrological troop with BMETS, a radar troop and a UAV troop.

(3) Area Air Defence (AAD) is provided by Rapier.

(4) The staff of a UK division includes a Brigadier of Artillery known as the Commander Royal Artillery (CRA). The CRA acts as the Offensive Support Advisor to the Divisional Commander and could normally assign one of his Close Support Regiments to support each of the Brigades in the division. These regiments would be situated in positions that would allow all of their batteries to fire across the complete divisional front. Therefore, in the very best case, a battlegroup under extreme threat could be supported by the fire of more than 36 guns and 18 GMLRS.

ARTILLERY FIRE MISSIONS

A brigade (of three infantry battalions and one armoured regiments) will probably have a Close Support Regiment of four batteries in support, and the CO of this regiment will act as the Offensive Support Advisor to the Brigade Commander.

It would be usual to expect that each of the Battlegroups in the brigade would have a Battery Commander / Artillery Officer acting as the Offensive Support Advisor to the Battlegroup Commander. Squadron / Company Groups in the Battlegroup would each be provided with a Forward Observation

Officer (FOO), who is responsible for fire planning and directing the fire of the guns onto the target. The FOO and his party travel in equivalent vehicles to the supported troops to enable them to keep up with the formation being supported and are usually in contact with:

(a) The Gun Positions
(b) The Battery Commander at BGHQ
(c) The Regimental Fire Direction Centre
(d) The Company Group being supported.

Having identified and applied prioritisation of targets, the FOO will call for fire from the guns, and he will then adjust the fall of shot to cover the target area. The FOO will be assisted in this task by the use of a Warrior FCLV OP vehicle containing the computerised fire control equipment which provides accurate data of the target location. The FOO would also have access to reports from overflying UAVs.

Given a vehicle with its surveillance and target acquisition suite the FOO can almost instantly obtain the correct grid of the target and without calling for corrections, order 'one round fire for effect'.

AIR DEFENCE

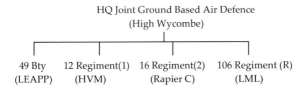

HQ Joint Ground Based Air Defence
(High Wycombe)

| 49 Bty | 12 Regiment(1) | 16 Regiment(2) | 106 Regiment (R) |
| (LEAPP) | (HVM) | (Rapier C) | (LML) |

(1) 12 Regiment has 3 x HVM batteries mounted on Stormer.
(2) 16 Regiment has 4 x Rapier batteries.

49 Battery

Stationed at Thorney Island 49 Battery is an independent Royal Artillery Battery composed of both RA and RAF personnel.

The battery is equipped with the Land Enviroment Air Picture Provision (LEAPP) designed to enhance battlespace (air defence) management using SAAB G-AMB radars to detect, track and identify air contacts and produce a local air picture.

12 Battery

12 Battery, (under command 12 Regiment) based at Thorney Island, has recently taken on the role of providing air defence to 16 Air Assault Brigade, who maintain a very high readiness battlegroup capable of deploying anywhere in the world to conduct the full range of military operations. Currently 12 Battery is able to deploy by helicopter and in the longer term may have an airborne (parachute) capability.

ARTILLERY SYSTEMS

AS90

(90 available – probably 50+ in store): Crew 5; Length 9.07 m; Width 3.3 m; Height 3.0 m overall; Ground Clearance 0.41 m; Turret Ring Diameter 2.7 m; Armour 17 mm; Calibre 155 mm; Range (39 cal) 24.7 kms (52 cal) 30 kms; Recoil Length 780 mm; Rate of Fire 3 rounds in 10 secs (burst) 6 rounds per minute (intense) 2 rounds per minute (sustained); Secondary Armament 7.62 mm MG; Traverse 6,400 mills; Elevation -89/ +1.244 mills; Ammunition Carried 48 x 155 mm projectiles and charges (31 turret & 17 hull); Engine Cumminis VTA903T turbo-charged V8 diesel 660 hp; Max Speed 53 kph; Gradient 60%; Vertical Obstacle 0.75 m; Trench Crossing 2.8 m; Fording Depth 1.5 m; Road Range 420 kms.

AS 90 was manufactured by Vickers Shipbuilding and Engineering (VSEL) at Barrow in Furness. 179 Guns were delivered under a fixed price contract for £300 million. These 179 guns completely equipped six field regiments replacing the older 120 mm Abbot and 155 mm M109 in British service. At the beginning of 2015 there remains three Regiments of 1 Artillery Brigade equipped with the system.

AS 90 is equipped with a 39 calibre gun fires the NATO L15 unassisted projectile out to a range of 24.7 kms (Base Bleed ERA range is 30 kms).

AS90 of 3 RHA firing in Iraq during 2008. (Pfc. Rhonda J. Roth-Cameron, U.S. Army)

The gun has been fitted with an autonomous navigation and gunlaying system (AGLS), enabling it to work independently of external sighting references. Central to the system is an inertial dynamic reference unit (DRU) taken from the US Army's MAPS (Modular Azimuth Positioning System). The bulk of the turret electronics are housed in the Turret Control Computer (TCC) which controls the main turret functions, including gunlaying, magazine control, loading systems control, power distribution and testing.

Artillery has always been a cost effective way of destroying or neutralising targets in the forward edge of the battlespace. When the cost of a battery of guns, (approx £40 million) is compared with the cost of a modern close air support aircraft, (£100 million – Lightning II estimate) plus and the cost of training each pilot, (£5 million +) the way ahead for governments with less and less to spend on defence is clear.

105 mm Light Gun

(Approximately 100 available) Crew 6; Weight 1,858 kg; Length 8.8 m; Width 1.78 m; Height 21.3 m; Ammunition HE, HEAT, WP, Smoke, Illuminating, Target Marking; Maximum Range (HE) 17.2 kms; Anti Tank Range 800 m; Muzzle Velocity 709m/s; Shell Weight HE 15.1 kg; Rate of Fire 6 rounds per minute.

The 105 mm Light Gun has been in service with the Royal Artillery for over 40 years, and has recently received a major upgrade. The enhancement is an Auto Pointing System (APS) which performs the same function as the DRU on the AS 90. The APS is based on an inertial navigation system which enables it to be unhooked and into action in 30 seconds. The APS replaces the traditional dial sight and takes into account trunion tilt without the requirement to level any spirit level bubbles as before.

The gun was first delivered to the British Army in 1975 when it replaced the 105 mm Pack Howitzer. A robust, reliable system, the Light Gun proved its worth in the Falklands, where guns were sometimes firing up to 400 rounds per day. Since then the gun has seen operational service in Kuwait, Bosnia, Iraq and Afghanistan.

105 mm Light Gun. (Copyright BAe Systems)

The Light Gun is in service with four Artillery Regiments (4 x Regular and 2 Reserve) as a go-anywhere, airportable weapon which can be carried around the battlefield underslung on a Puma or Chinook.

During March 2005 the UK MoD placed a contract for an advanced and more effective light artillery shell. This contract for 105 mm Improved Ammunition that was awarded to BAE Systems led to an initial buy of 50,000 High Explosive rounds, and was worth around £17 million.

The new High Explosive munitions are more effective against a range of targets and incorporates Insensitive Munitions (IM) technology, making them even safer to transport and handle.

The Light Gun has been extremely successful in the international market with sales to Australia (59), Botswana (6), Brunei (6), Ireland (12), Kenya (40), Malawi (12), Malaysia (20), Morocco (36), New Zealand (34), Oman (39), Switzerland (6), UAE (50), United States (548) and Zimbabwe (12).

227 mm GMLRS

(50 launchers available) Crew 3; Weight loaded 24,756 kg; Weight Unloaded 19,573 kg; Length 7.167 m; Width 2.97 m; Height (stowed) 2.57 m; Height (max elevation) 5.92 m; Ground Clearance 0.43 m; Max Road Speed 64 kph; Road Range 480 km; Fuel Capacity 617 litres; Fording 1.02 m; Vertical Obstacle 0.76 m; Engine Cummings VTA-903 turbo-charged 8 cylinder diesel developing 500 bhp at 2,300 rpm; Rocket Diameter 227 mm;

The MLRS launch vehicle is based on the US M2 Bradley (M270) chassis and the system is self loaded with 2 x rocket pod containers, each containing 6 x rockets. The whole loading sequence is power assisted and loading takes between 20 and 40 minutes. There is no manual procedure. Currently the MLRS vehicle is used operationally to fire the GMLRS rocket.

GMLRS firing during acceptance trials. *(MoD Crown Copyright 2015)*

GMLRS rockets contain Global Positioning System (GPS) elements and the latest advanced computer technology giving them accuracy out to a range of up to 70 kms. Armed with a 200 lb (90 kg) high explosive warhead which carries a payload of 404 Dual Purpose Improved Conventional Munition (DPICM) submunitions, the improved missile can engage more targets with a lower risk of collateral damage and with a smaller logistical burden.

The GMLRS rocket has been developed by a five-nation collaboration of the UK, France Germany, Italy and the US. The overall programme was worth over £250 million and the UK took delivery of several thousand rockets. The approximate (2010) cost per GMLRS Rocket was £68,000.

Following a series of successful trials the Guided Multiple Rocket Launch System (GMLRS) was declared fit for deployment with UK troops in Afghanistan in mid 2007.

The US Army is currently operating 830 MLRS, the French have 58, the West Germans 154 and the Italians 21.

Starstreak HVM

(135 fire units available and some carried on Stormer): Missile Length 1.39 m; Missile Diameter 0.27m; Missile Speed Mach 3+; Maximum Range 5.5 kms; Missile ceiling 1,000 m; Flight time to max rang is 8 secs.

Short Missile Systems of Belfast were the prime contractors for the HVM (High Velocity Missile) which continues along the development path of both Blowpipe and Javelin. The system can be shoulder launched by mounting on the LML (lightweight multiple launcher) or vehicle borne on the Alvis Stormer APC. The Stormer APC has an eight round launcher and 12 reload missiles can be carried inside the vehicle.

HVM has been optimised to counter threats from fast pop-up type strikes by attack helicopters and low flying aircraft. The missile employs a system of three dart type projectiles which can make multiple hits on the target. Each of these darts has an explosive warhead. It is believed that the HVM has an SSK (single shot to kill) probability of over 95%.

Using the HVM Thermal Sighting System (TSS) the system has the capability to operate at night, through cloud or in poor visibility. Some 84 x TSS are believed to be in service.

HVM on Stormer. (MoD Crown Copyright 2015)

During late 2011 the Mod announced the procurement of an additional 200 Starstreak to be delivered to both regular and reserve units.

12 Regiment RA stationed at Thorney Island are equipped with HVM and Stormer with 1 x Reserve Artillery Regiment similarly equipped. On mobilisation for general war an HVM Regiment is believed to be configured as follows:

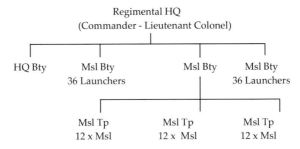

Note: An HVM detachment is carried in a Stormer armoured vehicle and in each vehicle there are four personnel. In general, inside the vehicle there are twelve ready to use missiles with a further eight stored inside as reloads.

12 Battery of 12 Regiment supports 24 Airmobile Brigade and can us the lightweight mobile launcher as appropriate.

Rapier (FSC)

(Possibly 24 fire units in service) Guidance Semi Automatic to Line of Sight (SACLOS); Missile Diameter 13.3 cm; Missile Length 2.35 m; Rocket Solid Fuelled; Warhead High Explosive; Launch Weight 42 kg; Speed Mach 2+; Ceiling 3,000 m; Maximum Range 9,000 m; Fire Unit Height 2.13 m; Fire Unit Weight 1,227 kg; Radar Height (in action) 3.37 m; Radar Weight 1,186 kg; Radar Range 16 kms; Optical Tracker Height 1.54 m; Optical Tracker Weight 119 kg; Generator Weight 243 kg; Generator Height 0.91 m.

The Rapier system provides area 24 hour through cloud, Low Level Air Defence (LLAD) over the battlefield.

Rapier Field standard C (FSC) incorporates a range of technological improvements over its predecessor including an advanced three dimensional radar tracker acquisition system designed by Plessey. The towed system launcher mounts eight missiles (able to fire two simultaneously) which are manufactured in two warhead versions. One of these is a proximity explosive round and the other a kinetic energy round. The total cost of the Rapier (FSC) programme was £1,886 million.

The UK's future Rapier air defence capability will be 16 Regiment Royal Artillery (Thorney Island). The possible configuration of a 16 Regiment on mobilisation will be four batteries each of two troops with three fire units per troop. In July 2004 the MoD announced the disbandment of the RAF Regiment Rapier squadrons.

Rapier. (Copyright BAe Systems)

During April 2014 the MoD awarded MBDA a £36 million contract for the assessment phase for the land version of FLAADS (Future Local Anti-Air Defence System) a possible replacement for Rapier.

Rapier in all of its versions has now been sold to the armed forces of at least 14 nations. We believe that sales have amounted to over 25,000 missiles, 600 launchers and about 350 radars.

Air Defence Alerting Device (ADAD)
An infra-red thermal imaging surveillance system that is used by close air defence units to detect hostile aircraft and helicopter targets and directs weapon systems into the target area. The air defence missile operators can be alerted to up to four targets in a priority order. This passive system which is built by Thorn EMI has an all weather, day and night capability.

MSTAR
Weight 30 kg; Wavelength J – Band; Range in excess of 20 kms.

MSTAR is a Lightweight Pulse Doppler J – Band All Weather Radar that has replaced the ZB 298 in the detection of helicopters, vehicles and infantry. Powered by a standard army field battery this radar will also assist the artillery observer in detecting the fall of shot. The electroluminescent display that shows dead ground relief and target track history, also has the ability to superimpose a map grid at the 1:50000 scale to ease transfer to military maps. MSTAR can be vehicle borne or broken down into three easily transportable loads for manpacking purposes.

MSTAR is used by Forward Observation Officers. There are believed to be around 100 MAOV (Warrior Mechanised Artillery Observation Vehicles) equipped with MSTAR. MSTAR is believed to cost about £50,000 per unit at mid 1999 prices and in total about 200 MSTAR equipments are in service throughout the British Army.

MAMBA – Mobile Artillery Monitoring Battlefield Radar (Ericsson ARTHUR)
(possibly 12 available)

In service with 5 Regiment this is an artillery hunting radar which was deployed operationally for the first time in April 2002. MAMBA automatically detects, locates and classifies artillery, rockets and mortars and carries out threat assessment based on weapon or impact position. All acquired data is automatically transmitted to a combat control centre. The equipment also incorporates its own basic command, control and communications system for direct control of counter-battery fire. The contract value was believed to be in the region of £30 million.

Mamba's detection range is 20 km (howitzer) and 30 km (rockets) with a circular error probable (CEP) of around 30 m at extreme range. The system can locate a maximum of eight targets simultaneously.

The system, which is mounted on a Alvis Hagglunds BV206 tracked vehicle is easily transportable by aircraft or helicopters. Reports from operational areas suggest that this system has been extremely successful.

Lightweight Counter-Mortar Radar (LCMR)

Also in service with 5 Regiment the LCMR provides continuous 3-D, 360-degree surveillance and 3-D rocket, artillery and mortar location using a non-rotating, electronically steered antenna. The radar perform with a track-while-scan capability allowing for the simultaneous detection and tracking of multiple threats fired from separate locations. Once a threat is detected, the radar sends an early warning message indicating that a round is incoming. After sufficient data is collected to enable an accurate point of origin, the weapon's location is reported back for a counterfire response from any other integrated systems.

LCMR is highly mobile, able to be carried in most in service vehicles and all fixed and rotary wing aircraft. An LCMR detachment is able to be in action in under 20 minutes and will provide a 24 hour, all weather capability. The radar range is in excess of 10 kms.

Sound Ranging

Sound Ranging (SR) locates the positions of enemy artillery from the sound of their guns firing. Microphones are positioned on a line extending over a couple of kilometres to approximately 12 kilometres. As each microphone detects the sound of enemy guns firing, the information is relayed to a Command Post which computes the location of the enemy battery. Enemy locations are then passed to Artillery Intelligence and counter battery tasks fired as necessary. Sound Ranging can identify an enemy position to within 50 m at 10 kms. The only Sound Ranging assets remaining in the Royal Artillery are those with 5 Regt RA at Catterick.

The UK has one battery in 5 Regiment equipped with Mark 2 HALO ASP (advanced sound ranging system), an acoustic weapons locating equipment specifically for use in out of area or sensitive operations where flying UAVs might be sensitive. The ASP system was first deployed in March 2003 and is expected to be in-service until 2020.

BMETS

The Battlefield Meteorological System BMETS came into service in 1999 and replaces AMETS which entered service in 1972 and provided met messages in NATO format.

With the extreme range of modern artillery and battlefield missiles, very precise calculations regarding wind and air density are needed to ensure that the target is accurately engaged. BMETS units can provide this information by releasing hydrogen filled balloons at regular intervals recording important information on weather conditions at various levels of the atmosphere.

To benefit from current technology BMETS uses commercially available equipment manufactured by VAISALA linked to the Battlefield Artillery Target Engagement System (BATES). It is a two vehicle system with a detachment of five in peace, six in war. It is deployed with all regular field artillery and MLRS regiments.

BMETS can operate in all possible theatres of conflict worldwide where the Meteorological Datum Plain (MDP) varies from 90 m below to 4000 m above sea level, and can be used with a variety of radiosonde types to sound the atmosphere to a height of up to 20 km. Measurements are made by an ascending radiosonde. This is tracked by a passive radiotheodolite which provides wind data, air temperature, atmospheric pressure and relative humidity from the datum plan for each sounding level, until flight termination. In addition virtual temperature, ballistic temperature and ballistic density are calculated to a high degree of accuracy. Cloud base is estimated by observation. The data is then processed by receiver equipment in the troop vehicles to provide formatted messages to user fire units via the existing military battlefield computer network.

UNMANNED AIR VEHICLES (UAV)

Watchkeeper

(54 on order); Take off weight 450 kg; Wingspan 10.51 m; Fuselage length 6.10 m; Max speed 175 kph; Operational ceiling 5,000 m plus; Endurance – more than 20 hours; Payload 150 kg.

In 2005 the MoD funded an £850 programme to procure the Watchkeeper unmanned aerial system (UAS) with Thales as the prime contractor.

Watchkeeper is a combination of two earlier army UAV programmes (Sender and Spectator) to meet the reconnaissance requirements of land commanders following the retirement of the Phoenix system. In service, Watchkeeper will replace the Hermes 450 system that will be phased out gradually as Watchkeeper systems enter service.

Watchkeeper. (Copyright Thales UK Ltd)

Watchkeeper is a system delivering an Intelligence, surveillance and reconnaissance capability and comprising a number of elements including air vehicles, ground control stations, data terminals, ground equipment and sensors, as well as infrastructure and training facilities. Watchkeeper has a endurance time of about 20 hours and a maximum payload of 150 kgs. The payload includes a range of sensors, a laser designator and a radar/ground moving target indicator.

Watchkeeper achieved its first initial operating capability in the summer of 2014 and was deployed to Afghanistan between August and October of 2014. A total of 54 systems have been ordered with 30 deployed in two regiments (32 and 47 Regiments) and a further 24 in reserve. Unit cost is believed to be in the area of £15 million. The system should be at full operating capability in April 2016.

Three UAS batteries from 32 Regiment will be aligned with the Reaction Force (3 United Kingdom Division) Armoured Infantry Brigades, and are likely to retain the full spectrum structure. They will get Warthog vehicles modified to act as carriers for the airframe detachments and they will also have Viking vehicles to transport the ground based Watchkeeper elements. Two batteries from 47 Regiment support the Adaptable Force (1 United Kingdom Division) with a third, 21 Battery, in the Very High Readiness role to support forces deployed at short notice. 21 Battery may well deploy with mini-UAVs and may be earmarked to support 16 Air Assault Brigade.

During early March 2014 approval was given for Royal Artillery pilots to begin live-flying Watchkeeper aircraft from Boscombe Down in Wiltshire. Since that time UAV pilots from 1st Artillery Brigade have been trained to fly Watchkeeper in a restricted airspace over the Salisbury Plain Training Area (SPTA). The flights take place between 8,000 and 16,000 feet, and will be overseen by military air traffic controllers.

Desert Hawk

Desert Hawk is a small and portable UAV surveillance system which provides aerial video reconnaissance. It has a flight time of approximately one hour, and can fly almost anywhere within a 10 km radius of its ground control station. Desert Hawk weighs 3.2 kg, has a length of 0.86 m and a wingspan of 1.32 m. The system can be used for a variety of tasks, such as force protection for convoys and patrols,

Desert Hawk. (Copyright Lockheed Martin)

route clearance, base security, reconnaissance or target tracking. It has both day and night time (thermal imaging) capability.

Total acquisition costs of the Desert Hawk UAVs are believed to be about £36 million and there are probably 176 Desert Hawk III airframes in service. Another 100 airframes are on order.

Desert Hawk has an extremely good record supporting UK forces in Afghanistan.

UAV OPERATED BY THE ROYAL AIR FORCE

Predator MR-9 Reaper
In service with:

13 Sqn	MR-9 Reaper	RAF Waddington (5)
39 Sqn	MR-9 Reaper	RAF Waddington (5)

Operated by one pilot and one sensor operator; Length 11m; Wingspan 20m; Weight 1,676kg (empty); 4,760kg (max); Operational Altitude 25,000ft; Endurance 16–28hrs; Range 3,682 miles; Payload 4,200lb; Max Speed 400kph/250mph; Cruise Speed 160kph/100mph; Engines 670 kW Honeywell TP331-10 turboprop; Armament 6 x hardpoints under the wings, can carry a payload mix of 1,500lb (680kg) on each of its two inboard weapons stations, 500–600lb (230–270kg) on the two middle stations and 150–200lb (68–91kg) on the outboard stations. Up to 14 x AGM-114 Hellfire air to ground missiles can be carried or four Hellfire missiles and two 500lb (230kg) GBU-12 Paveway II laser-guided bombs. The ability to carry the JDAM in the future is also possible, as well is the AIM 9X, Air to Air missile.

Reaper is a Remotely Piloted Air System (RPAS). The Reaper's primary mission is to act as an (intelligence, surveillance, target, acquisition and reconnaissance) platform. During Operation Herrick in Afghanistan Reaper has been used to provide close air support on opportunity targets to troops operating in the forward part of the battlespace. We believe that Reaper (RPAS) currently in RAF service employ two types of munitions; the Hellfire AGM 114 guided missile and the GBU 12 laser guided bomb.

MQ-9 Reaper. (MoD Crown Copyright 2015)

During April 2013 the RAF began operating Reaper RPAS from RAF Waddington in addition to those operated from Creech Air Force Base in Nevada by 39 Squadron. 'Operational since October 2012 at RAF Waddington, 13 Squadron has about 100 personnel including pilots, engineers and systems operators.

The UK MoD states that "Reaper is not an autonomous system and all weapons employment depends upon commands from the flight crew. The weapons may be released under the command of a pilot who uses Rules of Engagement that are no different to those used for manned UK combat aircraft. The targets are always positively identified as legitimate military objectives, and attacks are prosecuted in strict accordance with the Law of Armed Conflict and UK Rules of Engagement. Every effort is made to ensure the risk of collateral damage, including civilian casualties, is minimised." By the end of January 2013 approximately 365 weapons were launched by UK Reapers.

US sources suggest that the 'flyaway cost' of an MQ-9 Reaper is in the region of US$16.9 million (£11.2 million).

Taranis

The RAF has also taken the first steps towards developing its own Unmanned Combat Aircraft Systems (UCAS), Project "Taranis" was announced in 2008 and a demonstrator was flying in 2013 in Australia being used to evaluate how UCAVs will contribute to the RAF's future mix of aircraft.

The demonstrator is believed to be the size of a BAe Hawk, weighs about 8 tons and will be configured for reconnaissance and attack missions. Some analysts believe that a system developed from Project Taranis could be operational by 2020.

Taranis. (Photo BAe Systems)

Other than BAE Systems the project includes a teaming arrangement between Rolls-Royce, the Systems division of GE Aviation (formerly Smiths Aerospace) and QinetiQ who work alongside UK military personnel and scientists to develop and fly the system.

CHAPTER 12 – ENGINEERS

OVERVIEW

The engineer support for the Army is provided by the Corps of Royal Engineers (RE). Known as Sappers, the Royal Engineers are one of the Army's three Combat Support Arms, and are trained as fighting soldiers, combat engineers and artisan tradesmen as well as holding specialist qualifications within EOD, Search and Diving. The Corps of Royal Engineers performs highly specialised combat and non-combat tasks, and is active all over the world in conflict and during peace. The Corps has no battle honours, its motto *'ubique'* (everywhere), signifies that it has taken part in every battle fought by the British Army in all parts of the world.

FORCE STRUCTURE

As of late 2015, the RE had an approximate regular Army personnel strength of about 8,500. This large corps comprises 12 x Regular Regiments, 5 x Works Groups and 3 x Reserve Regiments.

The listing of major units by role is as follows:

		Regular	*Reserve*
Close Support Regiment	-	5	
Air Assault Regiment	-	1	
Commando Regiment	-	1	
Air Support Regiment	-	1	1
Force Support Regiment	-	1	1
EOD and Search Regiment	-	2	
Geographic Regiment	-	1	
Infrastructure Support (Works Groups)	-	5	1
Training Regiments	-	2	

Regular and Reserve units are listed in the following tables:

Regular Units	*Role*	*Location*
21 Engineer Regiment	Close Support	Catterick
22 Engineer Regiment	Close Support	Perham Down
23 Engineer Regiment	Air Assault	Woodbridge
24 Commando Regiment	Commando Support	Chivenor
26 Engineer Regiment	Close Support	Perham Down
32 Engineer Regiment	Close Support	Catterick
33 Engineer Regiment	EOD	Wimbish
35 Engineer Regiment	Close Support	Perham Down
36 Engineer Regiment	Force Support	Maidstone
39 Engineer Regiment	Air Support	Kinloss
42 Engineer Regiment	Geographic	RAF Wyton
101 Engineer Regiment	EOD	Wimbish
20 Works Group	Air Support	Wittering
62 Works Group	Infrastructure Support	Chilwell

63 Works Group	Infrastructure Support	Chilwell
64 Works Group	Infrastructure Support	Chilwell
66 Works Group	Infrastructure Support	Chilwell

Reserve Units	*HQ Location*	*Squadron Locations*
The Royal Monmouthshire Royal Engineers (Militia)	Monmouth	Jersey, Cwmbran, Swansea, Oldbury, Stoke-on-Trent
65 Works Group	Infrastructure Support	Chilwell
71 Engineer Regiment	RAF Leuchars	Paisley, Inchinnan, Cumbernauld, Orkney, Bangor
75 Engineer Regiment	Warrington	Birkenhead, Manchester, Holton
Reserve engineer units attached to regular units	At various UK locations	

8 ENGINEER BRIGADE

8 Engineer Brigade commands the majority of the Army's Royal Engineer capability. The Brigade is built around four Specialist Groups as follows:

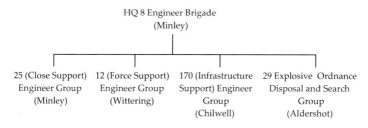

HQ 8 Engineer Brigade
(Minley)

25 (Close Support) Engineer Group (Minley) — 12 (Force Support) Engineer Group (Wittering) — 170 (Infrastructure Support) Engineer Group (Chilwell) — 29 Explosive Ordnance Disposal and Search Group (Aldershot)

25 (Close Support) Engineer Group provides mobility, counter-mobility and survivability for forces manoeuvring in the Land Environment. Both the Reaction Force and the Adaptable Force can be supported with systems such as Titan (gap crossing),Trojan (route opening and obstacle clearance) and Terrier (obstacle clearance, building anti-tank ditches, trenches etc.

12 (Force Support) Engineer Group provides support to Theatre Entry, including route maintenance and enabling airfield operations.

170 (Infrastructure Support) Engineer Group designs, resources and constructs the infrastructure to sustain a deployed force.

29 Explosive Ordnance Disposal and Search Group supports both deployed operations and Homeland Defence. The Group locates and disposes of conventional and improvised explosive threats using all forms of search capability including Military Working Dog support.

25 (Close Support) Engineer Group (Minley)

Unit	Role	Location	Affiliated reserve unit
21 Engineer Regiment	Close Support	Catterick	Hybrid – Composed of Regular and Reserve Squadrons
22 Engineer Regiment	Close Support	Perham Down	
26 Engineer Regiment	Close Support	Perham Down	
32 Engineer Regiment	Close Support	Catterick	Hybrid – Composed of Regular and Reserve Squadrons
35 Engineer Regiment	Close Support	Perham Down	

Note: 22, 26 and 35 Engineer Regiments support the Reaction Force (3 UK Division). 21 and 32 Regiments support the Adaptable Force (1 UK Division).

12 (Force Support) Engineer Group (Wittering)

Unit	Role	Location	Affiliated reserve unit
36 Engineer Regiment	Force Support	Maidstone	75 Engineer Regiment (R) (Maidstone) (1)
39 Engineer Regiment	Force Support	Kinloss	71 Engineer Regiment (R) (Leuchars)
20 Works Group	Force Support	Wittering	

Note: 75 Regiment (Reserve) is receiving the M3 rigs to become the Army's sole Wide Wet Gap Crossing Regiment.

170 (Infrastructure Support) Engineer Group (Chilwell)

Unit	Role	Location	Affiliated reserve unit
62 Works Group	Infrastructure Support	Chilwell	Hybrid – Composed of Regular and Reserve Squadrons
63 Works Group	Infrastructure Support	Chilwell	Hybrid – Composed of Regular and Reserve Squadrons
64 Works Group	Infrastructure Support	Chilwell	Hybrid – Composed of Regular and Reserve Squadrons
65 Works Group (R)	Infrastructure Support	Chilwell	Reserve Unit (STRE) (1)
66 Works Group	Infrastructure Support	Chilwell	Hybrid – Composed of Regular and Reserve Squadrons
Royal Monmouthshire Royal Engineers (R)	Infrastructure Support	Monmouth	Reserve Unit

Note:

(1) With 6 x STRE (Specialist Teams RE) providing specialist expertise on fuel, power, accommodation and storage, air and water etc.

29 Explosive Ordnance Disposal & Search Group (Aldershot)

Unit	Role	Location	Affiliated reserve unit
33 Engineer Regiment (EOD) (1)	Disposal & Search	Wimbish	Hybrid – Composed of Regular and Reserve Squadrons
101 Engineer Regiment (EOD) (2)	Disposal & Search	Wimbish	Hybrid – Composed of Regular and Reserve Squadrons
11 (EOD) Regiment RLC	Explosive Disposal	Didcot	
1 Military Working Dog Regiment	Search	North Luffenham	Hybrid – Composed of Regular and Reserve Squadrons

Note:

(1) 33 EOD Regiment is primarily tasked with EOD support to the Reaction Force (3 UK Division).

(2) 101 EOD Regiment supports the Adaptable Force (1 UK Division).

Engineer Units Under Other Commands

Unit	Role	Location	Headquarters
23 Engineer Regiment (Air Assault)	Close Support	Woodbridge	16 Air Assault Brigade
24 Commando Regiment	Commando Support	Chivenor	3 Commando Brigade
40 Engineer Regiment	Geographic	RAF Wyton	1 Intelligence and Surveillance Brigade

COMBAT ENGINEERING ROLES

Combat engineer support to military operations may be summarised under the following headings:

◆ Mobility
◆ Counter-mobility
◆ Protection

Mobility

The capability to deliver firepower, troops and supplies to any part of the battlefield is crucial to success. Combat engineers use their skills to overcome physical obstacles both natural and man-made, ensuring that armoured and mechanised troops can reach their targets and fight effectively.

Combat Engineers employ a wide variety of equipment, including tank-mounted, amphibious and girder bridges, to cross physical barriers. This equipment can be rapidly deployed to any part of the battlefield to ensure minimum interruption to progress.

Combat engineers are trained and equipped to clear enemy minefields which block or hinder movement. All combat engineers are trained to clear minefields by hand with the minimum risk. They also employ a number of explosive and mechanical devices to clear paths through minefields.

Combat engineers are also trained to detect and to destroy booby traps.

Improving the mobility of own and friendly forces may include the following tasks:

Route clearance and maintenance
Construction and maintenance of diversionary routes

Routes to and from hides
Bridging, rafting and assisting amphibious vehicles at water obstacles
Detection and clearance of mines and booby traps
Assisting the movement of heavy artillery and communications units
Preparation of landing sites for helicopters

Counter-mobility

Counter-mobility is the term used to describe efforts to hinder enemy movement. Combat engineers aim to ensure that hostile forces cannot have freedom of mobility. Combat engineers are trained in the use of explosive charges to create obstacles, crater roads and destroy bridges. In this role, the combat engineer may be required to delay detonation until the last possible moment to allow the withdrawal of friendly forces in the face of an advancing enemy.

Combat engineers are also responsible for laying anti-tank mines, either by hand or mechanically, to damage vehicles and disrupt enemy forces. Combat engineers are trained to handle these devices safely and deploy them to maximum effect. Combat engineers are also trained for setting booby traps.

Earthwork defences, ditches and obstacles – one of the earliest forms of battlefield engineering – are also used to prevent the advance of enemy vehicles. Hindering enemy movement may include the following tasks:

Construction of minefields
Improvement of natural obstacles by demolitions, cratering, and barricades
Nuisance mining and booby traps
Route denial
Construction of obstacles to armoured vehicle movement, such as tank ditches

Protection

Construction of field defences is a core task for combat engineers. The capability to protect troops, equipment and weapons is critical. Combat engineers provide advice and assistance to the other parts of the Land Forces and the other services on the best methods of concealment and camouflage, and use mechanised plant to construct defensive positions and blast-proof screens.

Protection for troops in defensive positions may include field defences, minefields, wire, and other obstacles. Because of their commitment to other primary roles, there may be little engineer assistance available for the construction of defensive positions. What assistance can be given would normally be in the form of earth-moving plant to assist in digging, and advice on the design and methods of construction of field defences and obstacles.

Combat Engineers Military Works Groups have design and management teams that can provide military infrastructure support to all armed services and other government departments. Secondary protection roles include:

Water and power supply in forward areas
Technical advice on counter-surveillance with particular reference to camouflage and deception
Destruction of equipment
Intelligence

A major Engineer commitment in the forward area is the construction, maintenance and repair, of dispersed airfields for aircraft and landing sites for helicopters.

Non-Combat Engineering

Combat engineers also perform non-combat tasks during national peacetime contingencies and multilateral peace support operations in foreign countries, including:

- General support engineering, including airfield damage repair and repair of ancillary installations for fuel and power, construction of temporary buildings, power and water supplies, repair and construction of POL pipelines and storage facilities, and construction and routine maintenance of airstrips and helicopter landing sites.
- Survey – including maps and aeronautical charts.
- Explosive Ordnance Disposal – including terrorist and insurgent bombs.
- Traffic Movement Lights for mobilisation and exercises.
- Postal and courier services for all the Armed Forces.

Recent coalition and peace support operations have highlighted the importance of combat engineers in all spheres of military activity. During the period 1993–2015, the multitude of tasks for which engineer support has been requested has stretched the resources of the Corps to its limit. Engineers are almost always among the first priorities in any call for support: tracks must be improved, roads built, accommodation constructed for soldiers and refugees, clean water provided and mined areas cleared. For example during 2003, 22 Engineer Regiment (operating in Iraq) was tasked to supply a quick fix to problem areas along the diesel pipeline for the Oil Security Force (OSF), and to ensure regular supplies of water for the Iraqi population in Basra and the surrounding urban areas.

CLOSE SUPPORT ENGINEER REGIMENT

Due to the current reorganisation exact details are still difficult to ascertain. However, we believe that the in-barracks organisation for a Close Support Engineer Regiment operating in support of the Reaction Force (3 UK Division) resembles the following:

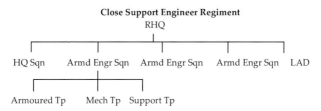

Close Support Engineer Regiment
RHQ
HQ Sqn   Armd Engr Sqn   Armd Engr Sqn   Armd Engr Sqn   LAD
Armoured Tp   Mech Tp   Support Tp

Strength: Approx 650 All Ranks

This whole organisation is highly mobile and built around the AFV 430, CVR(T), Panther series of vehicles with TITAN, TROJAN and TERRIER armoured vehicles. In addition to the Regimental REME LAD, each squadron has its own REME section of some 12-15 men. The smallest engineer unit is the Troop which is usually commanded by a Lieutenant and consists of approximately 30 men.

Following Future Army Structure changes, each Close Support Engineer Regiment is almost identical in structure irrespective of the type of brigade supported. Each Armoured Engineer Squadron will have at least one affiliated Battlegroup to which it offers engineer support by default, although the Regiment will flex engineer effort to where it is most required.

COMBAT ENGINEER TRAINING

All RE officers undergo officer training at RMA Sandhurst (44 weeks) before taking the Royal Engineers Troop Commanders Course (RETCC) with 1 and 3 RSME Regiments at the Royal School of Military Engineering (RSME). The RETCC is 27 weeks long. All RE officers are expected to have or to obtain university degree-level engineering qualifications, and many qualify for higher degrees in the course of their career.

Recruit training for other ranks involves three phases:

♦ Soldier training (12 to 32 weeks)
♦ Combat engineer training (10 weeks)
♦ Trade training (10–49 weeks)

For both officers and other ranks, specialist engineer training is mainly conducted by 1 and 3 Royal School of Military Engineer (RSME) Regiments based at Chatham and Blackwater. 1 RSME Regiment is the support regiment for training. During a year, some 8,000 students may pass through 1 RSME Regiment, many of whom have recently joined the army and who have arrived at Chatham for a long engineering course lasting, in some cases, up to 44 weeks. 1 RSME Regiment incorporates the Construction Engineer School at Chatham, where civil and mechanical engineering skills are taught.

3 RSME Regiment is responsible for combat engineer training. The Combat Engineer School is located at Minley responsible for Combat Engineer and Assault Pioneer training.

COMBAT ENGINEERING VEHICLES AND EQUIPMENT

Terrier

Terrier is an armoured, highly mobile, general support engineer vehicle optimised for battlefield support by providing mobility support (obstacle and route clearance), counter-mobility (digging of anti-tank ditches and creating other earthworks/obstacles) and survivability (digging of trenches and Armoured Fighting Vehicle slots).

Terrier is operated by a crew of two and has a remote control capability in particularly hazardous environments. The vehicle is able to tow the AVRE trailer carrying midi fascines, Class 70 trackway or general stores. It is also capable of towing and firing the Python minefield breaching system. The vehicle can also be fitted with an array of ancillaries including the Surface Clearance Device for the clearance of scatterable mines, earth orger, rippers and hammers. Terrier is also able to launch single midi fascines in order to breach shot gaps and therefore

Terrier with fascines. (Copyright BAe Systems)

establish routes while keeping pace with other armoured vehicles such as the Challenger 2 MBT, Warrior ICV and related Combat Engineer Vehicles Titan and Trojan. Terrier is fitted with day and night vision systems and is air-portable in a C17 or A400M transport aircraft. 60 Terrier vehicles were ordered in a contract that over the life of the Terrier programme is believed to be worth some £700 million.

Trojan and Titan

Trojan and Titan are Armoured Engineer Vehicles based on an improved Challenger 2 MBT chassis. These replacements of the Chieftain AVRE and AVLB systems means that the British Army has a common heavy armour fleet based on the Challenger 2 chassis. These vehicles represent the first armoured engineer vehicles specifically designed (rather than adapted from battle tank chassis) for their role and incorporate the very latest mobility and survivability features. Improved visibility is achieved by incorporating direct and indirect vision devices with low light, image intensifying and thermal imaging capabilities. The interior, and to some extent the exterior, of the vehicles have been designed around the crew station positions.

A contract worth £250 million was awarded during early 2001 for the supply of 66 vehicles – 33 x Trojan and 33 x Titan. Deliveries to the RE commenced in late 2006 and were completed, including final upgrade in late 2012.

Trojan Armoured Vehicle Royal Engineers (AVRE)

Trojan is designed as a breaching vehicle to open routes through complex battlefield obstacles and clear a path through minefields. Standard equipment includes a breaching-arm with opposing thumb that allows items such as trees and beams can be gripped and moved. A Full Width Mine Plough can be mounted as well as a Bulldozer blade to the vehicle as can a marking system. The breaching arm is also used to launch the midi-fascine, carried on the rear of the vehicle, into ditches enabling a short gap crossing capability. Trojan also tows the trailer-mounted Python mine-clearing system or AVRE trailer. Trojan has the flexibility to support a wide range of operations, including humanitarian missions.

Titan Armoured Vehicle Launcher Bridge (AVLB)

Titan is designed to provide a gap crossing capability of 45m, or less, using the in service Close Support Bridge (CSB) system (No 10,11 and 12 CSB) in combination or singly. It has a .8m step up and down capability in order to provide ground manoeuvre formations with improved capability over a greater range of terrain conditions. Titan can also be fitted with a dozer blade to prepare its own bank seats or Track Width Mine Plough.

Trojan minefield breaching system. (Copyright BAe Systems)

BR90 Bridges

The RE BR90 family of bridges are built from a range of seven modular panels of advanced aluminium alloy fabrication. These form two interconnecting trackways with a 4 m overall bridge width and a 1 m girder depth. BR90 is deployed with Royal Engineer units in both Germany and the UK with the bridges entering service in 1999 and comprising the following elements:

- General Support Bridge
- Close Support Bridge
- Two Span Bridge
- Long Span Bridge

Close Support Bridge – This consists of three tank-launched bridges capable of being carried on a tank bridgelayer and a Tank Bridge Transporter truck.

There are three basic Tank Launched Bridges (also known as Close Support or Assault Bridges): the No 10, No 11 and No 12.

General Support Bridge – This system utilises the Automated Bridge Launching Equipment (ABLE) that is capable of launching bridges up to 44 m in length. The ABLE vehicle is positioned with its rear

General Support Bridge Image. (Copyright BAe Systems)

pointing to the gap to be crossed and a lightweight launch rail extended across the gap. The bridge is then assembled and winched across the gap supported by the rail, with sections added until the gap is crossed. Once the bridge has crossed the gap the ABLE launch rail is recovered. A standard ABLE system set consists of an ABLE vehicle and 2 x TBT carrying a 32 m bridge set. A 32 m bridge can be built by 10 men in about 25 minutes.

Spanning Systems – There are two basic spanning systems. The long span system allows for lengthening a 32 m span to 44 m using ABLE and the two span system allows 2 x 32 m bridge sets to be constructed by ABLE and secured in the middle by piers or floating pontoons, crossing a gap of up to 60 m.

BR-90 carrier – The Unipower 8x8 TBT is an improved mobility transporter for the BR 90 bridging system. It can carry one No 10 bridge or two No 12 bridges. The TBT can self load from, and off-load to, the ground. The TBT task is to re-supply the Chieftain and Titan AVLB with replacement bridges.

Medium Girder Bridge (MGB)

The MGB is a simple system of lightweight components that can be easily manhandled to construct a bridge capable of taking the heaviest AFVs. The MGB has been largely replaced by the BR90 system, although some MGB have been retained for certain operational requirements. Two types of MGBs are fielded: Single span bridge – 30 m long which can be built by about 25 men in 45 minutes; Multi span bridge – a combination of 26.5 m spans: a two span bridge will cross a 51 m gap and a three span bridge a 76 m gap. If necessary, MGB pontoons can be also be joined together to form a ferry. MGB is deployed in support of operations in Afghanistan.

Class 16 Airportable Bridge

In service since 1974 and a much lighter bridge than the MGB, the Class 16 can be carried assembled under a Chinook helicopter or in 3 x 3/4 ton vehicles with trailers. A 15 m bridge can be constructed by 15 men in 20 minutes. The Class 16 can also be made into a ferry which is capable of carrying the heaviest AFVs. In the near future, the British Army will replace the Class 16 bridge with the Future Light Bridge (FLB) systems. This bridge will also be capable of being used as a ferry.

M3 Ferry

Weight 24,500 kg; Length 12.74 m; Height 3.93 m; Width 3.35 m; Max Road Speed 80 kph; Water Speed 14 kph; Road Range 725 kms; 3 Man crew.

The M3 can be driven into a river and used as a ferry or, when a number are joined together from bank to bank, as a bridge, capable of taking vehicles as heavy as the Challenger MBT. The M3 has a number of improvements over the M2 which it has replaced (the M2 was in service for over 25 years). The M3 can deploy pontoons on the move, in or out of water; it needs no on-site preparation to enter the water; it can be controlled from inside the cab when swimming and its control functions have been automated allowing the crew to be reduced from four to three.

A single two-bay M3 can carry a Class 70 tracked vehicle, where two M2s would have been required for this task with additional buoyancy bags. Eight M3 units and 24 soldiers can build a 100 m bridge in 30 minutes compared with 12 M2s, 48 soldiers and a construction time of 45 minutes. The M3 is only 1.4 m longer and 3,300 kg heavier than the M2. It is still faster and more manoeuvrable on land and in water. A four-wheel steering facility gives a turning diameter of 24 m.

Following the disbandment of 28 Engineer Regiment, 75 Regiment (Reserve) is receiving the M3 rigs to become the Army's sole Wide Wet Gap Crossing Regiment.

EOD and Mine Clearance

Talisman Route Clearance System: Following a successful introduction of the Talisman route clearance system into service in Afghanistan it would appear that the system has been retained. Some reports suggest that both 101 and 33 Engineer Regiments will each operate four enhanced Talisman Troops.

The Talisman system currently includes the following elements: Mastiff 2 command and control 'Protected Eyes'; Buffalo clearance vehicle; T-Hawk micro UAV system; Talon robotic vehicle; Mk 8 Wheelbarrow; High Mobility Engineer Excavator (HMEE). Terrier vehicles and Husky vehicles with ground penetrating radar are likely to be included.

T Hawk is a Vertical Take-Off Micro UAV that weighs about 8.5 kilos with an airborne endurance time of about 45 minutes. T Hawk can fly ahead of deploying troops or convoys and search for roadside bombs or IEDs. With its unique hovering ability suspicious areas or items can be inspected at close range.

Talisman troops operate on a convoy basis with integrated elements searching the route, inspecting and searching suspect area and where appropriate neutralising suspect devices.

Python
Python is a minefield breaching system that replaces the Giant Viper in RE service. The Python has the ability to clear a much longer 'safe lane' than its predecessor. It is also faster into action and far more accurate. It can clear a path 230 m long and 7 m wide through which vehicles are safe to pass.

The system works by firing a single rocket from a newly designed launcher trailer which has been towed to the edge of a mined area. Attached to the rocket is a coiled 230 m long hose packed with one and a half tons of powerful explosive. After the hose lands on the ground it detonates and destroys or clears any mines along its entire length. It is claimed that in a cleared lane, over 90% of anti-tank mines will have been destroyed. Python was deployed in support of operations in Afghanistan.

Mine Warfare
Anti-tank minefields laid by the Royal Engineers will usually contain Barmines (anti-tank) or Mk.7 (anti-tank) mines and anti-disturbance devices may be fitted to some Barmines. Minefields will always be recorded and marked; they should also be covered by artillery and mortar fire to delay enemy mine clearance operations and maximise the attrition of armour. ATGWs are often sited in positions covering the minefield that will give them flank shoots onto enemy armour; particularly the ploughs or rollers that might spearhead a minefield breaching operation. The future of UK mine warfare capability is currently under review.

CHAPTER 13 – COMMUNICATIONS

OVERVIEW

Royal Signals is the Combat Command Support Arm (CCS) that provides the Communications and Information Systems (CIS – the bearer network) and Information Communication Services (ICS – infrastructure and applications) used throughout the command structure of the Army, as well as supporting the other armed services and coalition partners. Traditionally this has been concentrated at Brigade level and above, but with the increasing hunger for information at the tactical level, this now stretches down to battle group level and below in direct support of the combat arms.

In addition to these tasks the Royal Signals also provide Electronic Warfare (EW) and Signals Intelligence (SIGINT). Life support and force protection duties also fall to Royal Signals units supporting certain formations.

Information is the lifeblood of any military formation in battle and it is the responsibility of the Royal Signals to ensure the speedy and accurate passage of information that enables commanders to make informed and timely decisions, and to ensure that those decisions are passed to the fighting troops in contact with the enemy. The rapid, accurate and secure employment of command, control and communications systems maximises the effect of the military force available and consequently the Royal Signals act as an extremely significant 'Force Multiplier'. The Corps motto is *'Certa Cito'* (Swift and Sure) and its soldiers are usually some of the first in and last out during any operation. The Corps possesses a large Special Forces element as well as air assault, air support and special communications units.

Several battle groups now deploy with a Royal Signals Regimental Signals Officer (RSO) and a highly trained multi-discipline Royal Signals Infantry Support Team (RSIST) in order to deliver the increasingly sophisticated and complex communications requirements at battle group level and below.

Royal Signals Mission: To deliver elements of deployable integrated Combat Command Support, Electronic Warfare and Force Protection in order to enable decisive command.

FORCE STRUCTURE

Royal Signals provides about 9 per cent of the Army's manpower with 11 x regular regiments, 1 x training regiment, and 4 x reserve regiments, each generally consisting of between three and six squadrons with between 400 and 600 personnel. There are also independent troops and detachments supporting various units around the world. Following the Strategic Defence and Security Review (SDSR), the Corps is restructuring to make most efficient use of its capabilities.

Regular and Reserve units are listed in the following tables:

Regular Units	Role	Location
1 Signal Regiment	Multi Role Signals Regiment	Stafford
2 Signal Regiment	Multi Role Signals Regiment	York
3 Signal Regiment	Multi Role Signals Regiment	Bulford
10 Signal Regiment	Specialist Support to UK and Expeditionary Operations	Corsham
11 Signal Regiment	Training & Training Support	Blandford
14 Signal Regiment (Electronic Warfare)	Electronic Warfare	St Athan

15 Signal Regiment (Information Systems)	Support to Information & Communications Systems	Blandford
16 Signal Regiment	Multi Role Signals Regiment	Stafford
18 (UKSF) Signal Regiment	Special Forces Support	Hereford
21 Signal Regiment	Multi Role Signals Regiment	Colerne
22 Signal Regiment	ARRC Support	Stafford
30 Signal Regiment	Supports ARRC, JHC, Joint Rapid Reaction Force (JRRF)	Bramcote
216 (Air Assault) Signal Squadron	Brigade Support	Colchester

Reserve Units	*HQ Location*	*Squadron Locations*
2 Signal Regiment	Glasgow	Belfast, Londonderry, Darlington, Leeds, Edinburgh, East Kilbride
37 Signal Regiment	Redditch	Birmingham, Coventry, Liverpool, Manchester Darlington, Leeds, Sheffield, Nottingham
39 Signal Regiment	Bristol	Bath, Windsor, Cardiff, Gloucester
71 (City of London) Signal Regiment	Bexleyheath	Lincoln's Inn, Whipps Cross, Colchester, Chelmsford, Uxbridge, Coulsdon

Royal Signals personnel are found wherever the Army is deployed including every UK and NATO headquarters in the world. The Headquarters and 'Home' of the Corps is at Blandford Camp in Dorset.

Royal Signals units based in the United Kingdom provide command and control communications for forces that have operational roles. There are a still a number of Royal Signals units or elements permanently based in Germany, Holland and Belgium from where they provide the necessary command support and Electronic Warfare (EW) support for both the British Army and other NATO forces based in Europe. Royal Signals personnel are also based in several other locations including Cyprus, the Falkland Islands, Kenya, Canada, and Gibraltar.

During late 2015 we believe that the approximate personnel strength of the Royal Signals was about 7,000.

ROLES OF MILITARY COMMUNICATIONS

Communications have enabling capabilities that support all military operations in war and peace. These roles may be summarised under the following headings:

Command and Control: Communications enable commanders at all levels to exercise command and control over their own forces. Communications enable commanders to receive information, convey orders and move men and materiel, and select and position their attacking and defensive forces to maximum effect in order to take advantage of their own strengths and enemy weaknesses.

The capacity to deliver firepower, troops and supplies to any part of the battlefield is crucial to success. From the earliest days of messengers, flags, bugles and hand signals, this has been vital to successful command. Modern electronic communications systems have vastly added to this capacity, increasing the distances over which Command and Control can be exercised – from line of sight or hearing to any geographical area where forces are deployed. The amount and type of information delivered for this purpose has also expanded massively.

Computerised Command Information: Communications enables commanders to receive information from the battlefield to build up a picture of the state and disposition of their own forces as well as enemy forces. Commanders have always sought to have the fullest possible information of both their own and enemy forces – but were typically limited by constraints of time, space and information carrying capacity.

Computer hardware and software – allied to the geographical spread, bandwidths and data-carrying capacity of modern military networks – have removed many of these constraints. Computer processing power enables information received from all sources to be sorted into meaningful patterns of use to commanders.

Such sources include:

Voice and data reports from troops in the field
Intelligence reports
Mapping
Battlefield sensors
Multi-spectral imaging from ground reconnaissance units
Reconnaissance and surveillance satellites, aircraft, helicopters and unmanned aerial vehicles
Electronic Warfare systems on ground, air and sea platforms

In modern war, to capture the full scope of computer information systems, this communications effect is typically described as Command, Control, Communications, Computers, Intelligence, Surveillance and Reconnaissance (C4ISR).

Electronic Warfare: Secure communications that deny the enemy knowledge of own and friendly force activities, capabilities and intelligence (Communications Security). Communications that enable the penetration, compromise and destruction of enemy communication systems (Electronic Warfare).

ROYAL SIGNALS OPERATIONAL MISSIONS

Royal Signals units have three principal operational missions:

Communications Engineering
Communications units design, build and dismantle the tactical communications networks used on operations.

Communications Operations
Communications units operate the tactical communications networks at division and brigade levels. Some communications are delivered by Royal Signals at battle group and even company or platoon level on many operations.

Communications Management
Communications units are responsible for the management of the whole communications nexus at division and brigade level, or across a designated area of operations.

These missions will need to be performed in all phases of battle:

Offensive: In the offensive: setting up command posts, setting up area communications networks and setting up networks to connect battalions to brigades and elsewhere as far as possible. Specialist units can set up air portable communications systems shortly after a foothold is secured on an air base or other point of entry.

Advance: In the advance: continuing to keep forward and area communications running and providing logistics and maintenance needs for company and brigade forces as appropriate. Running networked services forwards as far as possible with the advance. Setting up alternate HQs. Relocating and maintaining relay and retransmission points and ensuring communications to rear and flanks remain open.

Defensive: In the defence: re-enforcing command posts and relay points. Increasing the complexity and robustness of networks. Providing alternate and redundant communications for all users.

Withdrawal: In the withdrawal: Preventing communications assets falling into enemy hands, setting up alternate command posts on the line of withdrawal, running networks backwards to rear. Keeping nodes open and supplying logistics and maintenance support as required.

Non-Combat missions: Communications perform non-combat roles during peacetime, including national peacetime contingencies and multilateral peace support operations in foreign countries.

Functions of Military Communications

Military communications roles undertaken by the Royal Signals may be divided into three separate functions:

Strategic communications: Communications between the political leadership, military high command, and military administrative and field commands at the divisional level. In terms of capability as opposed to function, modern communications systems increasingly blur the distinction between strategic and tactical systems as a consequence of technological advance.

Tactical communications: Communications between field formations from corps to division through brigade down to battalion level.

Electronic Warfare: The security of own forces and friendly forces communications, and the penetration, compromise and degradation of hostile communications.

ORDER OF BATTLE

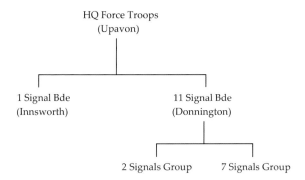

1 Signal Brigade

Units	Location	Role
22 Signal Regiment	Stafford	ARRC Formation Support
30 Signal Regiment	Bramcote	Supports ARRC, JHC, Joint Rapid Reaction Force (JRRF)
ARRC Support Battalion	Innsworth	ARRC Headquarters Support
299 Signal Squadron (SC)	Bletchley	Special Communications

11 Signal Brigade
2 Signals Group

Units	Location	Role
10 Signal Regiment	Corsham	Specialist Support to UK and Expeditionary Operations
15 Signal Regiment	Blandford	Support to Information & Communications Systems
32 Signal Regiment (R)	HQ Glasgow	UK National Communications
37 Signal Regiment (R)	HQ Redditch	UK National Communications
39 Signal Regiment (R)	Bristol	UK National Communications
71 Signal Regiment (R)	Bexleyheath	UK National Communications
CVHQ	Blandford	Specialist Support
7 Signals Group		
1 Signal Regiment	Stafford	Multi Role Signals Regiment (MRSR)
2 Signal Regiment	York	Multi Role Signals Regiment (MRSR)
3 Signal Regiment	Bulford	Multi Role Signals Regiment (MRSR)
16 Signal Regiment	Stafford	Multi Role Signals Regiment (MRSR)
21 Signal Regiment	Colerne	Multi Role Signals Regiment (MRSR)

Units Under Other Headquarters

Unit	Location	Role	Headquarters
11 Signal Regiment	Blandford	Training & Training Support	HQ Royal Signals
14 Signal Regiment (EW)	St Athan	Electronic Warfare	1 Int & Surveillance Brigade
18 (UKSF) Signal Regiment	Hereford	Special Forces Support	Director Special Forces
LIAG (1)	Blandford	Specialist Support	Joint Forces Command
216 Signal Squadron	Colchester	Brigade Comms	16 Air Assault Brigade
628 Signal Troop	Elmpt (Germany)	UK Contribution	1 NATO Signals Battalion
660 Signal Troop	Didcot	EOD Support	11 (EOD) Regiment RLC

Note: (1) LIAG (Land Information Assurance Group)

MULTI ROLE SIGNAL REGIMENTS (MRSR)

Support to the Reaction Force (3 UK Division) will be delivered by 5 x MRSR:

1 Signal Regiment
2 Signal Regiment
3 Signal Regiment
16 Signal Regiment
21 Signal Regiment

Once restructuring is complete, these five regiments will each have 3 x Field Squadrons and 1 x Support Squadron. Each MRSR is being equipped with the FALCON system, with at least 11 x FALCON detachments being assigned to each Regiment. Once deployed in the field, the MRSR will be tasked to provide the whole spectrum of communications needed by the Reaction Force and its HQs. It would appear that the exact nature of how support to the Reaction Force brigade and divisional HQs will be delivered has still be to worked out.

Three Signal Regiments (1, 16 and 21) will provide Command Support to the three Armoured Infantry Brigade, delivering small, medium and large points of presence, (nodes) providing tactical and operational communications.

Two Signal Regiments (2 and 3) will provide General Information and Communications Support to the Reaction Force HQ (HQ 3 UK Division) plus the Reaction Force Logistic Brigade HQ (HQ 101 Logistic Brigade). Equipped with a broad range of network assets to provide the flexibility required.

FALCON systems are installed on MAN 6-tonne trucks with FV-430 series communications vehicles plus a Mastiff communications variant. Other vehicles include land rovers and other assorted utility vehicles.

TRAINING

All Royal Signals officers undergo officer training at RMA Sandhurst (48 weeks) before taking the Royal Signals Troop Commanders Course at 11 (Royal School of Signals) Signal Regiment, Blandford Camp. Many Royal Signals officers have on entry, or obtain through the course of their careers, university degree-level engineering qualifications.

Recruit training for other ranks involves two phases:

Phase 1 – Soldier training (14 to 23 weeks)
Phase 2 – Trade training (7 to 50 weeks)

All Royal Signals soldiers, whether arriving from the Army Training Regiments at Pirbright, Winchester or Harrogate also complete trade, leadership, ethos and additional military training at 11 (Royal School of Signals) Signal Regiment. The length of the course depends on the trade chosen, varying from 7 weeks up to 50. Electronic Warfare operators also attend additional modules at the Defence Intelligence and Security Centre, Chicksands.

Soldiers will return to the Regiment for periods throughout their careers to complete Phase 3 trade upgrading courses and specialist operational pre-deployment or pre-employment training. The Regiment is also responsible for Royal Signals special-to-arm command, leadership and management training to qualify for junior and senior non-commissioned officer and warrant officer promotion. Soldier training provides modern apprenticeship and national vocational qualifications.

Supervisor training is also undertaken in Blandford Camp after a rigorous selection process. Supervisors are known as Yeoman, Foreman, Yeoman (EW) or Foreman (IS) of Signals depending on their specialism. On successful completion of training they receive degree level accreditation for their skills. Officers similarly return to complete additional career and specialised training up to masters degree level.

Over 100 different types of courses are delivered by 11 (Royal School of Signals) Signal Regiment, including to students from other Arms and Services and foreign and Commonwealth forces, in addition to those of the Corps itself. Over 700 courses are run per year. There are in excess of 7,000 students completing courses throughout the year with about 1,000 students on courses at any one time. These figures equate to approximately some 250,000 man training days a year.

EQUIPMENT

Royal Signals units are currently operating the following types of major equipment:

Static strategic communications
Mobile strategic satellite communications
Fixed and mobile electronic warfare (EW) systems
Tactical Area Communications – corps to brigade down to battalion HQ
VHF Combat Net Radios – battalion and sub-units
Tactical HF and UHF radios – battalion and sub-units
Teleprinters, Fax, CCTV and ADP Equipment
Computer Information Systems
Local area networks (LAN) and wide area networks (WAN) for computers

Tactical Area Communications

The principal tactical role of the Royal Signals is to provide corps to brigade level communications that link higher commands to battalion HQs. The area communications systems used by the Royal Signals include:

FALCON

FALCON is Royal Signals' replacement for Ptarmigan, the mobile, secure wide area battlefield CIS which was in service between 1986 and 2009. It also replaces the Royal Air Force's (RAF's) Tactical Trunk Communications System (RTTS) and the Deployed Local Area Network (DLAN) network. FALCON incorporates large elements of Commercial Off The Shelf (COTS) technologies and equipments including Internet Protocol (IP). Reflecting the growing importance of data over voice communications (although both are provided), FALCON has been designed to be the communications bearer and switching network for various command and control information infrastructures. FALCON may use its own line of sight radios as the bearer, with the range being extended by the use of satellite ground stations (including Reacher) or other bearers of opportunity (including landlines).

FALCON is provided in vehicle-mounted containers, dismounted containers and palletised boxes. The principal communications bearer detachments providing the wide area network are known as Wide Area Switching Points (WASPs). Headquarters and other command nodes are served by Command Post Support (CPS) detachments which provide the Local Area System (LAS). FALCON is being delivered by BAE Systems and is expected to enter service sometime in 2012.

Cormorant

Cormorant delivers CIS capabilities to both Royal Signals and the RAF. Cormorant is comprised of three primary equipments: a local access component, based on an Asynchronous Transfer Mode (ATM) switch, which provides digital voice subscriber facilities; a high speed data local area network (LAN) for headquarters; and a wide area component which provides the interconnection of these headquarters on a 'backbone' communications network across a large geographical area. The wide area component also provides the means to interconnect with single service and multinational systems.

Designed to link all components of a Joint Force, the system enables the force to deploy and operate its CIS Wide Area Network (WAN) across the spectrum of conflict (peacekeeping, military stabilisation or warfighting). The system is fully containerised and can be operated in either a (vehicle) mounted or dismounted mode.

A Cormorant network may consist of the following vehicle-mounted (or dismounted) installations:

◆ Local Area Support module
◆ Core Element
◆ Bearer Module

- Long-Range Bearer Module (Tropospheric)
- Management Information Systems
- Interoperable Gateways
- Tactical Fibre Optic cabling
- Short-Range Radio.

Promina

Promina networks deliver pulse code modulation (PCM) and compressed digital analogue voice, video conferencing, Internet Protocol (IP) frame relay, Asynchronous Transfer Mode (ATM) and legacy Synchronous and Asynchronous data services over satellite, microwave radio and leased line services. It is used to multiplex CIS infrastructure in use within the Land Environment.

Bowman

Bowman is the main radio system used by the Army and other ground forces. It is primarily a powerful combat network radio system sending secure digital voice and data around the battlefield. By enabling transmission of large quantities of electronic data Bowman can also provide information on the position of UK forces.

It also forms the underlying network to carry the CIP (Combat Infrastructure Programme). CIP is an automated battlefield command and control system. It is key to the concept of 'Network Enabled Capability'; joining up military communications and electronic systems in a 'network of networks'. The ability to see the position of UK forces, on screens in vehicles and headquarters, should amongst other benefits, help to reduce the frequency of 'friendly fire' incidents. An extremely capable system, regular updates continue to add extra utilities allowing better communications and more efficient command and control.

Satellite Communications (SATCOM)

Astrium Services operates the Skynet military satellite constellation on a concession basis and provides the three armed services with the ground terminals to provide all Beyond Line of Sight (BLOS) communications to the MoD.

Under a £4 billion Private Finance Initiative (PFI) Astrium is contracted to provide this service until 2022.

A number of Skynet satellites have been launched over the past decade and the fourth of the Skynet 5 series, Skynet 5D was launched from French Guiana (South America) in December 2012. Skynet 5A and Skynet 5B entered service in April 2007 and January 2008 respectively. Skynet 5C was launched in June 2008. Skynet 5D will travel at speeds of around 6,200 miles per hour in orbit.

The Land, Air and maritime environments utilise different equipment for their principal terminal capabilities. The Land and Air environments primarily use Reacher. The maritime environment uses the Satellite Communications Terminal (SCOT).

Reacher Satellite Ground Terminal

Reacher replaced the VSC 501 and is the main satellite ground terminal (SGT) used by the Army. It is delivered in three variants:

- Reacher Medium is a land terminal specifically designed for X-Band military satellite Communications. Designed to operate with a Forward Operating Headquarters unit, it is mounted on a Bucher Duro 6 x 6 vehicle and has a detachable Intermediate Group cabin and associated trailer.
- Reacher Large is mounted on the same vehicle as the Reacher Medium. The equipment has a larger antenna for greater bandwidth capacity.
- Reacher All Terrain is mounted on 2 x BV206 vehicles with associated trailers. It is used by the Royal Marines (RM) and is sometimes referred to as Reacher (RM).

All Reacher terminals are transportable using Chinook helicopters, C130 Aircraft, sea and rail.

Other SGTs used by the Army include Tacsat 117F, SWE-DISH (SMALL SATCOM) and V-Sat.

DII
The Defence Information Infrastructure (DII) is a Communications Information System (CIS) replacement for the numerous networks currently connected via the Restricted LAN Interface (RLI) and is currently being rolled out in phases across the armed forces and on operations. There is also a version that can connect to the Secret LAN Interface (SLI).

Electronic Warfare Systems

SEER
SEER is a lightweight man-portable EW system able to prosecute a wide range of electronic communications targets whilst static, on a vehicle or within a dismounted patrol. It comprises of both an Electronic Surveillance sensor and an Electronic Attack system (capable of undertaking simple jamming missions). The Electronic Surveillance sensors can be networked in order to allow the establishment of a fully interconnected and automated sensor baseline that is capable of providing an effective position fix for any intercepted electronic target. It is supported by a system laptop which has a sophisticated software suite that can provide technical analysis and geographic representation of target.

LANDSEEKER
LANDSEEKER will provide a family of (modular) EW capabilities able to conduct Electronic Surveillance for the full range of electronic target sets (both communications and non-communications) and undertake complex Electronic Attack tasks. It will provide an interface with other government departments in order to allow a fully integrated approach to the prosecution of EW missions under the framework of the Single SIGINT Battlespace. It will replace all existing EW equipment including SEER, the medium-weight Odette Electronic Surveillance communications system and the Ince non-communications Electronic Surveillance system. The system will provide modules that are optimised for light (dismounted), medium and heavy forces and will be introduced into the Service from 2018.

Odette
Odette provides electronic support measures within the overall EW capability and operates from both armoured and light utility vehicle. The systems identifies radio targets.

ECM Force Protection Suite: A range of devices are used in order to protect forces from the threat caused by radio-controlled explosive devices.

CHAPTER 14 – COMBAT SERVICE SUPPORT

LOGISTIC OVERVIEW

In the British Army logistic support is based upon the twin pillars of service support (the supply chain) and equipment support (the maintenance of equipment).

Combat Service Support within the British Army is provided by the Royal Logistic Corps (RLC), the Royal Electrical and Mechanical Engineers (REME) and the Royal Army Medical Corps (RAMC).

Within any fighting formation units from these Corps typically represent about 30 per cent of the manpower total of a division, and with the exception of certain members of the RAMC all are trained fighting soldiers.

The task of the logistic units on operations is to maintain the combat units in the field which entails:

◆ Supply and Distribution – of ammunition, fuel, lubricants, rations and spare parts.
◆ Recovery and Repair – of battle damaged and unserviceable equipment.
◆ Treatment and Evacuation – of casualties.

In an operational division the commanders of the logistic units all operate from a separate, self contained headquarters under the command of a Brigadier (or Colonel) who holds the appointment of the Division's Deputy Chief of Staff (DCOS). This headquarters, usually known as the Divisional Headquarters (Rear), co-ordinates the whole of the logistic support of the Division in battle.

Supplies, reinforcements and returning casualties pass through an area located to the rear of the division where some of the less mobile logistic units are located. This area is known as the Divisional Admin Area (DAA) and the staff are responsible for co-ordinating the flow of all materiel and personnel into and out of the Divisional Area.

LOGISTIC BRIGADES

Three Logistic Formations support HQ Land Forces (Andover):

HQ 101 Logistic Brigade (Aldershot) supports 3 UK Division (Reaction Force).
HQ 102 Logistic Brigade (Grantham) supports 1 UK Division (Adaptable Force).
HQ 104 Logistic Brigade (South Cerney) supports Force Troops.

Details of these three formations are as follows:

101 Logistic Brigade (Aldershot)

Unit	Role	Location	Affiliated reserve unit
1st Regiment RLC	Close Support	Bicester	
3rd Regiment RLC	Close Support	Aldershot	
4th Regiment RLC	Close Support	Abingdon	
9th Regiment RLC	Theatre Support	Hullavington	157 (Welsh) Transport Regiment RLC (R) (Cardiff)
10th Queens Own Gurkha Regiment RLC	Theatre Support	Aldershot	151 Transport Regiment RLC (R) (Croydon)
27th Regiment RLC	Theatre Support	Abingdon	154 (Scottish) Transport Regiment RLC (R) (Dunfermline) & 156 Supply Regiment RLC (R) (Liverpool)

1st Armoured Medical Regiment	Casevac	Tidworth	
4th Armoured Medical Regiment	Casevac	Aldershot	
5th Armoured Medical Regiment	Casevac	Tidworth	
3rd Armoured Close Support Bn REME	Close Support	Tidworth	105 Bn REME (R) (Bristol)
4th Armoured Close Support Bn REME	Close Support	Tidworth	103 Bn REME (R) (Crawley)
6th Armoured Close Support Bn REME	Close Support	Tidworth	
5th Force Support Bn REME	Force Support	Cottesmore	

HQ 102 Logistic Brigade (Grantham)

Unit	Role	Location	Affiliated reserve unit
6 Regiment RLC	Force Logistic Regiment	Dishforth	150 Transport Regiment (R) (Hull)
7 Regiment RLC	Force Logistic Regiment	Cottesmore	158 Transport Regiment (R) (Peterborough)
159 Supply Regiment RLC (R)	Reserve Supply Regiment	Coventry	
2 Medical Regiment RAMC	Hybrid Regiment	North Luffenham	Comprises Reserves & Regulars
3 Medical Regiment RAMC	Hybrid Regiment	Preston	Comprises Reserves & Regulars
225 (Scottish) Medical Regiment RAMC (R)	Reserve Medical Regiment	Dundee	
225 (Scottish) Medical Regiment RAMC (R)	Reserve Medical Regiment	Dundee	
254 (East of England) Medical Regiment RAMC (R)	Reserve Medical Regiment	Cambridge	
1 Close Support Battalion REME	Close Support	Catterick	102 Battalion REME (R) (Newton Aycliffe)
2 Close Support Battalion REME	Close Support	Leuchars	106 Battalion REME (R) (Glascow)
104 Battalion REME (R)	Reserve Equipment Support	Northampton	

HQ 104th Logistic Brigade (South Cerney)

Unit	Role	Location	Affiliated reserve unit
17 Port & Maritime Regiment RLC	Port & Maritime	Marchwood	165 Port and Enabling Regiment RLC (R) (Plymouth)
29 Regiment RLC	Postal, Courier & Movements	South Cerney	162 Postal & Courier Regiment RLC (R) (Nottingham)
152 Fuel Support Regiment RLC (R)	Reserve Unit	Belfast	
167 Catering Support Regiment RLC (R)	Reserve Unit	Grantham	
2 Operational Support Group RLC (R)	Reserve Unit	Grantham	

Logistics within the Army is becoming increasingly complex due to the multi-dimensional threat faced in conflict. Close combat is often needed to achieve the logistic mission and a flexible, highly responsive logistic support network is needed to maintain the momentum for the fighting troops. Defence does not exclusively use army logistics for the replenishment of our own troops and manoeuvrability to enable our sustainment role to work for others, such as local government and security forces, is becoming increasingly important. The use of the logistic capability to reinforce and assist with local infrastructure issues can be just as vital to winning the battle as the troops closing with the enemy in a more traditional role.

THE ROYAL LOGISTIC CORPS

The Royal Logistic Corps (RLC) is the youngest Corps in the Army and was formed in April 1993. The Corps was formed from an amalgamation of the Royal Corps of Transport, the Royal Army Ordnance Corps, the Army Catering Corps, the Royal Pioneer Corps and the postal and courier element of the Royal Engineers.

As at late 2015, the RLC makes up almost 15 per cent of the Regular Army, comprising of about 14,000 personnel, serving across approximately 800 different units. About 60 per cent of officers and soldiers serve within RLC units, with the remaining 40 per cent serving throughout the Ministry of Defence. The RLC Reserve component makes up about 15 per cent of the total Reserve strength.

The RLC is formed of 12 major regular units, and 12 major reserve units. RLC Regular and Reserve units are listed in the following tables:

Regular Units	Role	Location
1 Close Support Regiment	Close Support	Bicester
3 Close Support Regiment	Close Support	Aldershot
4 Close Support Regiment	Close Support	Abingdon
6 Force Logistic Regiment	Force Logistic Support	Dishforth
7 Force Logistic Regiment	Force Logistic Support	Cottesmore
9 Theatre Logistic Regiment	Theatre Logistics	Hullavington
10 The Queen's Own Gurkha Logistic Regiment	Theatre Logistics	Aldershot
11 EOD Regiment	Explosive Ordnance Disposal	Didcot
13 Air Assault Support Regiment	Air Assault Close Support	Colchester

17 Port and Maritime Regiment	Maritime Support	Marchwood
27 Theatre Logistic Regiment	Theatre Logistics	Abingdon
29 Regiment	Postal, Courier and Movements	South Cerney

Note: The Commando Logistic Regiment stationed at Barnstaple in Devon is a hybrid unit composed of personnel from the Royal Marines and personnel from the Royal Logistic Corps.

Reserve Units	HQ Location	Squadron Locations
150 Transport Regiment	Hull	Leeds, Hull, Doncaster
151 Transport Regiment	Croydon	Brentwood, Maidstone, Sutton, Barnett, Southall,
152 Fuel Support Regiment	Belfast	Londonderry, Coleraine, Belfast,
154 (Scottish) Transport Regiment	Dunfermline	Dunfermline, Glasgow, Edinburgh, Irvine,
156 Supply Regiment	Liverpool	Birkenhead, Salford, Bootle, Lancaster
157 (Welsh) Transport Regiment	Cardiff	Queensferry, Swansea, Haverfordwest, Carmarthen, Cardiff
158 Transport Regiment	Peterborough	Bedford, Ipswich, Colchester, Loughborough, Lincoln
159 Supply Regiment	Canley	Telford, Tynemouth, West Bromwich, Coventry
162 Postal Courier & Movements Regiment	Nottingham	Swindon, Nottingham, Coulby Newham,
165 (Wessex) Port & Enabling Regiment	Plymouth	Plymouth, Southampton,
166 Supply Regiment	Grantham	Banbury, Grantham, Aylesbury
167 Catering Support Regiment	Grantham	Grantham
2 Operational Support Group	Grantham	Grantham

LOGISTIC SUPPORT REGIMENTS

Close Support Regiments

Every Close Support Regiment (CSR) is affiliated to a deployable Brigade within the Army. A CSR is comprised 1 x General Support Squadron which looks after the supply function and 2 x Close Support Squadrons which execute distribution. On operations each CSR also deploys up to 6 Logistic Support Detachments (LSDs) who work with the formation Battlegroups and form the logistic link back to the CSR. 13 Air Assault Support Regiment and the Commando Logistic Regiment perform the same role as the CSRs for their specialist Brigades, 16 Air Assault Brigade and 3 Commando Brigade respectively.

Force and Theatre Support Regiments

Force and Theatre Support Regiments undertake more specialist roles, such as the control and distribution of supplies and materiel moving in and out of the theatre of conflict and specialist transport and distribution requirements, for example movement of heavy equipment over land. On operations they retain responsibility for these areas and may also encompass contractor management, the management of logistic support at unit level and the deployment and command of Logistic Support Teams, working with forward based sub-units from Battle Groups in the Brigade. The specialist Medical Supply Squadron is also within the Theatre Logistic Regiment.

Enablers

The final group of major units within the RLC are the 'enablers'. The enablers consist of 11 Explosive Ordnance Disposal (EOD) Regiment, 17 Port and Maritime Regiment, and 29 Postal, Courier and Movement Regiment. The majority of these units come under the command of 104 Logistic Support Brigade, with the exception of 11 EOD Regiment. These regiments provide specialist support from the home base and elements are routinely deployed to the theatre of operations. Some niche capabilities have personnel deployed on operations continuously, such as the Ammunition Technical officers and soldiers from 11 EOD Regiment, Movement Controllers and Postal and Courier operators from 29 Regiment.

Due to the ever changing nature of conflict, the RLC doctrine undergoes constant review and remains flexible to suit the requirement of the fighting force. Supplies are held both within supply areas across the theatre of operations, and on wheels, ready for rapid deployment forwards to the operational area. This is facilitated by intelligent, computerised provisioning and forecasting, allowing movement of materiel and combat supplies as needed, removing the requirement for vast stores of equipment and supplies at the forward edge of the battle. Where urgent supplies are identified, or a short notice replenishment is to be undertaken, the RLC has the ability to move stocks forward to the fighting troops through combat logistic patrols on the ground or by air, using the air despatch capability.

The Army do not just use the RLC for movement of supplies and materiel for our own force – the protected distribution capability has also been used for infrastructure re-building for nations such as Iraq and Afghanistan. For example the movement of the Kajaki Dam equipment in Afghanistan was completed by an RLC combat logistic patrol.

Due to the specialist nature of many aspects of the RLC and the importance of logistics within an armed force, the RLC have also become involved in the training and mentoring of a number of foreign armies, including the Afghan National Army. This has included training in the provisioning and accounting of stores, distribution through logistic patrols and specialist functions such as counter-Improvised Explosive Device (c-IED) work with 11 EOD Regiment.

With the threat from improvised explosive devices prevalent in operational theatres the RLC are developing vehicles and equipment to combat the threat. Protected mobility platforms are driven by the RLC for the command and control of convoys using platforms such as PANTHER and RIDGEBACK, with convoy protection being delivered by RLC soldiers from the standard armoured infantry wheeled vehicle such as MASTIFF. For distribution, the RLC use the MAN Support Vehicle EPLS (Enhanced Palletised Load System) which has replaced the previous DROPS load carrying vehicle. The MAN Support Vehicle also comes in a standard 15 ton variant with loads greater than the capacity of the MAN SV carried on the Heavy Equipment Transporter (HET). For liquid loads, such as water and fuel, the Close Support Tanker provides protection and mobility to allow replenishment forward to the fighting troops.

VEHICLES

Although many of the vehicles operated by the RLC are common to all arms, RLC units are in the main the majority users.

A rather dated vehicle fleet listing from 2011 remains interesting and will be updated as soon as the requirements for Army 2020 are announced.

Logistics vehicle in service (2011)

Vehicle type	Number in service
Bulk Fuel	1,189
Cargo	12,446
Container Handler	23
Crane	92
Equipment Transporter	732
Forklift	649
Medical	915
Recovery	466
Bulk Water	57
Airfield Support	631
Fire Vehicles	162

ROLES, FUNCTIONS AND TRADES IN THE RLC.

The primary roles of the RLC are supply, distribution and specialist logistic functions. Within these functions, soldiers are employed within trade groups, known as Main Trades For Pay. These RLC functions and the list of soldier trades are as follows:

Roles and Functions of the RLC

Role	Function	Trade
Supply	Materiel	Logistic Specialist (supply)
	Combat Supplies	Petroleum Operator
	Medical Stores	Vehicle support specialist
	Vehicles	
Distribution	Road	Driver
	Rail	Driver Tank Transporter
	Air Despatch	Driver Air Despatch
	Maritime – littoral	Driver Communications Specialist
Specialist	Explosive Ordnance Disposal	Ammunition Technician
	Postal and Courier	Postal and Courier Operator
	Movement Control	Movement Controller
	Port and Maritime	Marine Engineer
	Catering	Mariner
	Pioneer	Port Operator
	Photography	Chef
	Labour Support	Pioneer
	Systems Analysis	Photographer
	Contract Management	Systems Analyst

DAILY MESSING RATES

The allowances per day for catering purposes are based on a ration scale costed at current prices and known as the daily messing rate (DMR). The ration scale is the same for all three services and contrary to popular army belief the RAF are not supplied with caviar and fine wine etc at public expense. The rate per day is the amount that the catering organisation has to feed each individual serviceman or servicewoman.

The scale is costed to the supply source of the food items. When the source of supply is more expensive due to local conditions the DMR is set higher to take account of local costs. A general overseas ration scale exists for overseas bases and attachments. This scale has a higher calorific value to take into account the conditions of heat, cold or humidity that can be encountered.

RLC Catering Units feed the Army generally using detachments of cooks attached to units.

During mid 2015 the daily messing rate (DMR) was approximately £2.54 per day per soldier in the UK. With this amount RLC cooks, in barracks have to provide three meals per day as follows:

Breakfast £0.38
Main Meal £1.27
Third Meal £0.89

These figures are adjusted on a monthly basis.

Ration scales vary according to location. The home ration scale in the UK is designed to provide 2,900 kilo-calories nett – that is, after loss through preparation and cooking. The general overseas ration scale used in overseas bases, includes an arduous duty allowance, to allow for climate and provides 3,400 kilo-calories nett. In field conditions, where personnel are fed from operational ration packs, 3,800 kilo-calories are provided.

Army cooks are trained at the Defence Food Services School – Army (DFSS (A)) which was established in April 2004 as part of an organisation to serve the Army, Royal Navy and Royal Air Force. Before this, it was known as The Army School of Catering, founded in 1943, as part of the Army Catering Corps. DFSS (A) is located at Aldershot.

Postal
The Central Army Post Office (APO) is located in London and there are individual British Forces Post Offices (BFPO) wherever British Forces are stationed, plus Postal and Courier Squadrons with 29 Regiment (UK).

THE ROYAL ELECTRICAL & MECHANICAL ENGINEERS – REME

Equipment Support remains separate from the other logistic pillar of Service Support and consequently the REME has retained not only its own identity but expanded its responsibilities. Equipment Support encompasses equipment management, engineering support, supply management, provisioning for vehicle and technical spares and financial management responsibilities for in-service equipment.

The aim of the REME is "To keep operationally fit equipment in the hands of the troops" and in the current financial environment it is important that this is carried out at the minimum possible cost. The equipment that REME is responsible for ranges from small arms and trucks to helicopters and main battle tanks. All field force units have some integral REME support (first line support) which will vary, depending on the size of the unit and the equipment held, from a few attached tradesmen up to a large Regimental Workshop of over 200 men. In war, REME is responsible for the recovery and repair of battle damaged and unserviceable equipment.

The development of highly technical weapon systems and other equipment has meant that REME has had to balance engineering and tactical considerations. On the one hand the increased scope for forward repair of equipment reduces the time out of action, but on the other hand engineering stability is required for the repair of complex systems.

Seven REME Equipment Support Battalions have been established. Six of these battalions provide second line support for the Reaction and Adaptable Divisions. An Equipment Support Aviation Battalion in the UK supports 16 Air Assault Brigade.

We estimate that during late 2015 the REME had a total of about 9,000 regular personnel.

Regular Units	Role	Location
1 Close Support Battalion	Supports 102 Logistic Bde	Catterick
2 Close Support Battalion	Supports 102 Logistic Bde	Leuchars
3 Armoured Close Support Battalion	Supports 101 Logistic Bde	Tidworth (2017 – from Paderborn, Germany)
4 Armoured Close Support Battalion	Supports 101 Logistic Bde	Tidworth
5 Force Support Battalion	Supports 101 Logistic Bde	Cottesmore
4 Armoured Close Support Battalion	Supports 101 Logistic Bde	Tidworth
7 (Air Assault) Battalion	Supports 16 Air Assault Bde	Wattisham

Reserve Units	HQ Location	Squadron Locations
101 Battalion REME	Wrexham	Prestatyn, Liverpool, Manchester, West Bromwich, Telford
102 Battalion REME	Newton Aycliffe	Newcastle upon Tyne, Scunthorpe, Rotherham, Sheffield, Newton Aycliffe
103 Battalion REME	Crawley	Croydon, Portsmouth, Ashford, Bexleyheath, Barnett, Brentwood
104 Battalion REME	Northampton	Corby, Coventry, Redditch, Swindon, Nottingham, Derby
105 Battalion REME	Bristol	Yeovil, Taunton, Gloucester, Bristol, Bridgend, Cwmbran
106 Battalion REME	East Kilbride	Belfast, Lisburn, Dunfermline, Edinburgh, Grangemouth

Note: With the exception of 101 Battalion these battalions are paired with regular REME battalions (see Chapter 2).

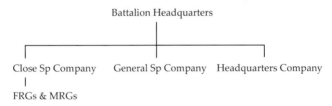

Note: Approx 450 personnel.

The Close Support Company will normally deploy a number of FRG's (Forward Repair Groups) and MRGs (Medium Repair Groups) in support of brigades. The company is mobile with armoured repair and recovery vehicles able to operate in the forward areas, carrying out forward repair of key nominated equipment often by the exchange of major assemblies. It is also capable of carrying out field repairs on priority equipment including telecommunications equipment, and the repair of damage sustained by critical battle winning equipments.

The role of the General Support Company is to support the Close Support Companies and Divisional Troops. Tasks include the regeneration of fit power packs for use in forward repair and the repair of equipment back loaded from Close Support Companies. The General Support Company will normally be located to the rear of the divisional area in order to maximise productivity and minimise vulnerability.

Expect an Equipment Support Battalion to have approximately 450 personnel.

REME LAD (Light Aid Detachment)

Major divisional units have their own REME support organisation generally called the LAD which can vary in size from about 60 to 120 personnel. Usually commanded by a Captain, LADs are capable of quick repairs at the point of failure.

In manpower terms the REME LAD support available to the units of a division might resemble the following:

Armoured Regiment (T56)	120
Armoured Cavalry Regiment	90
Armoured Infantry Battalion	90
Close Support Engineer Regiment	85
Field Regiment Royal Artillery	115
Air Defence Regiment Royal Artillery	160
Army Air Corps Regiment	130
Signals Regiment	60
RLC Logistic Support Regiment	75

ARMY MEDICAL SERVICES (AMS)

Medical support to members of the British Army is provided by the Army Medical Services which consists of the following Corps:

Royal Army Medical Corps
Queen Alexandra's Royal Army Nursing Corps
Royal Army Dental Corps
Royal Army Veterinary Corps

The Army Medical Services is the army single service element of the Defence Medical Services (DMS). There is more information regarding the Defence Medical Services in the Joint Service Chapter.

It is certain that without the superb support provided by the Defence Medical Services in both Iraq and Afghanistan, a large number of service personnel who would have been unlikely to have survived their wounds in earlier conflicts are still alive today.

THE ROYAL ARMY MEDICAL CORPS (RAMC)

In peace, the personnel of the RAMC are based at the various medical installations throughout the world or in field force units and they are responsible for the health of the Army.

There are 6 x regular medical regiments and 3 x field hospitals. The reserves provide 13 x field hospitals, 1 x Support Medical Regiment and 1 x Casualty Evacuation Regiment.

In late 2015 our estimate of the regular personnel strength of the RAMC is 2,900 officers and soldiers.

During late 2015 the structure of the regular and reserve units of the RAMC is as follows:

Regular Units	Role	Location
1 Armoured Medical Regiment	101 Logistic Brigade	Tidworth (from Germany by 2017)
2 Medical Regiment	102 Logistic Brigade	North Luffenham
3 Medical Regiment	102 Logistic Brigade	Preston
4 Armoured Medical Regiment	101 Logistic Brigade	Aldershot
5 Armoured Medical Regiment	101 Logistic Brigade	Tidworth
16 Close Support Medical Regiment	16 Air Assault Brigade	Colchester
22 Field Hospital	2 Medical Brigade	Aldershot
33 Field Hospital	2 Medical Brigade	Gosport
34 Field Hospital	2 Medical Brigade	Strensall

Reserve Units	HQ Location	Squadron Locations
225 (Scottish) Medical Regiment	Dundee	Stirling, Glenrothes, Dundee
253 (North Irish) Medical Regiment	Belfast	Limavady, Enniskillen, Belfast
254 (East of England) Medical Regiment	Cambridge	Ditton, Colchester, Norwich, Hitchin, Brentwood
201 (Northern) Field Hospital	Newcastle	Newton Aycliffe, Stockton on Tees, Newcastle
202 (Midlands) Field Hospital	Birmingham	Coventry, Stoke-on-Trent, Shrewsbury, Abingdon
203 (Welsh) Field Hospital	Cardiff	Swansea, Crickhowell, Colwyn Bay, Cardiff
204 (North Irish) Field Hospital	Belfast	Portadown, Belfast
205 (Scottish) Field Hospital	Glasgow	Aberdeen, Dundee, Edinburgh, Inverness, Glasgow
207 (Manchester) Field Hospital	Manchester	Stockport, Bury, Chorley, Manchester
208 (Liverpool) Field Hospital	Liverpool	Liverpool, Chester, Blackpool, Lancaster
212 (Yorkshire) Field Hospital	Sheffield	Leeds, York, Nottingham, Lincoln, Hull
243 (Wessex) Field Hospital	Keynsham	Gloucester, Exeter, Plymouth, Truro, Portsmouth
256 (City of London) Field Hospital	Walworth	Kensington, Kingston upon Thames, Brighton
306 Hospital Support Regiment	Strensall	Strensall
335 Medical Evacuation Regiment	Strensall	Strensall
Army Medical Services Operational Support Group	Strensall	Strensall

The majority of the reserve units are part of 2 Medical Brigade and many are paired with regular units (See Chapter 2 Organisations).

HQ 2nd Medical Brigade (Strensall)

Unit	Role	Location	Affiliated reserve unit
22 Field Hospital	Major Medical Facility	Aldershot	202 (Midlands) Field Hospital (R) (Birmingham); 207 (Manchester) Field Hospital (R) (Manchester); 208 (Liverpool) Field Hospital (R) (Liverpool)
33 Field Hospital	Major Medical Facility	Gosport	203 (Welsh) Field Hospital (R) (Cardiff); 243 (Wessex) Field Hospital (R) (Bristol); 256 (City of London) Field Hospital (R) (Walworth)
34 Field Hospital	Major Medical Facility	Strensall	201 (Northern) Field Hospital (R) (Newcastle-upon-Tyne); 204 (North Irish) Field Hospital (R) (Belfast); 205 (Scottish) Field Hospital (R) (Glasgow); 212 (Yorkshire) Field Hospital (R) (Sheffield)
306 Hospital Support Regiment (R)	Reserve Unit	Strensall	
335 Medical Evacuation Regiment (R)	Reserve Unit	Strensall	
Operational HQ Support Group (R)	Reserve Unit	Strensall	

Note: 225 Field Hospital (Dundee) and 254 Field Hospital (Cambridge) are both under the command of 102 Logistic Brigade (part of the Adaptable Force – 1 UK Division).

On operations, the RAMC is responsible for the care of the sick and wounded, with the subsequent evacuation of the wounded to hospitals in the rear areas. This is achieved by the provision of Close Support Medical Regiments (to treat front line casualties) and General Support Medical Regiments where more major procedures can be carried out some distance behind the front line, before evacuation to a Field Hospital where a full range of medical facilities is available.

Each Brigade in 3 UK Division (the Reaction Force) has a medical regiment which is generally a regular unit (in some cases this may be a hybrid unit) that operates in direct support of the battle groups. These units are either armoured, airmobile or parachute trained. There are generally extra medical squadrons that provide support at the divisional level; once again these squadrons can be either regular or reserve. These squadrons provide medical support for the divisional troops and can act as manoeuvre units for the forward brigades when required.

All medical squadrons have medical sections that consist of a Medical Officer and a number of Combat Medical Technicians (eight). These sub-units are located with the battlegroup or units being supported and they provide the necessary first line medical support. In addition, the field hospitals provide a dressing station where casualties are treated and may be resuscitated or stabilised before transfer to a field hospital. These units have the necessary integral ambulance support both armoured and wheeled, to transfer casualties from the first to second line medical units.

Field hospitals may be regular or reserve and are generally 200 bed facilities with a maximum of eight surgical teams capable of carrying out life saving operations on some of the most difficult surgical cases. Since 1990 regular medical units have been deployed on operations in the Persian Gulf, the Former Yugoslavia, Sierra Leone, Afghanistan and Iraq.

Casualty Evacuation (CASEVAC) is by ambulance, either armoured or wheeled and driven by RLC personnel, or by helicopter when such aircraft are available. A Chinook helicopter is capable of carrying 24 stretcher cases and a Puma can carry six stretcher cases and six sitting cases.

THE QUEEN ALEXANDRA'S ROYAL ARMY NURSING CORPS (QARANC)

The QARANC is an all-nursing and totally professionally qualified Corps. Its male and female, officer and other rank personnel, provide the necessary qualified nursing support at all levels and cover a wide variety of nursing specialities. QARANC personnel can be found anywhere in the world where Army Medical Services are required.

The QARANC personnel total is believed to be approximately 800.

ROYAL ARMY DENTAL CORPS (RADC)

The RADC is a professional corps that fulfils the essential role of maintaining the dental health of the Army in peace and war, both at home and overseas. Qualified dentists and oral surgeons, hygienists, technicians and support ancillaries work in a wide variety of military units – from static and mobile dental clinics to field medical units, military hospitals and dental laboratories.

The RADC personnel total is believed to be approximately 300.

THE ROYAL ARMY VETERINARY CORPS (RAVC)

The RAVC look after the many animals that the Army has on strength. Veterinary tasks in today's army are mainly directed towards the army's 550 guard or search dogs, and its 460 horses for ceremonial duties. Personnel totals believed to be in the region of 320.

THE ADJUTANT GENERAL'S CORPS (AGC)

The Adjutant General's Corps formed on 1 April 1992 and its sole task is the management of the Army's most precious resource, its soldiers. The Corps absorbed the functions of six existing smaller corps; the Royal Military Police, the Royal Army Pay Corps, the Royal Army Educational Corps, the Royal Army Chaplains Department, the Army Legal Corps and the Military Provost Staff Corps.

The Corps is organised into four branches with our late 2015 estimates of personnel totals (trained) as follows:

Staff and Personnel Support (SPS)	– 3,500
Provost	– 1,600
Educational and Training Services	– 320
Army Legal Services	– 130

THE ROLE OF SPS BRANCH

The role of SPS Branch is to ensure the efficient and smooth delivery of Personnel Administration to the Army. This includes support to individual officers and soldiers in units by processing pay and Service documentation, first line provision of financial, welfare, education and resettlement guidance to individuals and the provision of clerical skills and information management to ensure the smooth day to day running of the unit or department.

AGC (SPS) officers are employed throughout the Army, in direct support of units as Regimental Administrative Officers or AGC Detachment Commanders. They hold Commander AGC (SPS) and SO2 AGC (SPS) posts in district/Divisional and Brigade HQs and fill posts at the Adjutant General's Information Centre (AGIC) and general staff appointment throughout the Army headquarters locations.

AGC (SPS) soldiers are employed as Military Clerks in direct support of units within the AGC Field Detachments, in fixed centre pay offices, in headquarters to provide staff support and in miscellaneous posts such as embassy clerks, as management accountants or in AGIC as programmer analysts.

The principal functional tasks of AGC (SPS) personnel on operations are:

◆ The maintenance of Field Records, including the soldiers 'Record of Service', casualty reporting and disciplinary documentation.
◆ Clerical and staff support to Battlegroup HQs and independent Sub Units such as Engineer and Logistic Squadrons.
◆ The issue of pay and allowances to personnel.
◆ The maintenance of Imprest Accounts (the MoD Public Accounts) which involve paying local suppliers for services, receiving cash from non-Army agencies such as NAAFI and Forces Post Office receipts.
◆ The deployment of a Field Records Cell which co-ordinates all personnel administration in the field.

AGC (SPS) personnel play a full part in operational duties by undertaking such tasks as local defence, guard and command post duties. In addition, Command Officers can employ any soldier in their unit as they see fit and may require AGC (SPS) personnel to undertake appropriate additional training to allow them to be used in some specialist roles specific to the unit, or as radio operators or drivers.

Currently, about 70 per cent of AGC (SPS) personnel are serving with field force units, with the remaining 30 per cent in base and training units or HQs, such as the MoD.

Members of AGC (SPS) are first trained as soldiers and then specialise as Military Clerks. AGC (SPS) officers complete the same military training as their counterparts in other Arms and Services, starting as the Royal Military Academy, Sandhurst. They are required to attend all promotion courses and the Army Staff Course.

The Role of the ETS Branch

The AGC (ETS) Branch has the responsibility of improving the efficiency, effectiveness and morale of the Army by providing support to operations and the developmental education, training, support and resettlement services that the Army requires to carry out its task. ETS personnel provide assistance at almost all levels of command but their most visible task is the manning of Army Education Centres wherever the Army is stationed. At these centres officers and soldiers receive the educational support necessary for them to achieve both civilian and military qualifications.

The Role of the ALS Branch

The AGC (ALS) Branch advises on all aspects of service and civilian law that may affect every level of the Army from General to Private soldiers. Members of the branch are usually qualified as solicitors or barristers.

The Role of the Provost Branch

Provost comprises the Royal Military Police (RMP), the Military Provost Staff (MPS) and the Military Provost Guard Service (MPGS). The main role of the RMP is to 'Police the Force', and 'provide Police Support to the Force'. The MPS provide advice and support to Commanders on all custody and detention issues. The MPGS is the Army's professional armed guarding service, established to release general service personnel from armed guarding duties.

Provost Mission: To provide the necessary military police, custodial and guarding service to the Army in order to ensure military effectiveness.

THE ROYAL MILITARY POLICE (RMP)

The RMP is a regulatory body with unique investigative and policing skills and competencies which also undertakes military tasks complementary to its specialist role.

Regular Units	Location	Attached Reserve Unit Locations
1 Regiment RMP	Catterick	Livingston and Stockton on Tees
3 Regiment RMP	Bulford	Cannock and Manchester
4 Regiment RMP	Aldershot	Tulse Hill
Special Investigation Branch Regiment RMP	Bulford	Bulford
Special Operations Unit RMP	Longmoor	

The RMP has three specialist areas:

Investigations: Supporting the Military Criminal Justice System is the highest priority for the RMP, who alone have the unique capability to deliver the full range of policing functions throughout the spectrum of conflict at home, in overseas garrisons and on operations. This police support is both proactive and visible, contributing to success on operations by enforcing the law, deterring crime and thus underpinning the Military Criminal Justice System.

Special Investigations: The Special Investigations Branch (SIB) of the RMP is responsible for all special and sensitive investigations. In high intensity conflict they continue to police, investigating a range of offences ranging from murder to fratricide; the investigative procedure is the same, only the operational context changes.

Close Protection (CP): RMP provide CP personnel and training for others on CP duties, both for at risk military personnel and those of other government departments. The RMP provides a core of trained manpower at high readiness to cover contingencies and can also generate Short Term Training Teams.

In addition, the RMP also provide:

◆ The provision of a specialist Crime Reduction service to reduce the opportunities for crime, to shape attitudes and to maintain morale.
◆ The regulation of movement and manoeuvre, such as route reconnaissance, route selection, signing and manning of routes, and the establishment of Military Police Stations and Posts.
◆ The training and mentoring of indigenous Civilian and Police Forces through the provision of basic police training in the form of an investigative capability with crime scene management, interviewing skills, file preparation and possibly forensics.
◆ Special to arm advice directly to the operational commanders on: arrest and detention, searches of people, property or vehicles, incident control, and crime scene management. They will also provide surety to correct handling of evidence in support of pre-planned operations.

THE MILITARY PROVOST STAFF (MPS)

The principal function of the MPS at the Military Corrective Training Centre (MCTC) at Colchester, Essex, is to detain personnel, both male and female, of the three Services and civilians subject to the Services Disciplinary Acts, in accordance with the provisions of the Imprisonment and Detention (Army) Rules 1979. The MCTC is an establishment that provides corrective training for those servicemen and women sentenced to periods of detention; it is not a prison. The MCTC takes servicemen and women who have been sentenced to periods of detention from 14 days to two years. Up to 316 detainees can be held at the MCTC. The MCTC has extensive Military Training facilities and an Education Wing that includes trade training. The MPS has approximately 100 personnel from all three services.

THE MILITARY PROVOST GUARD SERVICES (MPGS)

The Military Provost Guard Service (MPGS) was established in 1997 as the Army's professional armed guarding service to relieve the Ministry of Defence Police and general service personnel from armed guarding duties at nominated Tri-Service locations.

The MPGS comprises regular soldiers employed on a Military Local Service Engagement that is restricted to the United Kingdom. All MPGS soldiers have had previous service experience and service may be up to the age of 55. The MPGS has approximately 1500 personnel and patrols over 100 sites.

MPGS duties include:

♦ Controlling entry and exit to a site.
♦ Managing control room operations and ensuring all visitors are dealt with efficiently.
♦ Patrolling site perimeters and taking necessary action to preserve perimeter security.
♦ Security incident management, such as suspicious packages, bomb threats, protests, etc.
♦ Military Working Dog services at some sites.
♦ The MPGS is part of the Provost Branch of the Adjutant General's Corps and is under the direction of Provost Marshal (Army), who is the Director and Head of Service. MPGS units are formed under the command of their respective Head of Establishment, with Provost Marshal (Army) maintaining technical standards through annual inspections.
♦ Each MPGS unit has a structured rank system that provides opportunity for promotion to Senior Non-Commissioned Officer, and Warrant Officer Level 2 rank at some sites.
♦ Given the size of the MPGS, a number of Warrant Officer Level 1 opportunities exist across the country. Promotion is based on merit and uses the same system of annual performance appraisal in line with the current Tri-Service guidance for appraisal reporting.

SMALLER CORPS

THE INTELLIGENCE CORPS (Int Corps) – The Int Corps deals with operational intelligence, counter intelligence and security. There are 3 x regular battalions and 4 x reserve battalions. Our estimate of the current regular personnel strength of the Intelligence Corps was 1,500.

THE ARMY PHYSICAL TRAINING CORPS (APTC) – Consists mainly of SNCOs who are responsible for unit fitness. The majority of major units have a representative from this corps on their strength. Our estimate of the current personnel strength of APTC is 400.

Early 2011 personnel total was in the region of 480.

ROYAL ARMY CHAPLAIN'S DEPARTMENT (RAChD) – Provides officers and soldiers with religious and welfare support/advice. The RAChD has approximately 120 chaplains who represent all of the mainstream religions.

THE GENERAL SERVICE CORPS (GSC) – A holding unit for specialists. Personnel from this corps are generally members of the reserve army.

SMALL ARMS SCHOOL CORPS (SASC) – A small corps with the responsibility of training instructors in all aspects of weapon handling. Our estimate of the current personnel total is in the region of 140.

CHAPTER 15 – RECRUITING, SELECTION, TRAINING

OVERVIEW

Recruiting is carried out to attract sufficient men and women of the right quality to meet the Army's personnel requirements. Selection is the process that is carried out to ensure that those who are accepted into the Army have the potential to be good soldiers and are capable of being trained to carry out their chosen trade. Training is the process of preparing those men and women for their careers in the Army. Training is progressive and continues all the way through a soldier and an officers' career.

The Army Recruitment and Training Division is responsible for the delivery of army recruiting and training.

ARMY RECRUITMENT AND TRAINING DIVISION

The Army Recruitment and Training Division (ARTD) is responsible for each stage of a potential recruit's progress from the recruiting office, through a Recruit Selection Centre, into recruit training, through specialist courses before they are finally posted to their unit in the Field Army. The ARTD is headed by the Director General Army Recruitment and Training (DG ART), a Major General who is responsible for ensuring that sufficient men and women of the right quality are recruited and trained to meet the needs of the service.

The ARTD Headquarters is based at Upavon in Wiltshire, close to many of the training units. Recruiting is carried out from over 100 towns and cities throughout the country, and individual training is conducted at some 40 schools. With a permanent staff of about 10,000 across the whole of the recruiting and training organisation, the ARTD is responsible for Ministry of Defence land, buildings and field assets valued at more than one and a quarter billion pounds.

The ARTD is required to enlist between 7,000 and 10,000 recruits each year (depending upon the requirement) and to be involved in the training of about 60,000 officers and soldiers (regular and reserve). ARTD conducts over 1,000 different types of courses with about 8,000 officers and soldiers under training at any time. Across all training phases, the average annual unit cost of training a soldier or officer is believed to be in excess of £20,000.

ARTD operations are divided into four inter-related functions: Recruiting, Recruit training (Phase 1), Specialist training (Phase 2), and Career training (Phase 3).

ARTD was formerly named Army Training and Recruitment Agency. It was renamed ARTD on 1 July 2006.

RECRUITING

An MoD committee called the Standing Committee Army Manpower Forecasts (SCAMF) calculates the numbers that need to be enlisted to maintain the Army's personnel at the correct level. The Committee needs to take account of changing unit establishments, wastage caused by servicemen and women leaving the service at the end of their engagements, and those who might choose to leave before their engagements come to an end (PVR – Premature Voluntary Release). The number required in each trade in the Army is assessed and figures are published at six monthly intervals so that adjustments may be made during the year.

Within ARTD, the Recruiting Group (in association with Capita plc) runs all Army Recruiting from the headquarters in Upavon. Recruiting activities take place all over the country, using the network of Careers Offices, about 60 Schools Advisers, over 20 Army Youth Teams and Regimental Recruiting Teams. The Commander Recruiting Group, a Brigadier serving in ARTD and his staff, located throughout the United Kingdom are responsible for the recruiting and selection to meet the personnel targets.

Potential recruits are attracted into the Army in a number of ways including advertisements on the television, on the internet and in the press. Permanently established recruiting teams from many Regiments and Corps tour the country and staff from the Armed Forces Careers Offices (AFCO) and Army Careers Information Offices (ACIO) visit schools, youth clubs and job centres. There is a network of AFCOs and ACIOs located throughout the UK and Army Careers Advisers who access schools and universities throughout the country. Young, recently trained soldiers are also sent back to their home towns and schools to talk to their friends about life in the Army and are regularly interviewed by the local press.

The overall army recruiting cost for 2012–2013 was in the region of £122 million (the latest figure available). The advertising cost for reserve recruitment during 2014–2015 was £3.8 million.

Annual Army recruiting figures (intake to untrained strength) during the recent past are as follows:

	2012/2013	2013/2014	2014/2015
Army Total	10,300	7,020	6,890

Outflow figures (trained and untrained personnel leaving the army) in the recent past are:

	2012/2013	2013/2014	2014/2015
Army Total	14,890	15,740	11,180

Note: The excess in outflow against intake reflects the SDSR personnel reduction targets. The intake figures include an average of about 800 officers per year.

SOLDIER SELECTION

Potential recruits are normally aged between 16 years and nine months and 32 years (can be older for some specialist skills), except when they are applying for a vacancy as a junior soldier when the age limits are from 16 years to 18 years and six months. As a trained soldier the minimum length of service will be four years from the age of 18, or from the start of training, if over 18.

Under the selection system, a potential recruit will have a two day assessment at an Army Assessment Centre. There are Assessment Centres at Pirbright, Lichfield, Penicuik (near Edinburgh) and Ballymena in Northern Ireland.

At the Assessment Centre he or she will take the Army Entrance Test which is designed to assess ability to assimilate the training required for the candidate's chosen trade. The staff at the Assessment Centre will then conduct a number of interviews to decide on overall suitability for the Army. A medical examination will also be carried out that checks on weight, eyesight and hearing. The potential recruit will also see at first hand the type of training that they will undergo, and the sort of life that they will lead in barracks if successful in getting into the Army. Physical fitness is assessed based on a 'best effort' 1.5 mile timed run and some gymnasium exercises. After further interviews the candidate is informed if he or she is successful and if so is offered a vacancy in a particular trade and Regiment or Corps.

PHASE 1 BASIC TRAINING FOR RECRUITS

Basic Recruit or Phase 1 training comprises the Combat Infantryman's Course (CIC) for infantry and the Common Military Syllabus Recruit (CMSR) for all other British Army regiments and corps.

As part of ARDT, the Initial Training Group (ITG) is responsible for Phase 1 (Basic) Training of the majority of soldier recruits, which is undertaken primarily at the Army Training Centre Pirbright in Surrey. Exceptions to this are the adult Infantry recruits who go direct to the School of Infantry at Catterick in Yorkshire.

Recent figures suggest that training a recruit on the CMSR at the ATC Pirbright costs £20,200.

The CMSR includes training in the basic military skills required of all soldiers and incorporates weapon handling and shooting, drill, physical fitness, field tactics, map reading, survival in nuclear chemical and biological warfare and general military knowledge. It is an intensive course and requires the recruit to show considerable determination and courage to succeed.

There is an Army Technical Foundation College at Winchester in Hampshire and the Army Foundation College at Harrogate in Yorkshire.

ARTD has its own Staff Leadership School (ASLS), at Alexander Barracks, Pirbright. ASLS has the task of training the Army's trainers, from corporal section commanders and trade instructors to Commanding Officers, as well as administrative and support staff. In all, about 2,000 military and civilian training, supervisory and support staff are trained each year.

SCHOOL OF INFANTRY, CATTERICK

Catterick is the home of all Infantry Training at Phase 1 and Phase 2, except Junior soldiers destined for the Infantry who continue to receive Phase 1 training the Army Foundation College. Catterick comprises the Headquarters School of Infantry and the Infantry Training Centre, Catterick. Also under its Command are the Infantry Battle School at Brecon and the Infantry Training Centre at Warminster, which both provide Phase 3 training for Infantry officers and soldiers.

Combat Infantryman's Course

The Combat Infantryman's Course (CIC) is the framework upon which all regular infantry recruit training is based. The course equips recruits with infantry special to arms skills needed for a rifle platoon ready to deploy on an operational tour after minimal further appropriate pre-operational training in the Field Army. Successful completion of the CIC marks the end of initial army training.

The majority of recruits joining the infantry choose line infantry regiments; they undertake the standard CIC which lasts for 26 weeks. Recruits joining the Foot Guards, Parachute Regiment and the Gurkhas, carry out additional training to meet the particular needs of these regiments. Similarly, recruits from the Army Foundation College at Harrogate undertake a specially adapted, but shorter CIC.

The Combat Infantryman's Course (Single) is structured around three phases as follows:

Weeks 1–6 Individual skills, drill, weapons training, fitness and fieldcraft.
Weeks 7–21 Team skills, endurance training including long runs, patrolling skills.
Weeks 22–26 Live firing and battle camp at Sennybridge in Wales followed by Passout Parade preparations.

Recent figures suggest that training a recruit on the CIC at the ITC Catterick costs £33,700. Parachute Regiment recruits cost about £10,000 more and their course is longer.

GURKHAS

Recruits from Nepal joining the Royal Gurkha Rifles, Queen's Gurkha Engineers, Queen's Gurkha Signals and the Queen's Own Gurkha Transport Regiment are trained at the ITC on a 38 week CIC (G). This combines the normal Common Military Syllabus Recruits (CMS(R)) course taught at the Army Training Regiments with the CIC course and it includes a special English language and British culture package.

As many as 30,000 potential Gurkha recruits apply to join the British Army each year and between 150 and 200 are selected.

Army Foundation College – Harrogate

The Army Foundation College (AFC) at Harrogate delivers Phase 1 (initial military) training to Junior Entry recruits destined for the Royal Armoured Corps, Royal Artillery and Infantry. Recruits make their final capbadge selection after week 21. The aim of the course is to develop the qualities of leadership, character, and team spirit required of a soldier to achieve a full career in the Army. The 42-week course is a progressive and integrated package divided into three 14-week terms. It combines the Common Military Syllabus (Recruits) with Vocational Education and Leadership and Initiative Training. Recruits achieve a Foundation Modern Apprenticeship and up to Key Skills Level 3.

Entrants to the college are aged between 16 and 17 years. At the College, they undertake a course that provides a supportive environment allowing students to develop a broad range of skills and qualifications that are equally valuable, in both Army and civilian life. There are three main elements to the course:

There are 23 weeks of military training, which include basic or advanced soldiering, progressive physical training, infantry weapons, grenades, military leadership, marksmanship, parade ground drill. There is also a two week final exercise in the field.

There are five weeks of leadership and initiative training which takes in hill walking, hiking, caving, rock climbing, abseiling, and all kind of leadership and command tasks.

Lastly, there are 14 weeks of vocational education which can result in an NVQ or SVQ in Information Technology.

The latest figures show that training a recruit at the Army Foundation College Harrogate cost about £68,700 per recruit.

ARMY TECHNICAL FOUNDATION COLLEGE – WINCHESTER

The Army Technical Foundation College Winchester was opened in 2010 and provides basic training to Junior Entry recruits wishing to join the Technical Corps. Recruits are found from the following: Royal Engineers; Royal Signals; Army Air Corps; Royal Logistics Corps; Army Medical Services; Royal Electrical and Mechanical Engineers; Adjutant General's Corps.

This is a 23-week course, designed to develop the Junior Soldiers' individual and team skills in a progressive manner, preparing them for Phase 2 training, where they will lean the specific skills for their chosen Army trade. Course modules include: Fieldcraft; Skill at Arms; Fitness Training; Qualities of a Soldier; Military Knowledge; Battlefield Casualty Drills; Individual Health; Education.

PHASE 2 SPECIAL TO ARM RECRUIT TRAINING

Phase 2 training is the 'Special to Arm' training that is required to prepare soldiers who have recently completed their basic Phase 1 training, to enable them to take their place in field force units of their Regiment or Corps. This phase of training has no fixed period and courses vary considerably in length.

From 2005 Phase 2 training for the major Arms and Services of the British Army has been carried out as follows:

Infantry – Infantry recruits do all of their recruit training (Phase 1 and Phase 2) at the Infantry Training Centre at Catterick.

The Royal Armoured Corps – Training takes place at the Armour Centre at Bovington Camp and Lulworth. Recruits for the Household Cavalry Regiment also undergo equitation training.

The Royal Artillery – Training takes place at the Royal School of Artillery at Larkhill in Wiltshire.

The Royal Engineers – Training takes place at the Combat Engineering School at Minley, the Construction Engineer School in Chatham and Blackwater and the Defence Explosive Ordnance Disposal School.

Royal Signals – Training takes place at 11 (Royal School of Signals) Regiment at Blandford Camp in Dorset. Since April 2004, the Defence College of CIS (DCCIS), also based at Blandford Camp, assumed the responsibility for Royal Signals training as well as that for the Royal Navy and Royal Air Force Signals communications specialists.

Army Air Corps – Training takes place at the School of Army Aviation in Middle Wallop

The Royal Logistic Corps – Training takes place at the RLC Training Regiment and Depot at Deepcut and the School of Logistics at Marchwood – previously under the joint Defence Logistic Support Training Group (DLSTG) and since April 2004 under Defence College of Logistics (DCL), also based at Deepcut. Under these new arrangements, ARTD is also responsible for Royal Navy and Royal Air Force Logistics training. The Army School of Catering, Aldershot, the Army School of Ammunition at Kineton and the School of Petroleum, West Moors are also ARTD logistics training facilities, as is the Defence School of Transport at Leconfield.

Royal Electrical and Mechanical Engineers – Vehicle Mechanics are trained at Bordon and other trades at Arborfield. Since April 2004, the Electro Mechanical elements of the ARTD REME Training Group transferred to the new Defence College of Electro Mechanical Engineering under the command of the Naval Recruiting and Training Agency (NRTA). The Aeronautical elements of the REME Training Group transferred to the Defence College of Aeronautical Engineering under the command of the RAF Training Group Defence Agency (TGDA). The ARTD REME Training Group ceased to exist in name at the end of 2003.

The Adjutant General's Corps – Pay and Clerks are trained at the AGC Depot at Worthy Down near Winchester; Defence School of Languages at Beaconsfield and the Defence Animal Centre at Melton Mowbray. From April 2002, the School of Finance and Management, previously part of the Group and located at Worthy Down, became part of the Defence Academy. From April 2004, the Royal Military Police (RMP) training school transferred to the Defence College of Policing and Guarding (DCPG) at Southwick Park, Portsmouth.

Intelligence Corps – Have trained since 1997 at the Defence Intelligence and Security Centre (DISC) in Chicksands in Bedfordshire. The DISC is responsible for training all personnel in intelligence, security and information support. In June 2003, command of the Defence School of Languages transferred to DISC, although the school remained at Beaconsfield.

Army Medical Services (AMS) – Made up of the Royal Army Medical Corps (RAMC), Royal Army Dental Corps (RADC), Queen Alexandra's Royal Army Nursing Corps (QARANC), and the Royal Army Veterinary Corps (RAVC). Training is conducted by the joint service Defence Medical Training Organisation at Aldershot and Birmingham, the Defence Dental Agency in Birmingham, and the RAVC training centre at Melton Mowbray respectively.

Recruit Physical Training Assessments – During Recruit Training personnel are assessed at different stages of training as follows:

Test	Introduction	Interim	Final
Heaves	2	4	6
Sit Up Test	1 Min (20 reps)	2 min (42 reps)	3 min (65 reps)
1.5 Mile Run	11 min 30 sec	11 mins	10 min 30 sec

CONDITIONS OF SERVICE – SOLDIERS AND OFFICERS

Length of Service – Soldiers
As a general rule, all recruits enlist on an Open Engagement. This allows a recruit to serve for 22 years from their 18th birthday or date of attestation, whichever is the later, and so qualify for a pension.

A soldier enlisted on this engagement has a statutory right to leave after four years reckoned from the 18th birthday or from three months after attestation, whichever is the later, subject to giving 12 months notice of intention to leave and providing the soldier is not restricted from leaving in any way. Certain employments, particularly those involving a lengthy training, carry a time bar which requires a longer period before soldiers have the statutory right to leave.

If a soldier is enlisted between l7.5 and 18 years of age; on payment of 7 days gross pay at any time after 28 days service, but only in his first six months of service or by age 18.25 years, whichever is earlier. If enlisted at 18 years of age or over; on payment of seven days gross pay between the end of the eight week and the third month of service. Individuals after this time are committed to serve for a minimum engagement of four years. There are of course allowances made for medical and exceptional compassionate circumstances.

OFFICER COMMISSIONS

There are five main types of commission in the Army. These are:

The Short Service Commission (SSC) – the SSC is the normal first commission for those who become an officer in the Army. It is a commission for those who do not wish to commit to a long career but would like to benefit from the high quality training and exceptional experience available to young officers. The SSC is also a first step to a mid-length or full career in the Army. SSCs are awarded for a minimum of three years (six years for the Army Air Corps on account of the length of pilot training) but can be extended to eight.

Candidates for commissions should be over 17 years and nine months and under 29 years old when they begin officer training.

The Intermediate Regular Commission (IRC) – The IRC offers a mid length career for a maximum of 18 years and can be applied for after two years SSC, subject to being recommended. On completion of 18 years after the age of 40 the officer will be entitled to a lump sum and regular monthly payments, which will convert at 65 to a further lump sum and pension.

The Regular Commission (Reg C) – The Reg C offers a full career of 35 years or to age 60 whichever is first. It can be applied for after two years IRC, subject to recommendation. Those completing a full career will receive an immediate lump sum and pension from age 55.

Undergraduate Army Placement (UGAP) – UGAP is a Commission for highly motivated undergraduates studying at UK universities requiring a placement as part of their degree. Up to 10 places are available each year. In all other respects the commission is identical to the GYC.

Late Entry Commissions – A number of vacancies exist for senior Non Commissioned Officers and Warrant Officers to be granted commissions known as Late Entry Commissions. They attend the Late Officer Entry Course (LEOC) at Sandhurst before commencing their officer careers. Because of their age they generally do not rise above the rank of Lieutenant Colonel.

Educational Requirements

All except LE officers require an indicative level of 35 ALIS points (34 for Scottish Standards) gained from the best seven subjects at GCSE, or equivalent, which must include English language, mathematics and either a science subject or a foreign language.

In addition a score of 180 UCAS Tariff points must be acquired in separate subjects at AS and A level, or equivalent. These must include a minimum of two passes at A level, or equivalent, at grades A-E. Note that the General Studies paper does not qualify for UCAS Tariff points.
The attainment of a degree will normally override the requirement for UCAS Tariff points.

OFFICER SELECTION AND SANDHURST (RMAS)

Officer candidates are normally advised by an Army Careers Adviser of the options open to them and they will also arrange for interviews and familiarisation visits to an appropriate Regiment or Corps. If the Regiment or Corps is prepared to sponsor a candidate they then guide him or her through the rest of the selection procedure. All candidates, except those seeking an Army Sixth Form Scholarship or entry to Welbeck (The Defence Sixth Form College) are required to attend a briefing at the Army Officer Selection Board (AOSB) at Westbury, Wiltshire for psychometric tests and a two day briefing (AOSB Briefing). So long as they meet the minimum standards they will be invited back for another three and a half day assessment also at AOSB (AOSB Main Board). Here they will also undergo a medical examination.

AOSB Main Board consists of a series of interviews and tests that assess the personality and the leadership potential in applicants. Candidates need to be themselves, be prepared to discuss the issues of the day and be physically fit. Historical Main Board results are as follows:

	Attendees	Passes	Fails
2011	1190	620	570
2012	990	490	500
2013	600	350	250

All potential officers accepted for training attend the RMAS (Royal Military Academy Sandhurst) Commissioning Course which lasts for 44 weeks with three entries a year in January, May and September. After successfully completing the Sandhurst course a young officer then completes a further specialist course with his or her chosen Regiment or Corps. Females cannot be accepted in the Household Cavalry, The Royal Armoured Corps or the Infantry although a policy review was underway in 2015.

In the 12 months to 31 December 2014, the RMAS commissioned 540 Direct Entry Regular Officers into the British Army.

Welbeck – The Defence Sixth Form College/Army Sixth Form Scholarship
Welbeck DSFC offers a two year residential A level course to motivated young people who would like, in the future, a commission in one of the more technical branches of the three Services, as well as the MoD Civil Service. Of those destined for the Army, most Welbexians will be commissioned into the Royal Engineers, the Royal Signals, the Royal Logistic Corps or the Royal Electrical and Mechanical Engineers. Both potential Welbexians and those seeking an Army Sixth Form Scholarship attend a similar 24 hour selection board at AOSB.

PHASE 3 IN-SERVICE TRAINING

An officer or soldier will spend as much as one third of their career attending training courses. Following basic Phase 1 and Phase 2 training soldiers are posted to their units and progressive training is carried out on a continual basis. Training is geared to individual, sub-unit or formation level and units regularly train outside of the UK and Germany. As would be expected there are specialist unit training packages for specific operational commitments such as Afghanistan.

For example the training package for personnel warned off for deployment to Afghanistan included a special-to-mission package. The training was carried out by specialist training advisory teams at in the UK and in Germany.

Phase 3 training facilities are the same as those listed under Phase 2, and also include the Defence Academy located mainly at Shrivenham. Defence Academy training and education facilities incorporate the Joint Services Command and Staff College at Shrivenham; The Defence Academy College of Management and Technology (previously known as the Royal Military College of Science, Shrivenham); The Royal College of Defence Studies; The Defence Leadership Centre, and The Defence School of Finance and Management. The Joint Doctrine and Concepts Centre is collocated at

Shrivenham. A Joint Services Warrant Officer's School is part of the Joint Services Command and Staff College at Shrivenham.

THE JOINT SERVICES COMMAND AND STAFF COLLEGE (JSCSC)

The JSCSC at Shrivenham trains the future commanders and staff officers of all three UK Armed Services and those of many allied and friendly countries from around the world.

As an element of the UK Defence Academy the Commandant (Major General J R Free – from August 2014) is a two star officer.

Within the JSCSC structure each single service is represented by an Assistant Commandant (Brigadier equivalent) each of them responsible for both single service issues and delivery of training.

The Advanced Command and Staff Course (ACSC) is a 46 week residential course designed to provide professional education covering a wide spectrum of military defence and security issues for selected UK, international military and civilian officers. The Higher Command and Staff Course (HCSC) is a Joint Service course that assists senior officers who may be destined for high command to acquire a deeper understanding of the fundamentals of military theory and practice.

Overseas Students

During any one year, as many as 4,000 students from over 90 different countries take part in training in the United Kingdom. The charges for training depend on the length of the course, its syllabus and the number taking part. Receipts from overseas governments for this training are believed to be in the region of £50 million annually.

TRAINING AREAS OUTSIDE THE UK AND EUROPE

The British Army's main training areas outside of the Europe are:

Canada – Suffield

British Army Training Unit Suffield (BATUS) has the responsibility to train battlegroups in the planning and execution of armoured operations through the medium of live firing and tactical test exercise. There are 6 x 'Medicine Man' battlegroup exercises each year in a training season that lasts from March to November.

Canada – Wainwright

The British Army Training Support Unit at Wainwright (BATSU(W)) provides the logistic and administrative support for Infantry units at the Canadian Forces training base in Western Canada.

Kenya

British Army Training and Liaison Staff Kenya (BATLSK) is responsible for supporting Infantry battalion group exercises and approximately 3,000 British troops train in Kenya each year in a harsh unforgiving terrain ranging in altitude from 8,000 feet down to 2,300 feet. BATLSK has been based at its present site in Kahawa Barracks since Kenya's independence in 1963.

Belize

The British Army Training Support unit Belize (BATSUB) was formed on 1 October 1994. Its role is to give training and logistic support to Land Command units training in a tropical jungle environment. In general terms BATSUB costs about £3 million per year.

Jungle Warfare School

The Jungle Warfare Wing (JWW) is located at Brunei on the island of Borneo close to the border with Sarawak (Malaysia) and is supported by the British Army's Brunei Garrison. JWW exists to provide a jungle training facility to meet the requirement to train jungle warfare instructors for the Field Army of the United Kingdom's Land Forces.

Note: Some training was conducted on Polish training areas from 1993 to 2007. Following the latest security problems in Eastern Europe it is possible that these areas may used again.

FITNESS REQUIREMENTS

All recruits and soldiers of all ranks and ages are required to take a basic fitness test. At the Recruiting Selection Centres, potential recruits undergo a series of tests known as Physical Standards Selection for Recruits (PSSR). These are 'best effort' tests that take place in the gymnasium. Recruits are required to complete the 1.5 mile (2.4 km) run.

Adult Entry candidates have to complete the run within 14 minutes or less. All Junior Entrants – Army Foundation College, Army Technical Foundation College or the School Leavers Scheme – are required to complete the run in 14 minutes 30 seconds or less. Officer candidates at the AOSB have to undertake a multi stage fitness test (known as the Beep Test) and aim to achieve a personal standard of 10.2 for males and 8.1 for females, as well as a number of sit-ups and press-ups.

In-service fitness requirements seek to maintain these standards. Tests typically require a 2.4 km run on level ground and in training shoes, in 10.5 minutes for those under 30. There are gradually rising time limits for older personnel. For women the requirement for the 2.4 km run is 13 minutes.

Standard fitness tests currently applied for infantry personnel include:

◆ BPFA Basic Personal Fitness Assessment. Sit-ups, press-ups, and a 1.5 mile (2.4km) run, all carried out against the clock. This tests individual fitness generally. The minimum fitness goals are: 54 continuous sit ups (with feet supported) and a 2.4 km (1.5 mile) run in 11 minutes 45 seconds.
◆ ICFT Infantry Combat Fitness Test. A distance of three miles as a squad carrying 56 pounds of kit each, including personal weapon. Timed to be completed in one hour, individuals must stay with the squad, or be failed.

CHAPTER 16 – MISCELLANEOUS

THE SERVICES HIERARCHY

Officer Ranks

Army	Navy	Air Force	NATO Code
Field Marshal	Admiral of the Fleet	Marshal of the RAF	OF-10
General	Admiral	Air Chief Marshal	OF-9
Lieutenant-General	Vice-Admiral	Air Marshal	OF-8
Major-General	Rear-Admiral	Air Vice Marshal	OF-7
Brigadier	Commodore	Air Commodore	OF-6
Colonel	Captain	Group Captain	OF-5
Lieutenant-Colonel	Commander	Wing Commander	OF-4
Major	Lieutenant-Commander	Squadron Leader	OF-3
Captain	Lieutenant	Flight-Lieutenant	OF-2
Lieutenant/2Lt	Sub-Lieutenant	Flying/Pilot Officer	OF-1
Officer Cadet	Midshipman	Officer Cadet	OF (D)

Note: OF-10 Commanders have 5 stars xxxxx; OF-9 Commanders have 4 stars xxxx; OF-8 Commanders 3 stars xxx; OF-7 Commanders 2 stars xx and OF-6 Commanders 1 star x.

Non Commissioned Ranks

Army	Navy	Air Force	NATO Code
Warrant Officer 1	Warrant Officer 1	Warrant Officer	OR-9
Warrant Officer 2	Warrant Officer 2		OR-8
Staff/Colour Sergeant	Chief Petty Officer	Flight Sergeant/Ch Tech (1)	OR-7
Sergeant	Petty Officer	Sergeant	OR-6
Corporal	Leading Rate	Corporal	OR-4
Lance Corporal	Able Rating		OR-3
Private Cl 1 -3		Leading Aircraftsman (2)	OR-2
Private Cl 4/Junior		Aircraftsman	OR-1

Note:

(1) Chief Technician

(2) May include Junior Technician and Senior Aircraftsman

UK ARMED FORCES PAY 2015–2016

The following table shows the average pay based on pay rates for 2015–2016.

Other ranks are allocated to either higher or lower pay spines in accordance with their trade. These are Army rates. For other service rates consult the table of ranks above.

Rank	Pay from 1 April 2015 (£)
New Entrant Rate	14,637
Private (Level 4)	20,727–22,531
Lance Corporal (Level 4)	21,816–24,913
Corporal (Level 4)	30,176–32,147
Sergeant (Level 4)	32,675–36,105
WO2 (Level 4)	36,804–41,029
WO1 (Level 4)	42,364–45,995
Officer Cadet	16,633
Lieutenant	30,670–33,842
Captain	39,236–46,660
Major	49,424–59,191
Lieutenant Colonel	69,366–80,320
Colonel	84,037–92,381
Brigadier	100,146–104,198

This table does not include the specialist pay rates for medical officers, chaplins, pilots etc.

MODES OF ADDRESS

Where appropriate officers and soldiers are addressed by their generic rank without any qualifications, therefore Generals, Lieutenant Generals and Major Generals are all addressed as 'General'. Colonels and Lieutenant Colonels as 'Colonel', Corporals and Lance Corporals as ' Corporal'. Staff Sergeants and Colour Sergeants are usually addressed as 'Staff' or 'Colour' and CSMs as Sergeant Major. It would almost certainly be prudent to address the RSM as 'Sir'.

Private Soldiers should always be addressed by their title and then their surname. For example: Rifleman Harris, Private Jones, Bugler Bygrave, Gunner Smith, Guardsman Thelwell, Sapper Williams, Trooper White, Kingsman Boddington, Signalman Robinson, Ranger Murphy, Fusilier Ramsbotham, Driver Wheel, Craftsman Grease or Air Trooper Rotor. However, it should be remembered that regiments and corps have different customs and although the above is a reasonable guide it may not always be correct. You are almost certain to enrage someone!

REGIMENTAL HEAD-DRESS

The normal everyday head-dress of NCOs and Soldiers (and in some regiments of all ranks) is the beret or national equivalent. The norm is the dark blue beret. Exceptions are as follows:

a.	Grey Beret	The Royal Scots Dragoon Guards
		Queen Alexandra's Royal Army Nursing Corps
b.	Brown Beret	The King's Royal Hussars
		The Royal Wessex Yeomanry
c.	Khaki Beret	All Regiments of Foot Guards
		The Honourable Artillery Company
		The Royal Anglian Regiment
		The Duke of Lancaster's Regiment
		The Yorkshire Regiment
d.	Black Beret	The Royal Tank Regiment

e.	Rifle Green Beret	The Rifles
		The Brigade of Gurkhas
		Adjutant General's Corps
f.	Maroon Beret	The Parachute Regiment
g.	Beige Beret	The Special Air Service Regiment
h.	Light Blue Beret	The Army Air Corps
i.	Scarlet Beret	Royal Military Police
j.	Cypress Green Beret	The Intelligence Corps

The Royal Regiment of Scotland wear the Tam-O-Shanter (TOS) and the Royal Irish Regiment wear the Corbeen.

THE MOD'S CIVILIAN STAFF

The three uniformed services are supported by the civilian staff of the MoD. At the beginning of 2015 the MoD employed 61,630 civilians, down from 83,000 during early 2010. This is a dramatic fall from the figure of 316,700 civilian personnel who were employed by the MoD in 1980.

During early 2015 MoD some of the areas where civilian staff were employed are as follows:

Navy (Fleet)	2,510
Army (Land Forces)	10,750
RAF (Air Command)	5,140
Joint Forces Command	5,840
Defence Equipment & Support	10.660
Defence Infrastructure Organisation	4,220
Head Office & Corporate Services	7,360
Royal Fleet Auxiliary	1,840
Defence Science & Technology Laboratory	3,660
Defence Support Group	2,410
Locally Engaged Civilians Overseas	6,290 (1)

Notes:

(1) The overwhelming majority of this figure are locally entered civilians supporting BFG (British Forces Germany).

Earlier in the decade the UK MoD stated that " The Department remains committed to a process of civilianisation. Increasingly, it makes no sense to employ expensively trained and highly professional military personnel in jobs which civilians could do equally well. Civilians are generally cheaper than their military counterparts and as they often remain longer in post, can provide greater continuity. For these reasons, it is our long-standing policy to civilianise posts and so release valuable military resources to the front line whenever it makes operational and economic sense to do so".

In general, MoD Civil Servants work in a parallel stream with their respective uniformed counterparts. There are some 'stand alone' civilian agencies of which the QinetiQ is probably the largest.

THE UNITED KINGDOM DEFENCE INDUSTRY

Despite uncertainties over future defence strategy and pressure on defence spending, the United Kingdom's Defence Industry has proved to be a remarkably resilient and successful element of our national manufacturing base.

Despite the rationalisation which is still taking place within the defence sector it is generally accepted that defence employment continues to provide a significant element of the broader UK economy via salaries paid throughout the supply chain.

Historically, the UK defence industry has possessed the capability and competence to provide a wide range of advanced systems and equipment to support our own Armed Forces. This capability, matched with their competitiveness, has enabled UK companies to command a sizeable share of those overseas markets for which export licence approvals are available. At home, UK industry has consistently provided some 75 per cent by value of the equipment requirements of The Ministry of Defence. In simple terms, in recent years UK industry has supplied £9–£10 billion worth of goods and services for our Armed Forces annually while a further £2–4 billion worth of business has accrued to the UK defence industry from sales to approved overseas customers.

The United Kingdom's defence companies are justifiably proud of their record in recent years in the face of fierce overseas competition. Reductions in the UK's Armed Forces and the heavy demands on our remaining Service personnel, who face an unpredictable international security environment, make it inevitable that considerable reliance will be placed upon the support and surge capacity offered by the UK's comprehensive indigenous defence industrial base. Without this effective industrial base, the ability of UK to exert independence of action or influence over collective security arrangements would be constrained. It is essential that government policies ensure that industry retains the necessary capabilities to support our forces in a changing world.

As importantly, the defence industry is not only a major employer but it is also the generator of high technology that is readily adaptable to civilian use in fields such as avionics and engine technology. The future of the UK's defence industry will almost certainly have to be property planned if it to remain an efficient and essential national support organisation in times of crisis. A look at MoD payments to contractors during FY 2009–2010 identifies some of the larger manufacturers.

Major Contractors paid over £500 million in FY 2013–2014 (Listing by Holding Company)
AWE Management Ltd
Agustawestland Ltd
BAE Systems (Operations) Ltd
BAE Systems Marine Ltd
BAE Systems Surface Ships Ltd
Devonport Royal Dockyard Ltd
HP Enterprise Services Defence & Security UK Ltd
NETMA (NATO Eurofighter and Tornado Management Agency)

Note: Payments to the companies listed may include payments made to subsidiaries or contractors.

QINETIQ

(Formerly known as the Defence Evaluation & Research Agency)

From 1 April 1995, the Defence Evaluation & Research Agency (DERA) assumed the responsibilities of its predecessor the Defence Research Agency (DRA). DERA changed its title to QinetiQ on 2 July 2001.

The name QinetiQ has been derived from the scientific term, kinetic (phonetic: ki'ne tik), which means 'relating to or caused by motion'. This in turn comes from the Greek, kinetikos based on 'kineo' which means 'to move'.

Following the 2001 restructuring, certain functions of DERA, encompassing the majority of the organisation's capabilities for defence and security and amounting to approximately three quarters of DERA, were formed into QinetiQ Limited, an entity which is a wholly-owned subsidiary of QinetiQ Group plc. In February 2006 QinetiQ was listed on the London Stock Exchange with a market capitalisation of £1.3 billion.

A quarter of QinetiQ has been retained within the MOD as the Defence Science and Technology Laboratory (DSTL) to manage the research programme and the International Research Collaboration, along with other sensitive areas such as CBD (Chemical & Biological Defence), Porton Down.

The Group employs over 14,000 people of which some 6,400 are in North America, and operates over 40 UK sites with major technology facilities at Farnborough, Boscombe Down and Malvern.

Since 2004 QinetiQ has acquired 13 companies in North America including five during FY 2008–2009 and the company is expanding into Australia.

About 60 per cent of the group's UK employees are graduates and more than 700 hold PhDs. More than half of the employees in the UK are focussed on research, invention, development and application of new technology. There are strategic partnerships with 13 UK universities, and 30 QinetiQ staff have visiting professorships.

QinetiQ is organised into six major operational divisions.

CODEWORDS AND NICKNAMES

A Codeword is a single word used to provide security cover for reference to a particular classified matter, eg 'CORPORATE' was the Codeword for the recovery of the Falklands in 1982. In 1990 'GRANBY' was used to refer to operations in the Gulf and 'Op HERRICK' is used for current UK operations in support of NATO forces in Afghanistan. 'Op ELLAMY' was the Codeword for UK participation in the military intervention in Libya during 2011. A Nickname consists of two words and may be used for reference to an unclassified matter, eg 'Lean Look' referred to an investigation into various military organisations in order to identify savings in manpower.

DATES AND TIMINGS

When referring to timings the British Army uses the 24 hour clock. This means that 2015 hours (pronounced twenty fifteen hours) is in fact 8.15pm. Soldiers usually avoid midnight and refer to 2359 or 0001 hours. Time zones present plenty of scope for confusion! Exercise and Operational times are expressed in Greenwich Mean Time (GMT) which may differ from the local time. The suffix Z (Zulu) denotes GMT and A (Alpha) GMT + 1 hour. B (Bravo) means GMT + 2 hours and so on.

The Date Time Group or DTG can be seen on military documents and is a point of further confusion for many. Using the military DTG 1030 GMT on 20 April 2007 is written as 201030Z APR 07. When the Armed Forces relate a days and hours to operations a simple system is used:

a. D Day is the day an operation begins.
b. H Hour is the hour a specific operation begins.
c. Days and hours can be represented by numbers plus or minus of D Day for planning purposes. Therefore if D Day is 20 April 2016, D-2 is 18 April and D + 2 is 22 April. If H Hour is 0600 hours then H+2 is 0800 hours.

PHONETIC ALPHABET

To ensure minimum confusion during radio or telephone conversations difficult words or names are spelt out letter by letter using the following NATO standard phonetic alphabet.

ALPHA – BRAVO – CHARLIE – DELTA – ECHO – FOXTROT – GOLF – HOTEL-INDIA – JULIET – KILO – LIMA – MIKE – NOVEMBER – OSCAR – PAPA-QUEBEC – ROMEO – SIERRA – TANGO – UNIFORM – VICTOR – WHISKEY – X RAY – YANKEE – ZULU.

THE ROYAL MARINES

The Royal Marines (RM) are specialists in Amphibious Warfare and the personnel total is approximately 7,000 (including 760 officers).

Royal Marine Major Units

Headquarters Royal Marines	(Portsmouth)
HQ 3 Commando Brigade Plymouth	(Stonehouse)
3 Commando Bde HQ & Signal Squadron	(Stonehouse)
3 Commando Bde Air Sqn	(Yeovilton)
30 Commando	(Stonehouse)
40 Commando	(Taunton)
42 Commando	(Plymouth)
43 Commando	(Clyde)
45 Commando	(Arbroath)
Commando Logistic Regiment	(Barnstaple))
539 Assault Sqn Plymouth	(Barnstaple)
Commando Training Centre	(Lympstone)
Royal Marines Stonehouse	(Plymouth)
1 Assault Group	(Poole)

All Royal Marines, except those in the Royal Marines Band Service, are commando soldiers. They are required to undergo a 32 week initial training course at the Commando Training Centre at Lympstone in Devon. The titular head of the Royal Marines is always a Major General – Commandant General Royal Marines (CGRM).

The Royal Marines have small detachments in ships at sea and other units worldwide with widely differing tasks. However, the bulk of the manpower of the Royal Marines is grouped in battalion-sized organisations known as Commandos (Cdo). There are 5 Commando Groups and they are part of a larger formation known as 3 Commando Brigade (3 Cdo Bde).

3 Cdo Bde Commando Organisation

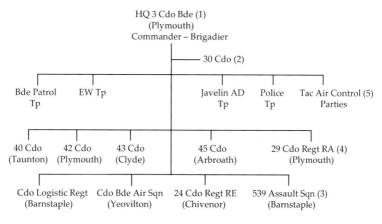

Notes:

(1) For operations expect 3 Commando Brigade to come under the command of the Joint Forces Command (JFC). An RM Commando will have approximately 650 personnel with 4 x manoeuvre companies.

(2) **30 Commando** – Information Exploitation Group is the organisation that provides command, communications, reconnaissance and intelligence capabilities to 3 Commando Brigade.

(3) **539 Assault Squadron** has the personnel that allows troops and equipment from 3 Commando Brigade to land from vessels at sea to the operational areas (mainly beaches) where operations are

to be conducted. 539 Assault Squadron is equipped with hovercraft, landing craft, raiding craft and Viking vehicles.

(4) **29 Cdo Regt RA** has one battery stationed at Arbroath with 45 Cdo.

(5) There are three regular Tactical Air Control Parties and one reserve.

(6) 1st Bn The Royal Netherlands Marine Corps can be part of 3 Cdo Bde for NATO assigned tasks.

43 Commando (Fleet Protection Group)

This specialist Commando group was originally formed in 1980 as Comacchio Group and has the task of guarding the UK's nuclear weapons, and other associated installations from a variety of threats, plus the security of UK oil rigs against terrorist attacks. Personnel are also deployed world-wide on specialist tasks.

During 2001 Comacchio Group was renamed as the Fleet Protection Group Royal Marines (FPGRM) and the unit moved from RM Condor to HMNB Clyde. In 2012 the unit adopted its current name and became part of 3 Commando Brigade.

43 Commando is structured around 3 x rifle squadrons and 1 x headquarters squadron. Personnel strength is in the region of 533 personnel.

1 Assault Group Royal Marines (1 AGRM)

1 AGRM provides the central expertise and training support for Amphibious Warfare and Royal Navy Board and Search Training and is located at Plymouth. A secondary role is the provision of training and advise to allied nations. 1 AGRM has 3 x sub-units:

10 Landing Craft Training Squadron (Poole).
11 Amphibious Trials and Training Squadron (Instow).
School of Board and Search (Torpoint),

Special Boat Service

This organisation is the Naval equivalent of the Army's SAS (Special Air Service). Personnel are all volunteers from the mainstream Royal Marines and vacancies are few with competition for entry fierce.

Generally speaking only about 30 per cent of volunteers manage to complete the entry course and qualify. The SBS specialises in mounting clandestine operations against targets at sea, in rivers or harbours and against occupied coastlines.

The SBS are a part of the UK Special Forces Group – see Chapter 5.

RAF REGIMENT

The need to raise a dedicated specialist force to protect air installations became apparent during WWII when unprotected aircraft on the ground were vulnerable to enemy air and ground attack. Consequently, the RAF Regiment was raised on 1 February 1942. At the end of WWII, there were over 85,000 personnel serving in the RAF Regiment manning 240 operational squadrons. As of 2015, the strength of the RAF Regiment is some around 2,000 airmen with approximately 300 officers and 500 part-time reservists. The Regiment is generally formed into Squadrons of 100 to 150 personnel. Currently the RAF Regiment exists to provide defence for RAF installations, and to train all the RAF's combatant personnel to enable them to contribute to the defence of their units. RAF Regiment units are under the operational command of No 2 Group.

As of late 2015 RAF Regiment Squadrons/units are as follows:

Squadrons & Wings

No 1 Squadron	Honington	Field Squadron
No 2 Squadron	Honington	Field / Parachute Sqn
No 15 Squadron	Honington	Field Squadron
No 34 Squadron	Leeming	Field Squadron
No 51 Squadron	Lossiemouth	Field Squadron
No 63 (QCS)	Uxbridge	Ceremonial / Field Sqn
RAF Regiment Depot	Honington	
RAF Force Protection HQ	Honington	

Specialist RAF Regiment training for gunners is given at the RAF Regiment Depot at Honington. On completion of training at the RAF College Cranwell officers also undergo further specialist training at RAF Honington and, in some cases, the School of Infantry at Warminster in Wiltshire.

The RAF Regiment also mans the Queen's Colour Squadron (QCS) which undertakes all major ceremonial duties for the Royal Air Force. These duties involve mounting the Guard at Buckingham Palace on an occasional basis, and providing Guards of Honour for visiting Heads of State. The Queen's Colour Squadron also has a war role as a field squadron.

The regiment is not alone in defending any RAF station. Every airman based at a station has a ground defence role and is trained to defend his place of work against ground attack and attack by NBC weapons. Training for this is given by RAF Regiment instructors who provide courses at station level for all personnel on various aspects of ground defence.

RAF Force Protection Wings

The former Survive to Operate HQ were restructured in 2006 to become rapidly deployable RAF Force Protection Wings (FPWs). The units integrated elements of the RAF Regiment, RAF Police, Intelligence and Support to deliver a full range of capability from policing and security (including dogs) to close combat. RAF FPWs have been extremely active in Afghanistan.

There are RAF Force Protection Wings at:

No 2 Force Protection Wing – RAF Leeming
No 3 Force Protection Wing – RAF Marham
No 5 Force Protection Wing – RAF Lossiemouth
No 7 Force Protection Wing – RAF Coningsby

No 20 Wing RAF Regiment

No 20 Wing at RAF Honnington is responsible for the Defence CBRN Wing. This organisation provides the CBRN (Chemical, biological, radiological and nuclear) reconnaissance, monitoring, detection and decontamination support required by the three armed services, and where necessary the civilian authorities. 20 Wing has two squadrons:

No 26 Squadron	Honington
No 27 Squadron	Honington

OPERATION BANNER – NORTHERN IRELAND

The 1st Bn The Prince of Wales' Own Regiment was the first unit to be deployed in Northern Ireland in August 1969 closely followed by The 1st Bn The Royal Green Jackets.

During the worst period of The Troubles between 1972 and 1973, 27,000 military personnel were stationed in Northern Ireland, the majority of them Army. These military personnel were supported by over 13,000 personnel from the Royal Ulster Constabulary.

Over the course of Operation Banner, 763 servicemen and women were killed as a direct result of terrorism. This includes 651 Army and Royal Marine personnel; one Royal Naval Serviceman; 50 members of the former Ulster Defence Regiment and later Royal Irish Regiment; 10 members of the Territorial Army and 51 military personnel were murdered outside Northern Ireland. Some 6,116 members of the Army and Royal Marines were wounded over the period.

At one stage there were 106 military bases or locations in Northern Ireland, however, following the first Provisional IRA cease-fire in September 1994, 80 per cent of these were closed. The closure of the bases was accelerated after the Good Friday Agreement of April 1998.

The process of steadily reducing military presence began on 1 August 2005 and Operation Banner officially ended on 31 July 2007. It was superseded on 1 August 2007 by Operation Helvetic, a garrison of no more than 5,000 military personnel in 10 locations, trained and ready for deployment worldwide.

The names of the UK service personnel who lost their lives during Operation Banner are listed on the Armed Forces Memorial, Staffordshire. The Memorial, which opened to the public in October 2007, remembers all those killed on duty in conflicts or on training exercises, by terrorist action or on peacekeeping missions – www.forcesmemorial.org

UK ARMED FORCES – FATAL CASUALTIES SINCE 1945

Korea: 765
Northern Ireland: 763 (1)
Malaya: 340
The Falklands: 255
Palestine: 784 (2)
Iraq 2003–2009: 179
Cyprus: 105
Aden: 68
Egypt: 54
Balkans: 48
The Gulf 1990: 47
Yangtse River: 46
Oman & Dhofar: 24
Suez: 22
Borneo: 126
Kenya: 12
Sierra Leone: 1

Notes:

(1) Figure for Northern Ireland includes military deaths on the UK mainland and Germany attributed to Irish terrorism). In 1972 171 service personnel were killed.
(2) Source Commonwealth War Graves Commission. The figure includes service personnel deaths by accident in theatre – about 80 per cent were killed in action and does not include deaths of members of the Palestinian Police.
(3) As of late 2015 a total of 453 UK Service personnel had been killed in Afghanistan since October 2001 as a result of enemy action. Operation Enduring Freedom continues with about 500 UK personnel involved in training.

HONOURS AND AWARDS

The following lists the hierarchy of gallantry, leadership and bravery awards for active operations (in the presence of the enemy):

Level 1	Victoria Cross (VC)		
Level 2	Distinguished Service Order (DSO) (for command and leadership)		Conspicuous Gallantry Cross (CGC) (for gallantry)
Level 3	Distinguished Service Cross (DSC) (at sea)	Military Cross (MC) (on land)	Distinguished Flying Cross (DFC) (in the air)
Level 4	Mention in Despatches (for bravery, no post-nominal)		

The hierarchy of gallantry and bravery awards for non-active operations (not in presence of the enemy):

Level 1	George Cross (GC)	
Level 2	George Medal (GM)	
Level 3	Queens's Gallantry Medal (QGM)	Air Force Cross (AFC)
Level 4	Queen's Commendation for Bravery (both for bravery, no post-nominal)	Queen's Commendation for Bravery in the Air

All awards, except for membership of Orders, can be given posthumously.

MAJOR ARMY CHARITIES

ABF – The Soldiers Charity

The Soldiers' Charity provides lifetime support to serving and retired soldiers and their families in times of need. The charity gives about half of the money donated to individuals with the remainder being given as grants to other charities.

Much of the support provided by the ABF falls into the following categories:

Annuities: Supporting service widows living alone and the income of older veterans living on basic pensions.

Bursaries: Helping with education and training including: funding for training colleges that help retrain soldiers with disabilities and training course fees and essential items for individual soldiers Support for ex-soldiers taking higher education courses to start on new careers after leaving the Army and providing assistance with funding for continuing education for the children of soldiers who have died or been severely disabled in service.

Care home fees: when local authority grants are insufficient providing modest top-up grants to help with cost of fees for older veterans or their widows.

General needs: Grants are made for a wide variety of purposes when there is a clear need that cannot be met from other sources – approximately one in five of these grants are made towards mobility aids such as wheelchairs, stairlifts, special beds etc.

Holiday schemes: Every year as many as 200 families benefit from short breaks at Pontins and Warner holiday resorts. In addition there is an annual grant to the Guild of St Helena that allows service children with special needs to have a holiday.

Special funds: The ABF administers special funds to assist soldiers who have been injured during active service in Northern Ireland, the Falklands Islands or The Gulf War. Dependants of those killed in these campaigns may also qualify for help from the funds. The George Purse Trust provides grants to those who live in South Wales and are in need of respite care.

Current operations fund: This was launched in 2007 and supports soldiers injured or families of those killed as a result of their service during the operations in Iraq and Afghanistan. The Fund was set up as a direct response to the mounting numbers of serving soldiers and their families in great need who require immediate help. The grants cover everything from retraining a disabled soldier for a new career to providing holiday funds for a war widow and her children.

Contact Details:
Email: info@soldierscharity.org
Tel: 020-7901-8900

Help for Heroes (H4H)
The Help for Heroes mission is to deliver an enduring national network of support for wounded UK service personnel and their families, inspiring those who have made sacrifices on our behalf to achieve their full potential. Although combat operations in Afghanistan are over, for those who have suffered life-changing injuries, their battles are continuing.

Help for Heroes estimate that of the 220,560 individuals deployed to Afghanistan and Iraq between 2001 and 2014, up to 75,000 servicemen and women (and their families) may need support in the future. Help for Heroes are determined to ensure that they will not let them fight these battles alone.

In the main the charity raises funds through supporters organising special events that range from a cake sale to a marathon cycle ride or an exotic trek. Major activities include running recovery centres at Tidworth, Catterick, Colchester and Plymouth plus major involvement in the UK MoD's Battle Back Programme.

Help for Heroes also supports a wide range of other service charities.

Contact Details:
Telephone: 01980 844 280
Email: bandofbrothers@helpforheroes.org.uk / bandofsisters@helpforheroes.org.uk

Blind Veterans UK
Blind Veterans UK provide veterans much-needed support to adjust to sight loss, overcome the challenges of blindness and make the best of daily life. Blind Veterans UK provides blind veterans with training and rehabilitation, a safe and happy home in which to live, support for them and their families and a life after blindness.

Blind Veterans UK (formerly St Dunstans) was established in 1915 by Sir Arthur Pearson, who owned the *Evening Standard* and founded the *Daily Express* to care for personnel who had lost their vision in the First World War. Today Blind Veterans UK not only cares for ex-Service men and women blinded in action, but for veterans who have lost their sight through accident, illness or old age. There are three centres (in Brighton, Llandudno and Sheffield) that provide residential and respite care plus sports facilities, as well as qualified welfare staff who help blind veterans across the UK to live independently within their own communities.

Contact Details:
Telephone: 020 7723 5021
Fax: 020 7262 6199

The Veterans Charity (VC)
The Veterans Charity was founded in 2008 and focuses on providing fast, direct support to veterans of all generations who may be facing hardship and or crisis. The charity provides items like food shopping, clothing, basic furniture and household items and also helps with TVs, mobile phones, laptops and mobility/living aids – all of which can have a lasting and very positive effect on the well-being of beneficiaries.

The charity focuses on providing these essential items in the shortest possible time, ensuring that Veterans get the support they need when they need it most. The average turn-around time is just a few days and in many urgent cases, VC is able to get vital items like food delivered the next day.

VC receives referrals from government departments, welfare providers, care homes, housing centres and many other charities and also works hard to signpost veterans to other charities in cases where VC is unable to assist.

Contact Details:
Telephone: 01753 653772

British Limbless Ex-Service Men's Association (BLESMA)

Blesma is a national charity that directly supports all of our Service men and women who have lost limbs or the use of limbs or the loss of eyesight in the service of the United Kingdom. The charity understand the needs of a military amputee like no other national charity in the United Kingdom. Formerly known as The British Limbless Ex-Service Men's Association, BLESMA has existed in one guise or another since the First World War and have continued to support veterans ever since.

Blesma also exists to empower and promote the welfare and wellbeing of all serving and ex-service men and women who may have rehabilitative requirements post limb loss. The charity is also committed to supporting surviving partners and dependants of deceased military personnel.

BLESMA has also lobbied successive governments to achieve improvements in pensions, in standards of artificial limbs and in the provision of suitable transport and employment opportunities. Residential homes have been opened, wide ranging health and well-being services initiated, sporting activities undertaken and innovative research commissioned, all helped by the ceaseless fund-raising activities of associated members and supporters.

Contact Details:
Telephone: 020 8590 1124
Fax: 020 8599 2932
Email: ChadwellHeath@blesma.org

Combat Stress

Combat Stress is the UK's leading Veterans' mental health charity and is currently supporting over 5,000 veterans aged from 19 to 97. The mission of Combat Stress is to provide timely, effective clinical treatment and welfare support to Veterans who suffer from psychological wounds. The charity is a vital lifeline for these men and women, and their families who are in need of support with treatment and other support services provided free of charge.

Combat Stress currently spends over £15 million per annum delivering its unique range of specialist treatment and welfare support.

Telephone: 0800 138 1619 (24-hour Helpline for Veterans, serving personnel, and their families)

The Royal British Legion (RBL)

A major tri-service charity, The Royal British Legion helps the whole of the Armed Forces' community through welfare, comradeship and representation as well as being the Nation's custodian of Remembrance.

The RBL provides practical care, advice and support to the whole of the Armed Forces family all year round. Although welfare is at the heart of everything the RBL does, the charity works with all political parties, campaigning to improve the lives of all Service people - past, present and future.

The Royal British Legion is one of the UK's largest membership organisations with over 300,000 members.

Contact Details:
Telephone: 0808 802 8080

CENTRE FOR DEFENCE ENTERPRISE (CDE)

The Centre for Defence Enterprise (CDE) is a part of the Defence Science and Technology Laboratory (Dstl) and funds innovative research that could lead to a cost-effective capability advantage for UK armed forces and national security.

The CDE seeks applications for funding from small companies, academia and any individuals with a brilliant idea that has a potential defence application. CDE investments in science and technology research are high risk but always have a high potential benefit. CDE has a small staff based at Harwell in Oxfordshire and is aligned with the UK Government's Small Business Research Initiative.

CDE's major priorities are amongst the following:

◆ Extend CDE's reach to new small and medium sized companies with innovative ideas.
◆ Hold regular competitions to address specific defence and security challenges.
◆ Promote the monthly enduring challenge competition to address the most important problems in defence.
◆ Improve the routes to commercialisation following initial CDE proof-of-concept funding.
◆ Introduce a new, improved online portal for proposal submissions.

Contact:
Email: cde@dstl.gov.uk
Telephone: +44 (0)30 67704236

SOME UNUSUAL BRITISH OFFICERS

Lieutenant General Adrian Carton de Wiart VC, sacrificed many of his body parts in battle. He lost an eye fighting the "mad mullah" of Somaliland, was shot in the face, skull, stomach, ankle, leg, hip and ear and lost a hand. During World War One he was severely wounded on eight occasions, mentioned in despatches six times and won a VC commanding 8th Battalion, Gloucestershire Regiment on the Somme.

As a POW in the Second World War Carton de Wiart made five escape attempts, tunnelling out with his one arm. His only real fear, which surfaced when he was obliged to wear plain clothes following an escape attempt in Italy, was of Italian tailoring. He only finally agreed to a local suit "provided he did not resemble a gigolo".

Lieutenant Jack Churchill, DSO & Bar and MC & Bar, known as "Mad Jack" enjoyed his war and preferred to fight the Nazis with medieval weaponry. He was fond of saying, "Any officer who goes into action without his sword is improperly dressed." Throughout the Second World War he armed himself with a basket-hilted Scottish broadsword and as an accomplished archer he claimed the last recorded bow and arrow kill in action, shooting a German soldier in 1940.

As the ramps fell on the first landing craft in the invasion of Sicily, Churchill leapt forward playing "March Of The Cameron Men" on his bagpipes, broadsword sword slung around his waist, a longbow and quiver of arrows around his neck.

"If it wasn't for those damn Yanks we could have kept the war going another 10 years," he later regretted.

In 1944 Major Digby Tatham-Warter won the DSO commanding a company of 2 Para at Arnhem. when he led a bayonet charge wearing a bowler hat and carrying an umbrella. When he was told that it would be useless against German fire he replied "But what if it rains".

(The editor would be grateful for other stories relating to unusual British officers or soldiers – charles. heyman@yahoo.co.uk).

QUOTATIONS

Young officers and NCOs may find some of these quotations useful on briefings etc: There are two groups – Military and General.

Military

"The more ambitious the plans – the more god laughs".

Anon

General Tommy Franks head of the US Central Command in 2003, told a Defence Secretary (during planning for the invasion of Iraq) "I'll pay attention to the day and you pay attention to the day after".

The idea that the Iraqi Army – trained and equipped by the US to the tune of $17 billion – needs to be 'retrained' is absurd. It deserted en masse because it wasn't being paid, was badly led and badly supplied.

Roger Boyes – The Times 22 October 2014

"It's not the bullet that's got my name on it that concerns me; it's all them other ones flyin' around marked 'To Whom It May Concern.'"

Rifleman – Afghanistan 2011

"Young officers are always taught that the first battle they will fight is that for the respect of their men."

Anon

"Never be sad about becoming an old soldier – there are thousands who wished they had the chance."

Anon

"You build a better mousetrap and all you get is smarter mice".

Matt Scudder (fictional American private investigator)

"You may not be interested in war, but war is interested in you."

Leon Trotsky – 1879–1940

"All warfare Is based on deception."

Sun Tzu – about 600 BC

"Tactics without Strategy is just noise before defeat."

Sun-Tzu – about 600 BC

"Any government has as much of a duty to avoid war as a ship's captain as to avoid a shipwreck."

Guy de Maupassant 1850–1893

"The human factor will decide the fate of war, of all wars. Not the Mirage, nor any other plane, and not the screwdriver, or the wrench or radar or missiles or all the newest technology and electronic innovations. Men – and not just men of action, but men of thought. Men for whom the expression 'By ruses shall ye make war' is a philosophy of life, not just the object of lip service."

Israeli Air Force Commander Ezer Weizman 1924–2005

"It is the soldier, not the priest, who protects freedom of religion; the soldier, not the journalist, who protects freedom of speech. History teaches that a society that does not value its warriors will be destroyed by a society that does."

Jack Kelly (US Columnist for the Pittsburg Post Gazette 2004)

"Anyone wanting to commit American ground forces to the mainland of Asia should have his head examined."

General Douglas MacArthur 1880–1964

"They used to say professionals talk logistics and then tactics. Today, real professionals talk command, control and communications, then logistics and after that tactics."

General Sir David Richards to the House of Commons Defence Committee (February 2009)

"In 1920 King Amunullah of Afghanistan made a state visit to London. As his coach rolled down The Mall towards Buckingham Palace two Cockney bystanders watched proceedings:

First Cockney: 'ose that in the coach then?
Second Cockney: Its the King of Arfghanistan!
First Cockney: 'ose the King of the other Arf then?"

"Having lost sight of our objectives we need to redouble our efforts."

Anon

"During the Second World War Air Marshal Sir Arthur (Bomber) Harris was well known for his glorious capacity for rudeness, particularly to bureaucrats. "What are you doing to retard the war effort today" was his standard greeting to senior civil servants."

"The military value of a partisan's work is not measured by the amount of property destroyed, or the number of men killed or captured, but the number he keeps watching."

Confederate Cavalry Leader – John Singleton Mosby 1833-1916

"It is foolish to hunt the tiger when there are plenty of sheep around."

Al Qaeda Training Manual 2002

"Information is something that you do something with. Data is something that just makes officers feel good! I keep telling them but nobody listens to me."

US Army Intelligence specialist – CENTCOM Qatar 2003

"If you torture data sufficiently it will confess to almost anything."

Fred Menger – Chemistry Professor (1937–)

"If you tell someone what needs doing, as opposed to how to do it, they will surprise you with their ingenuity."

General Patton 1885–1945

"More delusion as a solution."

US State Department Official – Baghdad March 2005

"If you claim to understand what is happening in Iraq you haven't been properly briefed."

British Staff Officer at Coalition HQ 2004

"If you can keep your head when all about you are losing theirs and blaming it on you – you'll be a man my son."

Rudyard Kipling 1865–1936

"If you can keep your head when all about you are losing theirs – you may have missed something very important."

Royal Marine – Bagram Airfield 2002

"Admiral King commanded the US Navy during the Second World War. His daughter wrote – "He was the most even tempered man I ever met – he was always in a rage. In addition, he believed that civilians should be told nothing about a war until it was over and then only who won. Nothing more!"

"We trained very hard, but it seemed that every time we were beginning to form up in teams, we would be reorganised. I was to learn in later life that we tend to meet any new situation by reorganising, and a wonderful method it can be for creating an illusion of progress, while producing confusion, inefficiency and demoralisation."

Caius Petronius 66 AD

"The beatings will continue until morale improves."

Attributed to the Commander of the Japanese Submarine Force in 1944

"When other Generals make mistakes their armies are beaten; when I get into a hole, my men pull me out of it."

The Duke of Wellington 1759–1852

"Take short views, hope for the best and trust in God."

Sir Sydney Smith 1764–1840

"There is no beating these troops in spite of their generals. I always thought them bad soldiers, now I am sure of it. I turned their right, pierced their centre, broke them everywhere; the day was mine, and yet they did not know it and would not run."

Marshal Soult 1769–1851 (French Army) – Commenting on the British Infantry at Albuhera in 1811

"More powerful than the march of mighty armies is an idea whose time has come."

Victor Hugo 1802–1885

"Its always best to leave a party before the fight starts."

John Sergeant – 19 November 2008

"What experience and history teach us is this – that people and governments have never learned anything from history, or acted upon any lessons they might have drawn from it."

Georg Hegel 1770–1831

"Better ten years of repression than one night of mob mayhem."

Old Muslim proverb

"Why plan when panicking is so much more fun."

UN administrator in the Congo during 2006 when pressed for his lack of planning for an imminent operation

"You can get a lot more done with a kind word and a gun than you can with a kind word alone."

Attributed to Al Capone

"This is just something to be got round – like a bit of flak on the way to the target."
Group Captain Leonard Cheshire VC 1917–1992 – Speaking of his incurable illness in the week before he died.

"Pale Ebenezer thought it wrong to fight,
But roaring Bill, who killed him, thought it right."

Hiliare Belloc 1873–1952

"Everyone wants peace – and they will fight the most terrible war to get it."

Miles Kington – BBC Radio 4th February 1995

"War is a competition of incompetence – the least incompetent usually win."

General AAK Niazi (Pakistan) – after losing Bangladesh in 1971

"In war the outcome corresponds to expectations less than in any other activity."

Titus Livy 59 BC – 17AD

"Nothing is so good for the morale of the troops as occasionally to see a dead general."

Field Marshal Slim 1891–1970

"It makes no difference which side the general is on."

Unknown British Soldier

"The only time in his life that he ever put up a fight was when we asked for his resignation."

A comment from one of his staff officers following French General Joffre's resignation in 1916

"How can the enemy anticipate us when we haven't got a clue what we are doing?"

Pte Thomas Atkins (Basrah 2006)

"Never disturb your enemy while he is making a mistake."
Mrs Saatchi explained her 12 month silence after her husband started living with Nigela Lawson by quoting Napoleon's dictum

General Quotes
"Out of everything I've lost, I miss my mind the most!"

Ozzy Osbourne

"I believe that most of the world's problems can be solved by dancing."

James Brown (American singer 1933–2006)

While canvassing in Plymouth in 1919, Lady Astor (one of the first women to be elected to Parliament) was accompanied by a naval officer in uniform (some say a Rear Admiral). They knocked on the door of a rather run-down house and were greeted at the door by a young girl whose mother had gone shopping. The girl said that before her mother left home, she said that "if a lady comes with a sailor they're to use the upstairs room and leave ten bob on the bed". (Ten bob is 50 pence today).

My entire life can be described in one sentence. It didn't go entirely as planned and that's okay!

Peanuts (Charles Schulz 1922 –2000)

"All rumours are true, especially when your boss denies them."

Dogbert – Build a better life by stealing office supplies

"If a miracle occurs and your boss finally completes your performance appraisal, it will be hastily prepared, annoyingly vague and an insult to whatever dignity you still possess."

Dogbert – Clues for the clueless

"Put all your friends in private offices and all of your wretched slaves in open plan offices".

Roman General Dogbertius Dilbert – Thriving on vague objectives

"Don't worry about people stealing an idea. If it's original you will have to ram it down their throats."
Howard Aiken 1900–1973 (Howard Aiken completed the Harvard Mark II, a completely electronic computer, in 1947)

Homer Simpson's advice to his son Bart:
Homer to Bart: "These three little sentences will get you through life":

Number 1: "Oh, good idea boss".
Number 2: (whispers) "Cover for me".
Number 3: "It was like that when I got here".

"Democracy means government by the uneducated, while aristocracy means government by the badly educated.

GK Chesterton 1874–1936

Quite a lot of people will be relived to know that jellyfish have survived for about 650 million years despite having no brain.

Anon

"From the naturalistic point of view, all men are equal. There are only two exceptions to this rule of naturalistic equality: geniuses and idiots".

Mikhail Bakunin 1814–1876

"The greatest evil is not done in those sordid dens of evil that Dickens loved to paint ... but is conceived and ordered (moved, seconded, carried, and minuted) in clear, carpeted, warmed, well-lighted offices, by quiet men with white collars and cut fingernails and smooth-shaven cheeks who do not need to raise their voices. We should remember that...Evil flourishes where good men do nothing".

CS Lewis 1898–1963

'We're menaced by what I might call 'Fabio-Fascism', by the dictator-spirit working away quietly behind the facade of constitutional forms, passing a little law here, endorsing a departmental tyranny there, emphasizing the national need for secrecy elsewhere, and whispering and cooing the so-called 'news' every evening over the (BBC) radio, until opposition is tamed and gulled.'

EM Forster 1879–1970

"The incompetent always present themselves as experts, the cruel as pious, sinners as excessively devout, usurious as benefactors, the small minded as patriots, the arrogant as humble, the vulgar as elegant and the feebleminded as intellectual.

Carlos Ruiz Zafon – (from The Angels Game 2006)

"Tell the truth and run".

Old Yugoslav Proverb

"One of the great things about books is sometimes there are some fantastic pictures."

Attributed to US President George W Bush 3 January 2000

"The credit belongs to one who strives valiantly and errs often, because there is no effort without error or shortcoming. Even if such a person fails, he fails while daring greatly, so his place shall never be with those cold and timid souls who know neither victory nor defeat".

US President Theodore Roosevelt (1858–1919)

"All you need in this life is ignorance and confidence. Success is then assured."

Marl Twain 1835–1910

"In this country nobody really seems to know anything about anything anymore".

From the New York Times during the financial crisis of September 2008

"Avoid 'toxic colleagues' who stop you doing your job by whinging and complaining and diverting you from getting things done. Keep away from people who try to belittle your ambition. Small people always do that, but the really great make you feel that you too, can achieve something great".

Mark Twain 1835–1910

"The more corrupt a state; the more numerous its laws"

Tacitus AD 89

"Clear language, reflects clear thought."

George Orwell (1903–1950)

"It's like the old hooker said. I really enjoy the work – it's the stairs that are getting me down"

Elaine Stritch – Actress 2003

"The primary function of management is to create the chaos that only management can sort out. A secondary function is the expensive redecoration and refurnishing of offices, especially in times of the utmost financial stringency".

Theodore Dalrymple 'The Spectator' 6 November 1993.

"Success is generally 90% persistence".

Anon

"It is only worthless men who seek to excuse the deterioration of their character by pleading neglect in their early years".

Plutarch – Life of Coriolanus – Approx AD 80

"They say hard work never hurt anybody, but I figured why take the chance".

US President Ronald Regan 1911–2004

"To applaud as loudly as that for so stupid a proposal means that you are just trying to fill that gap between your ears".

David Starkey – BBC Radio 4 (Feb 1995)

"Ah, these diplomats! What chatterboxes! There's only one way to shut them up – cut them down with machine guns. Bulganin, go and get me one!"

Joseph Stalin 1878–1953 – As reported by De Gaulle during a long meeting

"Whenever I hear about a wave of public indignation I am filled with a massive calm".

Matthew Parris – The Times 24th October 1994

"It is a general popular error to imagine that the loudest complainers for the public to be the most anxious for its welfare."

Edmund Burke 1729–1797

"The men who really believe in themselves are all in lunatic asylums."

GK Chesterton 1874–1936

"What all the wise men promised has not happened and what all the dammed fools said would happen has come to pass".

Lord Melbourne 1779–1848

"Awards are like haemorrhoids: in the end every asshole gets one".

Frederick Raphae (author born 1931)

"When we have finally stirred ourselves to hang them all, I hope that our next step will be to outlaw political parties outside Parliament on the grounds that, like amusement arcades, they attract the least desirable members of our society."

Auberon Waugh 1939–2001 (in The Spectator 1984)

EXTRACTS FROM OFFICER'S ANNUAL CONFIDENTIAL REPORTS

"Works well when under constant supervision and cornered like a rat in a trap."

"He has the wisdom of youth, and the energy of old age."

"This Officer should go far – and the sooner he starts, the better."

"This officer is depriving a village somewhere of its idiot."

"Only occasionally wets himself under pressure."

"When she opens her mouth, it seems that this is only to change whichever foot was previously in there."

"He has carried out each and every one of his duties to his entire satisfaction."

"He would be out of his depth in a car park puddle."

"This young man has delusions of adequacy."

"When he joined my ship, this Officer was something of a granny; since then he has aged considerably."

"This Medical Officer has used my ship to carry his genitals from port to port, and my officers to carry him from bar to bar."

"Since my last report he has reached rock bottom, and has started to dig."

"She sets low personal standards and then consistently fails to achieve them."

"His men would follow him anywhere, but only out of curiosity."

"This officer has the astonishing ability to provoke something close to a mutiny every time he opens his mouth".

"His mother should have thrown him away and kept the stork".

"I cannot believe that out of 10,000 sperm his was the fastest".

"The most complimentary thing that I can say about this officer is that he is unbearable".

Finally
Drill instructor to an embarrassed officer cadet who appears to be completely incapable of identifying left from right – "Tell me Sir, as an outsider, what is your opinion of the human race?

Overheard at the RMA Sandhurst

EXTRACTS FROM THE DEVILS DICTIONARY 1911

Accuracy: A certain uninteresting quality generally excluded from human statements.

Armour: The kind of clothing worn by a man whose tailor is a blacksmith.

Colonel: The most gorgeously apparelled man in a regiment.

Education: That which discloses to the wise and disguised from the foolish their lack of understanding.

Enemy: A designing scoundrel who has done you some service which it is inconvenient to repay.

Foe: A person instigated by his wicked nature to deny one's merits or exhibit superior merits of his own.

Foreigner: A villain regarded with various degrees of toleration, according to his conformity to the eternal standard of our conceit and the shifting ones of our interest.

Freedom: A political condition that every nation supposes itself to enjoy in virtual monopoly.

Friendless: Having no favour to bestow. Destitute of fortune. Addicted to utterance of truth and common sense.

Man: An animal so lost in rapturous contemplation of what he thinks he is as to overlook what he ought to be. His chief occupation is the extermination of other animals and his own species,

Overwork: A dangerous disorder affecting high public functionaries who want to go fishing.

Peace: In international affairs a period of cheating between two periods of fighting.

Plunder: To wrest the wealth of A from B and leave C lamenting a vanished opportunity.

Republic: A form of government in which equal justice is available to all who can afford to pay for it.

Resign: A good thing to do when you are going to be kicked out.

Revelation: Discovering late in life that you are a fool.

Robber: Vulgar name for one who is successful in obtaining the property of others.

Zeal: A certain nervous disorder affecting the young and inexperienced.

ABBREVIATIONS

The following is a selection from the list of standard military abbreviations and should assist users of this handbook.

AWOL	Absent without leave
ACE	Allied Command Europe
Adjt	Adjutant
AD	Air Defence/Air Dispatch/Army Department
ADA	Air Defended Area
ADP	Automatic Data Processing
AFCENT	Allied Forces Central European Theatre
AIFV	Armoured Infantry Fighting Vehicle
Airmob	Airmobile
ATAF	Allied Tactical Air Force
armd	Armoured
ACV	Armoured Command Vehicle
AFV	Armoured Fighting Vehicle
AMF(L)	Allied Mobile Force (Land Element)
APC	Armoured Personnel Carrier
APDS	Armour Piercing Discarding Sabot
ARV	Armoured Recovery Vehicle
AVLB	Armoured Vehicle Launched Bridge
AP	Armour Piercing/Ammunition Point/Air Publication
APO	Army Post Office
ARRC	Allied Rapid Reaction Corps
ATGW	Anti Tank Guided Weapon
ATWM	Army Transition to War Measure
BE	Belgium (Belgian)
BEF	British Expeditionary Force (France – 1914)
BGHQ	Battlegroup Headquarters
bn	Battalion
bty	Battery
BG	Battle Group
bde	Brigade
BAOR	British Army of the Rhine
BFG	British Forces Germany
BFPO	British Forces Post Office
BMH	British Military Hospital
C3I	Command, Control, Communications & Intelligence.
CCP	Casualty Collecting Post
CCS	Casualty Clearing Station
CASEVAC	Casualty Evacuation
CAD	Central Ammunition Depot
CEP	Circular Error Probable/Central Engineer Park
CEPS	Central European Pipeline System
CET	Combat Engineer Tractor
CGS	Chief of the General Staff
CinC	Commander in Chief
CIMIC	Civil Military Co-operation
CIS	Communications and Information Systems
CLF	Commander Land Forces

CLV	Command and Liaison Vehicle
COMMS Z	Communications Zone
CVD	Central Vehicle Depot
CW	Chemical Warfare
COS	Chief of Staff
CP	Close Protection/Command Post
CAP	Combat Air Patrol
CV	Combat Vehicles
CVR(T) or (W)	Combat Vehicle Reconnaissance Tracked or Wheeled
CinC	Commander in Chief
CPO	Command Pay Office/Chief Petty Officer
CO	Commanding Officer
coy	Company
CQMS	Company Quartermaster Sergeant
COMSEN	Communications Centre
CCM	Counter Counter Measure
DAA	Divisional Administrative Area
DF	Defensive Fire
DPA	Defence Planning Assumptions
DK	Denmark
DISTAFF	Directing Staff (DS)
DAA	Divisional Administrative Area
DMA	Divisional Maintenance Area
DS	Direct Support/Dressing Station
DTG	Date Time Group
ECAB	Executive Committee of the Army Board
ECCM	Electronic Counter Measure
EDP	Emergency Defence Plan
EME	Electrical and Mechanical Engineers
EMP	Electro Magnetic Pulse
engr	Engineer
EOD	Explosive Ordnance Disposal
ETA	Estimated Time of Arrival
EW	Early Warning/Electronic Warfare
FRG	Federal Republic of Germany
FGA	Fighter Ground Attack
FUP	Forming Up Point
FAC	Forward Air Controller
FEBA	Forward Edge of the Battle Area
FLET	Forward Location Enemy Troops
FLOT	Forward Location Own Troops
FOO	Forward Observation Officer
FR	France (French)
FRT	Forward Repair Team
FUP	Forming Up Place
GDP	General Defence Plan
GE	German (Germany)
GR	Greece (Greek)
GOC	General Officer Commanding
GPMG	General Purpose Machine Gun
HAC	Honourable Artillery Company

HE	High Explosive
HEAT	High Explosive Anti Tank
HESH	High Explosive Squash Head
HVM	Hyper Velocity Missile
IFF	Identification Friend or Foe
II	Image Intensifier
IGB	Inner German Border
IO	Intelligence Officer
INTSUM	Intelligence Summary
ISTAR	Intelligence, Surveillance, Target Acquisition and Reconnaissance
IRG	Immediate Replenishment Group
IR	Individual Reservist
IS	Internal Security
ISAF	International Security Assistance Force (Kabul)
ISD	In Service Date
IT	Italy (Italian)
IW	Individual Weapon
JFHQ	Joint Force Headquarters
JHQ	Joint Headquarters
JSSU	Joint Services Signals Unit
KFOR	Kosovo Force (NATO in Kosovo)
LAD	Light Aid Detachment (REME)
L of C	Lines of Communication
LLAD	Low Level Air Defence
LO	Liaison Officer
LML	Light Mobile Launcher
LRATGW	Long Range Anti Tank Guided Weapon
LSW	Light Support Weapon
MAOT	Mobile Air Operations Team
MBT	Main Battle Tank
MFC	Mortar Fire Controller
MNAD	Multi National Airmobile Division
NE	Netherlands
MO	Medical Officer
MP	Military Police
MPSC	Military Provost Staff Corps
MOD	Ministry of Defence
MT	Military Tasks
MV	Military Vigilance
NAAFI	Navy, Army and Air Force Institutes
NADGE	NATO Air Defence Ground Environment
NATO	North Atlantic Treaty Organisation
NBC	Nuclear and Chemical Warfare
NCO	Non Commissioned Officer
NL	Netherlands
NO	Norway (Norwegian)
NOK	Next of Kin
NORTHAG	Northern Army Group
NRF	NATO Reaction Force
NSC	National Security Council
NTR	Nothing to Report

NYK	Not Yet Known
OP	Observation Post
OC	Officer Commanding
OCU	Operational Conversion Unit (RAF)
OIC	Officer in Charge
OOTW	Operations Other Than War
ORBAT	Order of Battle
POL	Petrol, Oil and Lubricants
PJHQ	Permanent Joint Head Quarters
PO	Portugal (Portuguese)
PPV	Protected Patrol Vehicle
PUS	Permanent Under Secretary
QGE	Queens Gurkha Engineers
QM	Quartermaster
(R)	Reserve Unit
RAP	Rocket Assisted Projectile/Regimental Aid Post
RJDF	Rapid Joint Deployment Force
RTM	Ready to Move
RCZ	Rear Combat Zone
R & D	Research and Development
Regt	Regiment
RHQ	Regimental Headquarters
RMA	Rear Maintenance Area/Royal Military Academy
RSA	Royal School of Artillery
RSME	Royal School of Mechanical Engineering
RTU	Return to Unit
SACUER	Supreme Allied Commander Europe
SATCOM	Satellite Communications
SDSR	Strategic Defence and Security Review
SFOR	Stabilisation Force (NATO in Bosnia)
2IC	Second in Command
SH	Support Helicopters
SHAPE	Supreme Headquarters Allied Powers Europe
SITREP	Situation Report
SIB	Special Investigation Branch
SMG	Sub Machine Gun
SLR	Self Loading Rifle
SMG	Sub Machine Gun
SNCO	Senior Non Commissioned Officer
SP	Spain (Spanish)
Sqn	Squadron
SP	Self Propelled/Start Point
SSM	Surface to Surface Missile
SSVC	Services Sound and Vision Corporation
STA	Surveillance and Target Acquisition
STOL	Short Take Off and Landing
TOT	Time on Target
TCP	Traffic Control Post
tp	Troop
TCV	Troop Carrying Vehicle
TLB	Top Level Budget

TU	Turkish (Turkey)
TUL	Truck Utility Light
TUM	Truck Utility Medium
UAV	Unmanned Air Vehicle
UCAV	Unmanned Combat Air Vehicle
UK	United Kingdom
UKMF	United Kingdom Mobile Force
UNCLASS	Unclassified
UNPROFOR	United Nations Protection Force
UXB	Unexploded Bomb
US	United States
U/S	Unserviceable
VCDS	Vice Chief of the Defence Staff
VJTF	Very High Readiness Joint Task Force
VOR	Vehicle off the Road
WE	War Establishment
WIMP	Whinging Incompetent Malingering Person
WMR	War Maintenance Reserve
WO	Warrant Officer

CHARLES HEYMAN (EDITOR)

A former infantry officer, Charles Heyman served in the British Army between 1962 and 1986, with tours of active service in Borneo, Cyprus, Malaysia and Northern Ireland. Between active service tours he served as a Regimental Officer (commanding a Combat Team in Germany) and as a General Staff Officer in the Headquarters of the 1st British Corps. Before leaving the British Army in 1986 he spent two years as a lecturer in Defence Studies at the Royal Air Force College (Cranwell).

Since leaving the British Army Charles Heyman has been specialising in threat and general military and security analysis. Initially working as a consultant for various NATO Defence Ministries, by the early 1990s he was leading research teams for Jane's Information Group. From 1995 until 2003 he was the editor of Jane's World Armies and from 1994 to 2000 the editor of Jane's Police and Security Handbook. In addition, from 1995 until 2004 he was the Senior Defence Analyst for Jane's Consultancy Group and took part in over 200 defence related consultancy projects.

Charles Heyman has extensive experience in the Balkans, and during the recent campaigns in Iraq and Afghanistan he has been a regular contributor to the BBC World Service, Sky News, National Public Radio in the USA and the Australian and Canadian Broadcasting Corporations. During the past five years he has written articles for a variety of newspapers that include The Times, The Scotsman, Sunday Express and the Sydney Morning Herald. He remains the author of the Armed Forces of the United Kingdom and The British Army Guide published by Pen & Sword.

During recent NATO operations in Libya and the recent crisis in both Syria and Iraq he has been a regular contributor for both the BBC and Sky News. During July 2014 he spent three days with Al Jazeera International explaining the intricacies of the ISIS related operations in Northern Iraqi.

He is a member of the International Institute for Strategic Studies (IISS) and the Royal United Services Institute (RUSI).

E Mail – Charles.Heyman@Yahoo.co.uk

This publication was produced by R&F (Defence) Publications
Editorial Office Tel 07889 886170
E Mail:Editorial@armedforces.co.uk
Website: www.armedforces.co.uk

Editor: Charles Heyman

Other publications in this series are:
The Royal Air Force Pocket Guide 1994-95
The Armed Forces of the United Kingdom 2014–2015 (Volume 7)
The Territorial Army – Volume 1 1999

Further copies can be obtained from:
Pen & Sword Books Ltd
47 Church Street
Barnsley S70 2AS

Telephone: 01226-734222   Fax: 01226-734438

First Edition of this publication was in September 1986

HMSO Core Licence Number CO2W0004896
Parliamentary License Number P2006000197
PSI Licence Number C2006009533